Frances P. Cobbe

The Modern Rack

Papers on vivisection

Frances P. Cobbe

The Modern Rack
Papers on vivisection

ISBN/EAN: 9783337255930

Printed in Europe, USA, Canada, Australia, Japan

Cover: Foto ©Andreas Hilbeck / pixelio.de

More available books at **www.hansebooks.com**

THE MODERN RACK

Papers on Vivisection

BY

FRANCES POWER COBBE

> Savage Tormentors of old
> Wrested with thumbscrew and rack
> Secrets of crime and blood and guile
> From traitors and murderers black—
> Lives there now in the world a man so bold
> Would call those torturers back?
>
> Baser Tormentors to-day
> Grope out with scalpel and knife
> In gruesome wound of faithful hound
> Fair Nature's secrets of life—
> Lives there yet in our land a man will say
> These meaner tormentors shall have their way?

ARDVA · QVÆ · PVLCRA

LONDON

SWAN SONNENSCHEIN & CO.

PATERNOSTER SQUARE

1889

CONTENTS.

PREFACE.

MESSRS. SWAN SONNENSCHEIN having done me the honour
to propose to republish my principal contributions to the
Vivisection controversy, I have gladly accepted their
offer, and have selected from the mass the speeches,
essays, and leaflets which constitute this small volume.
In this collected form these papers may, I would fain
hope, prove useful in supplying statements and arguments
to those who are now carrying on the agitation against
scientific cruelty, and who will continue, I doubt not, to fight
the good fight when my share of it is done. Perhaps others
also whose minds have never awakened to the meaning
of this dreadful subject may be touched by something
they may find in one or other of these varied discussions
and appeals, and thus be drawn to aid us.

The articles in this book (with the exception of the first,
which is of earlier date than those which follow it), have
not been arranged chronologically ; but, so far as was convenient, under the different departments of the controversy
with which they are respectively concerned. As regards
the scientific passages and descriptions of experiments in
these papers, they have all been written with the help
(or, at least, not without the revision) of men qualified to
judge of each question ; and I have no fears that their
accuracy will be seriously impugned. The moral arguments
have been the results of my own long and anxious reflections,

based on the chosen studies of my youth. When, more than thirty years ago, I wrote my *Essay on Intuitive Morals* (an attempt to present Kantian ethics in a popular and religious form) I did not anticipate that my old age would be devoted to an effort to apply those large principles solely to protect the science-tortured brutes from cruel wrong. But such has been the guidance of my life under pressure of claims from which I could not turn away ; and, sickening as is the retrospect which the reprinting of these papers has cost me of years filled with helpless indignation and pity, I do not regret that so it has been. It will be enough if I can close my work with the conviction that, sooner or later, the God-given consciences of men will surely revolt against this deadly practice, and make an end of it for ever.

FRANCES POWER COBBE.

HENGWRT, DOLGELLY,
   March, 1889.

THE MODERN RACK.

I.

THE MORAL ASPECTS OF VIVISECTION.

THE popular idea of the extreme tenderness and sensibility of early youth, especially in the male human creature, is almost as purely conventional and remote from experience as the poetic fiction of an English spring—all sunshine and flowers. That type of cruelty which comes of ignorance and recklessness, alike of their own suffering and that of others, and wherein Curiosity, not Malice, is the prevailing motive, is at its worst in adolescence; and only as years go by, and observations multiply, and the experience of pain ploughs up the heart, does sympathy grow by slow degrees, till at last, as Sir Arthur Helps has pointed out, it may be predicted with certainty that a jury of old men will take the most merciful view of every case brought for their verdict.

On the larger scale of nations and of humanity, the same process of initiation into the mysteries of suffering and of sympathy has gone forward; and we now behold society so far emerged from the age of barbarism that an English gentleman would no more insert nowadays in his account-book (like the pious and charitable Alleyne) an item for "Whipping of ye Blind Beare," than the stream of traffic would proceed peacefully over Westminster Bridge were a row of heads to be exhibited on the cornice. The influences of civilisation, of religion, of cultivation of all kinds, mental and moral, have softened, like the rain of heaven, the crust of our dry, hard world; and there is every reason to hope that, unless arrested or perverted, they will trickle downwards and permeate the whole soil of human society, till the "desert shall rejoice and blossom as the rose". When we think of what earth might become were the tiger passions within our race to be bred out at last, and the divine faculty of love and sympathy to attain its obviously-intended development, it would seem as if efforts for the improvement of our physical or sanitary conditions, or for the advance of arts, science, or laws, were scarcely worth making in comparison of any step which should bring us nearer to such an age of joy.

But it is by no means an even and unbroken line of progress which we can flatter ourselves our race is pursuing towards a millennium of mercy. While the general stream of tendency is undoubtedly in that direction, and may, indeed, be dimly traced so to have been since the beginning of history, yet there are certain counter currents observable which are setting altogether in an opposite direction. The great wars which the gigantic armies of modern European statecraft have made possible, and the dire legacy of national hatred which such conflicts bequeath to unborn generations, present formidable obstacles in our road. It may excite surprise, perhaps ridicule, if I point to another and apparently comparatively insignificant feature of modern life as no less threatening in another way. If, while a patient seems to be recovering from a long malady, a new and strange symptom should suddenly exhibit itself, the physician would unquestionably hold that there existed considerable latent danger. Much such a rapid development of peculiarly acrimonious moral disease appears to be taking place in that part of our social body which is just now the seat of highest vitality.

Science is undoubtedly at this hour the ruling pursuit of the age. What the Chase, War, Art, and Learning have been in various past epochs, so is the pursuit of Physical Knowledge in our generation. The triumphs thereby achieved have dazzled us, as the people of France were dazzled by the victories of the first

Napoleon; and even such of us as understand but very imperfectly wherein these boasted conquests consist, are ready, like our betters, to cast our palms in the way of the new Messiah and shout "Hosanna!" albeit we have too seldom reason to believe that he "cometh in the name of the Lord". If any men may claim to be more than others the representatives of the period, in the "foremost files of time," it is our men of science. Whether the rest of mankind will hereafter meekly follow in their mental track yet remains to be seen; but it is certain that no statesmen, no divines, no metaphysicians, offer themselves at the present day with such high pretensions to become our Moses and Aarons, and to lead us—it may be into a Canaan, it may be into a wilderness. What is done, thought, felt, by the men of science is of almost incalculable weight in determining the proximate tendencies of thousands of lesser spirits; the direction to be taken by all those innumerable minds which have no motor force of their own, but follow the *Zeit-Geist* whithersoever he goeth. A peculiar and abnormal manifestation of sentiment among the scientific class, or even of a certain small section of it,* is, therefore, quite otherwise significant than the rise of a silly or cruel fashion among the *jeunesse dorée* of the clubs and the race-course, or the prevalence of an idle delusion in urban coteries.

Such manifestation is, I apprehend, actually observable in the very rapid extension of the practice of painful Experiments on Animals. In the present paper I purpose studiously to avoid detailing, or even alluding specifically to any of the multiform

---

* Probably the great astronomers and geologists would be the very last to countenance such practices as those to which reference is made. Mrs. Somerville's expressions of abhorrence of them are repeated many times in her *Recollections;* and the late venerable Sir Charles Lyell, a short time before his death, answered the writer's inquiries as to his opinion with a shudder of disgust, and added: "I do not even like to think of all the *insects* I killed when I was a young man and made my entomological collection. Of course I did it with every precaution to save them pain, but I do not like to remember it now."

horrors which are classified under the name of Vivisections.
But without harrowing the reader by descriptions of them, I shall
merely point to such experiments as those singularly ingenious
varieties of torture which fill the large volumes of French,
German, and English physiological Handbooks, and suggest to
my readers the inquiry: Whether this sort of thing be not
strangely at variance with the tone of thought and practice which
at present prevail in other departments of human activity; and
whether such books, for example, as these English Catechisms of
the Art of Torture do not even stand unique in the literature of
the world? While our legislation tends to an almost excessive
lenity towards criminals; while our Art and our Letters become
yearly more refined and fastidious; while our manners grow
more uniformly courteous towards all classes; and while in a
very special manner we are beginning to take a new interest in
the intelligence and affections of the lower animals, and to visit
their occasional ill-treatment by the working classes with condign
punishment—in the midst of all this humanising process we
suddenly find a break, a pause, nay, a very decided retrograde
movement. It is at least fitting that we should inquire into the
meaning of this strange and startling phenomenon.

Let us suppose, to aid our imagination, that something
analogous to vivisection were going on in some other department
of modern activity. There are legends that *dilettante* sovereigns
in the Cinque-cento age, when Art was supreme as Science is
now, were so anxious to aid the great painters at their work
that they beheaded men to serve for models for John the
Baptist, and crucified boys to enable them to verify the details
of Calvary. Were a similar expedient suggested in our day in
the schools of the Royal Academy, can we conceive the tempest
of public indignation which would gather round the head of the
enthusiastic Art Director who deemed the "end" of producing
a noble and religious *picture* so sacred that all "means" were
lawful to attain it? Or suppose that, for the sanitary interests
of the community, it were proposed to stamp out small-pox by
administering poison to every person seized with the disease. Is

it imaginable that such a scheme would obtain a hearing? Or (to come to closer analogies) let us fancy that, in the progress of gastronomy, an experiment, to which we had not become hardened by custom, and no less cruel than the production of *foie gras*, or the old process for making white veal, were suddenly to be introduced from France; or that sportsmen adopted a fashion of merely mangling their game, or using red-hot or poisoned shot. How horrible and startling should we pronounce the novel indulgence of tastes so morbid and pastimes so atrocious!

Yet such indifference to suffering as we have imagined in our hypothetical cases of artists, or sanitary reformers, or cooks, or sportsmen would actually be less monstrous and anomalous than the passion for Vivisection among the men of science; and this for two noticeable reasons. In the first place, artists, sportsmen, and *bon-vivants* know comparatively little of the nature and extent of the suffering caused by lacerations of the living tissues or the production of morbid conditions, while the physiologists understand the matter to a nicety, and have the most perfect acquaintance with every pain which they cause—nay, the causation which is often the cause of their ingenious exertions. As the writer of a letter, bearing the well-known signature of "Lewis Carroll," expressed it: "What can teach the noble quality of mercy, of sensitiveness to every form of suffering, so powerfully as the knowledge of what suffering really is? Can the man who has once realised by minute study what the nerves are, what the brain is, and what waves of agony the one can convey to the other, go forth and wantonly inflict pain on any sentient being? A little while ago we should have confidently replied, 'He cannot do it'. In the light of modern revelations we must sorrowfully confess he can." Again, in a still more marked way the acts of the vivisectors are anomalous and out of character. It is the boast of the school of science to which they belong that it has exploded the old theory that man is unique in creation, with a higher origin than the brutes and a different destiny. They give us to understand that God—or, rather, the "Unknown and

Unknowable " — has " made of one blood " at least all the
Mammalia upon earth. Not merely our corporeal frames, but
Thought, Memory, Love, Hate, Hope, Fear, and even some shadowy
analogues of Conscience and Religion, have been traced by the
great thinker at the head of this school throughout the lower
realms of life upon this planet; and, in the eyes of most cultivated and thoughtful persons in these days, the claims of a dog,
an elephant, a seal, or a chimpanzee to consideration and compassion are at least as high as were those of a Negro a century
ago in the eyes of a Jamaica planter. To find a number of men
of science—disciples, it is believed, almost without exception, of
the doctrine of evolution—themselves pursuing, and teaching
their pupils to pursue, trains of physiological investigations involving unutterable suffering to these same " poor relations " of
our human family, is an appalling phenomenon. That Pope
Pius IX. should have refused the late Lord Ampthill's request
for permission to form in Rome a Society for Prevention of
Cruelty to Animals might, perhaps, be understood on the strange
ground his response assumed — viz., that it was a theological
error to suppose that man owes any duty to an animal.* But
that the disciples of Darwin should themselves be the teachers
and leaders in a new development of most exquisite cruelty to the
brutes whom they believe to share our blood, our intelligence,
and our affections, is indeed a portent of strange and threatening
augury. It involves no less than the adoption of a moral theory

* This expression has been perhaps scarcely rightly understood. His
Eminence Cardinal Manning, who has taken a lively interest in the subject
and most importantly served the cause of anti-vivisection, made the following
observations as a member of the deputation to the Home Secretary from the
Victoria Street Society : " I think it greatly to the honour of England that
there is a law in the statute-book punishing cruelty to animals. That law
seems to express the great moral principle that people have no right to inflict
needless pain. The plea of scientific inquiry and research appears to present
the most refined pretext of cruelty in violation of that law. The infliction of
needless pain is a moral wrong ; and to say that we owe no moral obligations
to the lower animals is simply odious and detestable, because a moral obligation is due to their Creator."

of boundless application—namely, that the weak have absolutely no claims at all against the strong, but may be tortured *ad infinitum* even on the chance of discovering something interesting to the lordlier race, or for the purpose of better fixing an impression by the sight of their agonies than could be effected by the verbal description of a lecturer.* "We ask, bewildered," says a writer in the *Daily News*, "how far, then, will these apologists of Vivisection go in approving of the sacrifice of the weak for the sake of the strong? If it be proper to torture a hundred affectionate dogs or intelligent chimpanzees to settle some curious problem about their brains, will they advocate doing the same to a score of Bosjesmen, to the idiots in our asylums, to criminals, to infants, to women?"

Truly, this mournful spectacle of the perpetration of cruelty by those who best understand what is cruel, and of the contemptuous disregard of the claims of the brutes by those who have taught us that the brutes are only undeveloped men, is one to fill us with sorrowful forebodings for that future of our race which, from other quarters, seems to promise so fairly. "The simultaneous loss," writes one of the deepest and most observant thinkers of the day, "from the morals of our 'advanced' scientific men of all reverent sentiments towards being *above* them, as towards being *below*, is a curious and instructive phenomenon, highly significant of the process which their natures are undergoing at *both ends*." †

Of course events like the sudden development of physiological cruelties do not take place without sufficient cause, and are not without some ostensible excuse on the part of those responsible for them. The common passion for science in general and for physiology in particular, and the prevalent materialistic belief that the secrets of Mind can best be explored in Matter, undoubtedly account in no small measure for the vehemence of the new pursuit of original physiological investigations. Then, for the instruction of students in agonising experiments, other causes

---

* Prof. Rutherford, at a meeting cf the British Medical Association at Edinburgh, expressly defended Vivisection on this ground.
† Dr. James Martineau.

may readily be found.   Young men at the age of ordinary
medical students are, as I began by remarking, filled with curiosity and exceedingly empty of sympathy and pity.   An eminent
physiologist recently bore testimony to his surprise when a whole
class of his pupils trooped out of his lecture-room on purpose to
see the assistant kill a creature which he had considerately intended should be despatched out of sight before dissection.   " I
remained alone in my chair," he observed, "a sadder and a wiser
man."   The same keenness of observation, or a memory of their
own youthful insensibility, ought to teach all professors of physiology that they are indulging a maleficent tendency which already
exists in their pupils' disposition when they invite mere lads of
the Bob Sawyer type to watch their frightful experiments — the
more frightful, so much, alas! the more attractive.*   And,
further still, the proclivity of the time to youthful independence
and raw incredulity of the experience of others adds strength to
the desire of students to see with their own eyes the phenomena
which their instructors might as thoroughly convey to them by

* Great indignation was expressed by Sir William Gull and Professor
Ferrier before the Royal Commission at the above remarks when they
appeared on the first publication of this paper in a monthly review.   Sir
William Gull said (Minutes of Evidence, 5502) that "he had never seen anything affording the remotest justification of the phraseology" of the passage;
and Professor Ferrier (*ibid.*, 3350) thought it "a gross libel upon a class".
   The opinion of two no less eminent men and much more experienced
teachers, Professor Rolleston, of Oxford, and Dr. Haughton, were somewhat
different.   Professor Rolleston remarked: "Kingsley speaks of 'the sleeping
devil that is in the heart of every man,' but you may say it is the lower nature
which we possess in common with the Carnivora.   It is just this, that the
sight of a living, bleeding, and quivering organism most undoubtedly does act
in a particular way upon what Dr. Carpenter calls the emotiono-motor nature
in us.   I know that many men are superior to it; but I beg to say that if we
are talking of legislation, we are not to legislate for the good, but for the mass,
who, I submit, are not always good" (1287).   Dr. Haughton said: "I would
shrink with horror from accustoming large classes of young men to the sight
of animals under vivisection.   I believe that many of them would become
cruel and hardened, and would go away and repeat those experiments reck-
lessly.   Science would gain nothing, and the world would have let loose upon
it *a set of young devils*" (1888).

means of descriptions and of the extraordinarily perfect models and diagrams now available.* There is nothing intrinsically blameworthy in this wish, which is, perhaps, an integral part of the scientific temperament. But its claims to be indulged, when indulgence means for a sensitive creature exquisite torture, and for the student such satisfaction as he may find in watching it, is another question.

Of the argumentative defences of Vivisection more must be said. The chief, I think, is a double-barrelled instrument, aimed at our selfishness (under the grandiloquent name of the Benefit of the Human Race) on the one side, and our bad conscience as regards various kinds of cruelty on the other. The latter, or *tu quoque* argument, which was set forth at large in a semi-jocose pamphlet by the assistant of M. Schiff, and published in Florence under the name of *Gli Animali Martiri*, refers us with a sneer to the cruelties of the chase and the shambles, and asks us whether, in a world where such things are done from the very lowest motives, it is worth while to dispute a few victims for those sacred Altars of Science which form the furniture of physiological laboratories? The answer to this appeal is not far to seek. One offence does not exculpate another, even if both be morally on the same level. But (as we have just seen) all other cruelties have some excuse in the ignorance or stupidity of those who inflict them, while those of the Physiologist alone bear the treble stigma of being done in the full light of knowledge, by singularly able men, and with the calmest forethought and deliberation. And while every other kind of cruelty is falling into disrepute if not into disuse, this alone is rising almost into the rank of a profession, like a superior sort of butchery. As to the argument

* And which *are* so conveyed in other branches of study when their exhibition would cause any serious inconvenience. What chemist thinks it needful to blow up a room to show his pupils the qualities of a detonating powder? Since the passing of the Act 39 and 40 Vict., cap. 77, demonstrations to students are required to be on animals under anæsthetics, and from the publicity of the case there may be ground to hope that this provision is generally observed.

that it "does not become people who eat animal flesh to demur to the torture of animals," it would have seemed that no one with common sense could have employed it, had we not found it repeatedly brought forward by the pro-vivisectors as if it possessed withering force. The cattle we use for food exist on the condition that we shall take their lives when we need them ; and in doing so in the ordinary, not unmerciful, manner, we save them the far worse miseries of old age and starvation. To end a creature's existence is one thing. To cause it to suffer torture which shall make that existence a curse is quite another matter.

Finally, for the tediously reiterated but more reasonable reproach that the opponents of Vivisection make no efforts to put down Field Sports, and count among their numbers many fox-hunters, deer-stalkers, fowlers, and anglers : what shall be answered ? My reply is, that the parallel between Vivisection and Field Sports is about as just and accurate as if a tyrant, accused of racking his prisoners in his secret dungeons, were to turn round and open a discussion on the Lawfulness of War. That creatures who chase and are chased all their days in fields and waters should have an arch-enemy and pursuer in man may be differently estimated as ill or well. But it is almost ludicrous to compare a fox-hunt, for example, with its free chances of escape and its almost instantaneous termination in the annihilation of the poor fox when captured, with the slow, long-drawn agonies of an affectionate, trustful dog, fastened down limb by limb and mangled on its torture-trough. An old-world passion, which had its place and use in another form of society, is running to seed in the modern fashion of field sports, such as *battues* and pigeon matches. A new passion, which scarcely had existence twenty years ago, is sprouting above ground and showing its bud in Vivisection.

Of course the motive of the sportsman, being usually merely sport, contrasts much to his disadvantage with that which the vivisector requires us to believe is his actuating principle. The latter, if an Englishman, tells us that it is for the exalted purpose of alleviating the sufferings of mankind (which touch his tender heart to the quick) that he puts himself and his brute victims to the pain of the experiments; whereas the sportsman can only sometimes plead that he kills game for food or to clear the land of noxious creatures, and must usually confess that he hunts, or shoots, or angles for his own pleasure, health, and amusement.

So far as the present writer's opinion is concerned, these latter motives do *not* justify such pursuits when they entail the death of animals neither hurtful to man nor wanted for his food; nor do any field sports seem to harmonise with the highest type of cultivated and humane feeling. But the men who follow them may plead at least the excuse of custom and of partial ignorance. Turn we, on the other hand, to those boasted motives of lofty and far-sighted philanthropy which are alleged to spur the vivisector to his ugly work in his laboratory, where no fern-brakes or heathery hills, no fresh breezes or murmuring streams, such as throw enchantment round the pursuits of the sportsman, are present to cast any glamour over the process of torture; and where no chance of escape on the part of the brute or risk to his own person may stir his pulse with the manly struggle for victory.

In the first place I may remark that the mental constitution of a man must be somewhat exceptional who is enthusiastically anxious to relieve the sufferings of unseen, and perhaps unborn, men and women, but who cares in comparison nothing at all for those agonies which are endured immediately under his eye by creatures who (according to his philosophy) are only a step lower in the scale of being. It verges truly on the gigantic and Promethean to talk of such devotion to the interests of Humanity *in the abstract;* and when we behold a cultivated and gifted gentleman selecting freely for his life-work the daily mangling of dogs and cats, we are quite at a loss to qualify the grandeur of his voluntary martyrdom. Perhaps it is not very astonishing that homely people, who do not feel in their breasts the vocation for such sublime devotion, should treat the boast of these motives as just a little partaking of the character of moonshine, and suppose, in a matter-of-fact way, that either the vivisector is a perfectly callous man, whose horrid work never cost him a pang,* or that, if he have any lingering feelings of compassion, he puts them aside in favour of sentiments rather more common in the world than such Curtius-like self-sacrifice. As very few of us would purchase immunity from our own diseases at the cost of the torture of a hundred dogs, we may be pardoned for doubting whether the vivisector who cuts them up (as he assures us) for our sakes, is really more interested on our behalf than we are for ourselves.

I believe, then, that we may not unjustifiably fall back on the conclusion that the real motives of vivisectors are of one or other of two less exalted kinds. The better class we may credit with a sincere ardour for Science, and that passion which has been well named the Dilletanteism of Discovery. And these belong precisely to that order of *hommes à grands desseins*, who are more than any others liable to overstep the bounds of justice and mercy, and who more than others need the restriction of the public conscience to check their recklessness. For a lower class we must, I fear, take the word of a man who worked for four months among them, in the laboratory of the greatest physiologist of his day, where from one to three dogs were sacrificed daily: "The idea of the good of humanity was simply out of the question, and would have been laughed at; the great aim being to keep up with or go ahead of our contemporaries in science, even at the price of an incalculable amount of needless torture to animals".†

But the motives which actually influence living vivisectors do

* I am compelled to testify that in wading through a mass of this Dead Sea literature, I have never been refreshed by a single passing expression of commiseration for the animals (whose signs of agony are recorded merely as interesting features of the experiments), or of regret that the higher scientific objects in view necessitated the prolongation of their tortures. If such feelings exist in the hearts of the operators, I congratulate them on the signal success wherewith they consistently eliminate the slightest trace of them from all their reports. Further, in perusing the books dedicated to the instruction of young students, I have looked equally in vain for any hint of caution or recommendation to parsimony in the use of the most excruciating experiments.

† Dr. Hoggan's letter to the *Morning Post.*

not, of course, determine the ethical lawfulness of the practice of Vivisection. Our real problem is : Whether the highest end to which it *may* conduce, and which they *may* possibly contemplate, —viz., either the direct benefit of mankind by special discovery, or the indirect benefit by the general advancement of science—morally justifies the means whereby it is to be obtained? Does the Good of Man justify the Torture of Brutes?

At this point we are commonly called upon to recognise with profound admiration and gratitude the immense value of discoveries said to be due to physiological experiment, and we are challenged to say whether, for example, Harvey's Circulation of the Blood, Bell's Double Function of the Nerves, and Simpson's Chloroform were not secrets worth buying at the price of a considerable amount of animal pain? The first answer to this "tall talk" is, that not one of these great discoveries appears to have been really made by the aid of Vivisection ; and that of the other reputed results of such experiments, it may be generally affirmed that they resemble the marvels said to have been wrought by the magicians of Pharaoh, who could *bring* the plagues upon Egypt, but remained quite powerless to *cure* them. Into such controversies, however, concerning the Utility of Vivisection, I, for one, refuse to enter. I am quite ready to admit that benefit has frequently resulted in all ages from a variety of evil deeds— from Rapine, Perjury, Infanticide, and especially from the sacrifice of "hecatombs" of women to spare "the smallest pain (or self-restraint) of men ". But not on account of such utility do I consider robbery and falsehood, the murder of infants or the prostitution of hapless women, right or lawful. Thus I refuse even to entertain the question whether the torture of animals can be justified on the plea of benefit to humanity. Repudiating the Jesuit principle that " The End justifies the Means," I am satisfied that the " Means " of Torture are morally forbidden and unlawful. To make the existence of a sentient creature such a misfortune and curse as that it should seem better it had never been born, is assuredly far beyond the exercise of any prerogative which man can claim for himself, either in virtue of any inherent superiority of his nature, or of any privilege he can conceive to have been granted to him by the Creator.

To affirm, then, as vivisectors are wont to do, that they would freely "sacrifice a hecatomb of dogs to save the smallest pain of a man," is merely an expression of contempt for the rights of beings feebler than themselves, and not yet advanced by evolution to the lordly class of "Bimana," or the genus "Homo". What are the moral grounds, we ask, for this astounding new principle of *Race Selfishness?* What is there in Man, either considered only as our fellow-bimanous animal, or as an immortal being whose body is but the garment of his soul, which should make his trifling pain so inexpressibly solemn a matter, and the agony of another animal, no less physically sensitive, insignificant by comparison? Of course we may naturally feel a little more spontaneous sympathy with a suffering man than with a suffering horse. But what is the ethical reason why we should prefer the pain of a thousand horses to that of a single man? Sir Henry Taylor has written noble lines on this matter, going deep into the heart of the question :

> " Pain, terror, mortal agonies that scare
> Thy heart in man, to brutes thou wilt not spare :
> Are theirs less sad and real? *Pain in man*
> *Bears the high mission of the flail and fan ;*
> *In brutes 'tis purely piteous."* *

There is no sight in all the world, to a thoughtful mind, more suggestive of harrowing reflection, no line of the long "riddle of the painful earth" more confounding to the religious soul, than the sufferings of creatures who have never sinned, and for whom (according to common belief) there will be no compensation for injustice in another life. While human pain has its plausible explanations and its possible beneficent results, animal pain seems (at least to our dim eyes) sheer unmitigated evil. I am at a loss then to conceive on what principle, deserving the name of moral, we are to speak and act as if such evil counted absolutely for nothing, while the aches and pains of men are to be so highly

* *Poems*, vol. iii.—" The Amphitheatre at Pozzuoli ".

esteemed, that the most cruel sacrifices must not be spared, if a chance exist of alleviating them. When we remember who are the teachers who talk about the "hecatomb," and what is their view of the relationship of man to the lower animals, we discover (as above remarked) that the only intelligible principle on which they proceed is that very ancient one—*le droit du plus fort.* As the main work of civilisation has been the vindication of the rights of the weak, it is not too much, I think, to insist that the practice of Vivisection in which this tyranny of strength culminates is a retrograde step in the progress of our race—a backwater in the onward flowing stream of justice and mercy, no less portentous than deplorable.

But it is impossible to regard this subject as if it were a mere abstract ethical problem. The vivisection of dull reptiles and wild rats and rabbits, wherewith the elder generation of students generally contented themselves, is not alone in question, nor even that of the heavy beasts in our pastures. By some strange and sinister fatality the chosen victims at present are the most intelligent and friendly of our domestic favourites—the cats who purr in love and confidence as they sit beside us on the hearth; the dogs whose faithful hearts glow with an affection for us, truer and fonder than we may easily find in any human breast. To disregard all the beautiful and noble moral qualities which such animals exhibit, and coldly contemplate them as if their quivering frames were mere machines of bone and tissue which it might be interesting and profitable to explore with forceps and scalpel, is to display heinous indifference to Love and Fidelity themselves, and surely to renounce our claim to be the object of such sentiments to brute or man. Our human race has for thousands of years trained these creatures to serve and trust us, till their natures are all bent towards us in love and confidence. So deeply rooted, indeed, is this faith in man in the case of the dogs that those who have witnessed the scenes in the laboratories of physiologists testify that the brutes can scarcely be made to understand that it is intended to hurt and kill them, but still try after hours of agony to lick the hands of their tormentor, and plead with him for mercy with their beseeching eyes when their limbs are all fastened down and immovable on the operating table. Will any one contend that it is not the vilest, the most odious treachery to betray and mock such faith of the dumb creature, and torture him to death for our purposes, while he—poor brute, whom we despise! would die freely to save us from fire or the waves, or perchance expire of grief upon our graves?

Nay, more; are we not altogether on a wrong track in arguing this question on the level to which we have descended? Are not Generosity, Self-sacrifice, the readiness to suffer for others, the very rudiments of all virtue and all nobility of character? Are we to go back to the condition of savages—nay, rather of those

> " Dragons of the prime
> Which tare each other in their slime,"

when we have boasted we had ascended to the rank of men, of Christians, of English Gentlemen? Is it a question for a man who aspires to be a brave or worthy, not to speak of a chivalrous or noble person, whether he *may*, within the limits of actual offence, spend his days in putting harmless animals on the rack for the benefit of himself and his kind? And are they our proper Teachers, those who are fit to guide and train young minds and direct the tendencies of future generations, who are striving to move us to condone and approve such deeds by cant about the "Glory of Science," and by appeals to our miserable, cowardly fears of disease and our selfish willingness to save "the smallest pain of a man at the cost of the torture of a hecatomb of brutes"?

To me it appears, I avow, that all this reveals a backsliding in feeling and moral aim almost measureless in the depth of its descent. The whole notion of Vivisection, as a legitimate exercise and mode of satisfying human desire of knowledge, seems to rest on a radically false conception of the proper ends of human life, and a no less erroneous idea of our relationship to those humbler tribes of creatures who are our fellow-lodgers in this planet-house of the Almighty. As life is more than meat, so are there better things to live for than Knowledge or escape from

Pain; nor is any fact which Science can reveal worth acquiring at the price of selfishness and cruelty. The brutes are not mere toys and puzzles, put here by their Creator and ours that we may freely divert ourselves by breaking them to pieces to see how His wisdom has made them. They are *fellow-creatures* with ourselves —*sinless* fellow-creatures, be it remembered, who have broken no divine law and deserved no punishment. If the day ever come (as it is my faith it will, hereafter) when all men shall look back upon the deeds done upon earth, and behold them in their true colours, must it not be that in the agonies of remorse and self-abhorrence in the vivisector's soul will be meted out the measure of justice he has dealt to his victims?

II.

WHAT IS VIVISECTION?

An Address

Delivered at a Meeting in Southampton.

The Right Rev. the Bishop of Winchester in the Chair.

We are come here to-night to discuss the best way to protect animals from cruelty. It is a sad thing that there should be any need to do this, to protect those beautiful, gentle, loving, and devoted creatures from sufferings always undeserved and sometimes so basely cowardly and ungrateful. But it is very slowly that men are learning to feel kindly to human beings of other races than their own, and we must have patience.

From *what* cruelty is it most important we should protect animals? Is it from the violence and ill-usage of ignorant and brutal men? This is bad enough. But every year this kind of cruelty is declining under the influence of advancing civilisation. There is a much worse kind of cruelty, alas! to be checked. Cruelty which is calm, deliberate, fully conscious of what agonies it inflicts, and which is so far from yielding before the progress of education that it actually claims to be a sort of education in itself; which is, in short, a *growing*, not a *dwindling*, evil, and which it behoves us accordingly to combat with all our strength, while yet there is time.

I speak, of course, of *Vivisection*—of the dissecting alive, cutting to pieces, baking, injecting with poisons, torturing in a thousand different ways, living horses, cats, rabbits, pigeons, and dogs.

I should think ill of any man who could hear of such things for the first time without passionate indignation. But this righteous feeling is not seldom quenched ere long by the calm assurances of the advocates of Vivisection that the practice is not half so bad as is represented; and that it is, moreover, absolutely *necessary* for the interests of mankind, and that, in the words of one of those gentlemen, " You cannot do justice to the men without it". And so the indignation against the vivisector quietly subsides into a sense of having been rather cheated into misapplied pity, and there is an end.

Now, I will ask those present to whom this sad subject is familiar to pardon me while I say a few words to explain to others the *raison d'être*, the why and wherefore, of Vivisection, and how it comes to be practised by men who are not wantonly cruel; that is to say, who do not take pleasure in inflicting pain, but only *disregard* the pain they inflict in pursuit of their own objects.

People sometimes ask : " Why do these physiologists not content themselves with dead subjects ? " Well, dead subjects are not all they want. Anatomical science—that is, the knowledge of the bodily frame of men and animals, of the form of the bones, position of the muscles, and so on— can be thoroughly studied on dead bodies, and is so, regularly, in all our schools. I may remind you, however, in passing, that fifty years ago, when dead corpses were scarce, Burke and Hare (whose effigies some of you have seen in Madame Tussaud's Chamber of Horrors) took an ingenious method of supplying students with them, by *burking* living men ; and those students (who were more than suspected of having connived at the murders) no doubt found them *necessary* in the sacred interests of science. The Legislature took a different view, however, of the matter, and speedily passed the Anatomy Act, which has ever since been a protection to men and women *liable to Dissection.*

Physiology differs from anatomy in being concerned with the functions, the operations, and modes of working of the organs of the living body ; how the heart beats ; how the food is digested ; how the nerves act, and so on. You will easily see that there is a temptation to try to obtain a sight of what is going on in the living body; and accordingly in old times physicians indulged their curiosity in the simplest way by cutting open unhappy slaves and prisoners, and peering into the poor wretches' entrails. But even by heathens this was condemned as too cruel; and now for a long time back such experiments have been pretty nearly confined to animals, and, unhappily, chiefly to the higher animals because they most nearly resemble men. Hundreds of thousands of these creatures have perished during the past century. Thousands perish every year. Many are perishing at this instant in 240 laboratories in Germany, France, and Italy; some slowly expiring with their brains dug out, and, as a German physiologist says, "resembling a newly-hoed potato field"; some mangled, with their nerves dissected out like strings drawn across where the flesh once covered them; some fastened down on their troughs like the one in this photograph, with a machine playing to force air into their lungs, while they were subjected to every kind of agonising experiment. Now, the question is for all men and women to decide : "Is this kind of thing to go on for ever?"

Of course we are told that it is no affair of ours, that we must leave the matter in the hands of men specially qualified to form a judgment. But, I ask, "Qualified to form a judgment about *what?* Is it about the *utility* of Vivisection for their own pursuits?" That is a point on which physiologists and medical men may well have the advantage of us. But about the *moral lawfulness* of the practice, that is another thing; one which I think you and I, my friends, and our Right Reverend Chairman, and the honoured President of this Society, and several gentlemen and ladies on this platform, are just as well qualified to form a judgment as any physiologist in the land. I should as soon have asked Burke and Hare whether it were *right* to smother men to furnish subjects for Dissection as ask a physiologist whether it were *right* to torture dogs by Vivisection.

There are three defences urged on behalf of Vivisection which it behoves you to take into fair consideration—

1st. You will be told that *very little pain* is inflicted on the animals ; the use of anæsthetics (chloroform and so on) rendering them insensible.

2nd. That other people do things quite as cruel.

3rd. That, whatever pain the animals suffer in Vivisection, it is *necessary* they should bear it in the interests of human beings.

Now, concerning the small degree of pain inflicted, I will at once say that a considerable number of vivisections *do* involve only a little, or a moderate degree, of pain. There is a mistake current on this subject which, like every exaggeration, it is well to avoid. But beside those comparatively mild experiments from which the animals recover, or under which they are killed while insensible, there are a vast number more involving horrible suffering, and for which the boasted anæsthetics offer no alleviation or only the alleviation of the first operation, while the long-drawn after-agony of the creature has no relief at all. All the now popular experiments on the nervous system would be vitiated by the use of anæsthetics, and so would many experiments on the digestive and other organs.

So much for *real* anæsthetics and how little they do to stop animal suffering, even when the physiologists are willing to go to the expense and considerable trouble of using them, and do not, like Dr. Klein, "only use them for convenience' sake !" We know he told the Royal Commission that "we chloroform a cat because we are *afraid of being scratched*" ; but not a small dog, because "if it is a small dog, *there is no fear of being bitten*" (3642).

But, though the genuine anæsthetics are of very little use, the *sham* anæsthetics, unhappily, are only too important a feature in Vivisection. There is a horrid drug called *curare* which entirely paralyses the power of motion, but leaves the power of suffering actually increased. This abominable curare is in constant use in Germany, few experiments being done without it. Claude Bernard also used it frequently in Paris, though he himself wrote of it (in the *Revue des Deux Mondes* for Sept. 1, 1864) that it causes the victim to suffer "the most atrocious tortures which the imagination of man can conceive !" Finally, I have to tell you that this curare is used *in this country*—used under the sanction of the law; for the Act of 1876 does not forbid its use, though it excludes it from the class of anæsthetics.

Now we come to the second excuse for Vivisection, namely, that "other people do things quite as cruel". This is constantly used as if it were a real argument on behalf of Vivisection, whereas, if it were actually a fact, it would only furnish an argument for correcting both cruelties at once, which, I think I can answer for us Anti-Vivisectors, we should be only too happy to do to-morrow. But is it really seriously that anybody compares the pain inflicted by either butchers and fishermen, or by fox-hunters and fowlers, with the long-drawn, exquisite agonies of the Vivisector's torture-trough? Believe me, my friends, the people who try to escape blame by this *tu-quoque* argument count upon your ignorance of what Vivisection really is, or they would never use it. I do not like sport myself; I cannot conceive what pleasure my countrymen take in it; but not till I see some joyous and open-hearted English gentleman tie a fox down to a table, and slowly dissect out its quivering nerves for ten hours at a time (as Paul Bert tormented a dog), or bake a rabbit alive (as Claude Bernard baked a score in this stove), shall I suffer anyone in my presence to compare the sportsman of the field with the sportsman of the laboratory. I should like to see how the members of a hunt would treat a man *suspected* of such doings as those which these physiologists unblushingly publish!

Now we turn to the third and grand excuse—"Vivisection," we are told, "whether cruel or not, is *Necessary!*"

My friends, I have often asked for some definition of that word "Necessary" in this connection. A poor costermonger, brought up for driving his donkey when it is not fit to work, pleads to the magistrate, "Please, sir, it was absolutely *necessary* for me to take out my cart and sell my apples or my shrimps. My wife and children are starving—I had no other way to feed them." The plea is a good and true one, but the magistrate never listens to it. Has any physiologist a greater "necessity" to urge than that of the costermonger?

What the Vivisector alleges is; that he expects to find some day or other some valuable secrets, and thus it is "necessary" he should be allowed to go on prying and ferreting for them in the brains and entrails of tortured brutes. Once I was told in Florence that it was the *Religion of the Future* which Professor Schiff was likely to find; but usually it is something less—the remedy for some disease of our bodies. It is not said the vivisectors have yet discovered any very important therapeutic agent, such as chloroform, or quinine, or iodine, for example, or the right method to cure any of the greater diseases, such as consumption, or cancer, or madness. If they had done so, you would have heard it long ago trumpeted abroad and proclaimed on the housetops. No, they have not done this, and the best improvements in modern medicine are due, not to their cruel researches, but to patient chemical and microscopical observation. For five hundred thousand animals sacrificed they can scarcely reckon one small discovery which you or I could be made to understand, or by which we could profit. The goddess who presides over these Altars of Science, like other false gods, takes many victims and returns few blessings. And no wonder it is so, for it is rather error and mistake than physiological truth which can be wrung from the poor agonised frames and ruined fragments of animals on which these vivisectors experiment; and, when all is said, the organisation of a brute is so different from that of a man that the surgeon who would act on the assumption that he could safely perform an operation on a woman because he had done it on a guinea-pig would deserve to be punished as a homicide. That celebrated Scotch physiologist who tortured the thirty-six dogs to ascertain the property of a drug was obliged to confesss to the Royal Commission that what happened to a dog could only *suggest* what would happen in the case of a man: to make anything certain it would be necessary to try it on a man (Minutes, 2966). But I refuse to base my argument about the lawfulness of Vivisection on the success or non-success of the vivisectors. Mr. Froude the historian told me the other day that Queen Elizabeth's life and her Protestant succession had been unquestionably saved several times by torturing suspected traitors; that is, putting them on the rack, as was the habit in those days, and forcing them to answer questions and reveal accomplices. If we had lived then we should have been told of course that it was *necessary* for the supreme interests of justice and of the nation to use the rack and the thumb-screw. Nevertheless I do not imagine any of us now think that it would be right and proper to employ those valuable instruments for the discovery of truth !

Almost every crime in history may be justified if we begin by adopting the abominable maxim that the end justifies the means, and that everything is right out of which Providence has permitted some good to somebody to arise. To my thinking, to inflict on a sensitive creature a torture worse than death, such as to make its whole existence to have been a curse instead of the blessing its Creator intended, is a great and grievous sin, and I am not concerned ever to learn the good consequences of sins.

But in truth the innocent public is much misled in imagining that physiologists are generally busy looking for remedies for their diseases at all. The *ideal* vivisector is a sort of Prometheus of the nineteenth century, borne away by his gigantic enthusiasm of humanity to spend his whole life in the most revolting pursuit conceivable, in the hopes of bringing balm to the woes of his kind. The *real* vivisector is a different kind of gentleman—who pursues his "Chamber Sport" (as Lord Shaftesbury has happily named it), sometimes, no doubt, from pure love of science, sometimes from desire to distinguish himself and *ex*tinguish rival physiologists; who (in short) *cuts his way to Knowledge and Notoriety* through the tissues of the hapless animals. Shall I give you just one glimpse into a laboratory? Here is a little scene which my friend Dr. Hoggan (who has done so much to reveal the secrets of these torture-dens) once told me quite incidentally. It was a mere mild and ordinary one, not what is called a severe experiment at all—in short, the every-day work in a certain celebrated foreign laboratory, to whose deceased master all our leading English physiologists have lately joined to raise a memorial.

The room is full of costly and delicate machines, expressly constructed for a hundred kinds of experiments. You may see the prints of them in this Atlas (Cyon's) and this English "Handbook," and then judge of the truth of the assertion, that it is a *rare* practice for which scores and hundreds of such expensive instruments are made! A little white fox-terrier has just been taken down off the torture-trough. Its sides have been mangled, and certain nerves cut across, so that, when it is placed on the floor, its slender hind legs only trail behind it. It will never stand on them and scour over the fields again. It crawls away, as stricken animals do, to hide itself in the darkest corner and cool its fever of agony by lying on the stones. Meanwhile a fine black retriever rises from the fireside. He has served for other experiments. He has had some ganglions at the base of the brain which are connected with the eyes severed, and the result is that his poor eyes, once so bright and keen, have been for several days slowly perishing and putrefying, to the great satisfaction of the physiologists, who thus know they have cut just the right spot. The poor brute feebly rises and meets the little white terrier. I do not know anything more; I could not bear quite to hear it. It was a very small incident, involving nothing like the extremes of suffering; but it gave me just a glimpse into a vivisector's workshop.

And then, to show you how little they reck what creatures they torture. I was dining last week with a friend (a lady well known in the literary world) and her husband. "My little girl," my friend said, "had two guinea-pigs of which we all made special pets. When we came to London we thought it best to give them away, and so we looked for the happiest place for them we could find, and at last left them with the children of Professor ——, with many recommendations to kindness. After a time we went back to X—— on a visit, and my child ran to ask her little friends about the guinea-pigs. 'Oh,' they said, 'one day, when we were out, *papa got them and cut them up!*'" Another friend was told by a student, who witnessed the scene in Edinburgh, that a little dog, brought into a certain professor's laboratory, took alarm at the awful preparations and, turning from one to another of the assistants, stood up and begged for its life. The lads were touched, and asked the professor to allow them to pay its price and set it free. The professor told them he would teach them to have no such maudlin sensibility, and not only vivisected the creature cruelly that day, but kept it till the following week's lecture and tortured it again, till death mercifully ended its poor little existence. *No* condition, indeed, of the animals suffices to soften the vivisector's heart. Dr. De Noë Walker has told me that he has seen one take up a mother from her young, cut off its mammary glands (its breasts), and put it down, mutilated, bleeding, and dying, among its little ones, whom it could no longer feed, but only licked in its last agony.

Here are some extracts from the principal German scientific Reports of last year—those reports which, Professor Haughton told the Royal Commission, English students constantly read *to copy the experiments* (1874). I take them from the admirable address of our Honorary Corresponding Member for Dresden, Baron von Weber, translated by our Society, and to be procured at this door and at our office in London.

Pflüger's Archives of Physiology, vol. xiv., pp. 412-43—"On the Destruction of the Brain," by Professor Goltz (of the Physiological Laboratory at Strasburg).—Fifty-one dogs had portions of the brain washed out of the head, which had been pierced in several places; this repeated three times, the creatures mutilated, and their behaviour studied for months. Most of the animals died at last of inflammation of the brain. P. 415.—"Interesting" experiment on a delicately-formed little bitch; left side of the brain extracted; wire pincers on the hind feet. Doleful whining—the little animal began again to howl piteously, soon afterwards foamed at the mouth. P. 417.—The same dog last operated upon on the 15th October; since then blind; died on November 10th. The dissected brain resembles a lately-hoed potato-field. P. 418.— Little bitch last operated upon on the 26th May, and made nearly

blind; dies on the 7th July of inflammation of the brain.   P. 420.—
A dog last operated upon on May 30th; blind since then; dies
on the 18th November.

Ibid., vol. xiii. (1876), pp. 1-44—Professor Goltz, Dr. Gergens,
and Dr. Tiegel (of the Physiological Institution at Strasburg).—
Mutilation of brains of dogs continued for six months.   As Hitzig,
Carville, Duret, Soltmann, Schiff, Hermann, and others had only
removed small portions of the brain from the heads of live dogs,
Goltz introduced a new method by which larger portions of the
brain were torn away and washed out, by means of heated spring-
water, after the skull had been pierced in several places.   The
crater-shaped cavities thus formed we washed out.   Of course the
more extensive the destruction of the brain, the less favourable
was the prospect of maintaining life.   P. 5.—A dog, with five holes
bored in the head and with the loss of nearly half the brain, lived
from February 14th to March 15th.   P. 7.—"We, as well as
other observers, have lost a large number of animals through inflammation of the brain."   P. 8.—Only young dogs are suitable
for these experiments.   "No one has succeeded in destroying
the brain so extensively and handling it so roughly, while still
preserving the creature's life, as myself."

P. 9.—"It does not often happen that two physiologists are of
one opinion in matters affecting the brain."   P. 17.—"In the
case of several mutilated dogs I decided to put out the left sound
eye in order to estimate correctly the functions of the eye maimed
by the loss of the brain."   On the 8th Nov., 1875, two holes
bored in the head of a bull-dog and the brain washed away.   The
animal becomes blind with the right eye.   On Dec. 11th I took
the left eyeball out.   Fresh disturbance of the brain on the 10th
Jan., 1876; a third on the 5th Feb., this time on the right side ;
dies on Feb. 15th.   P. 20.—On Nov. 29th, 1875, part of the left
side of the brain and the left eye of a young hound taken out.
On the 12th Jan., 1876, a second, and on the 29th a third, mutilation of the brain   On the 31st Jan. total blindness set in.   On
the 10th Feb. the brain further destroyed.   On the 4th March
again for the fifth time, causing death on March 8th.

P. 31.—" A very clever lively young female dog, which had learnt to shake hands with both fore-paws, had the left side of the brain washed out through two holes on the 1st Dec., 1875. This caused lameness in the right paw. On being asked for the left, the dog immediately laid it in my hand ; I now demand the right, but the creature only looks at me sorrowfully, for it cannot move it. On my continuing to press for it, the dog crosses the left paw over, and offers it to me on the right side, as if to make amends for not being able to give the right." On the 13th Jan. a second portion of the brain destroyed ; on Feb. 15th a third ; and on March 6th a fourth, this last operation causing death.

[The cynical humour with which Professor Goltz tries to make the description of his experiments amusing and tasteful to the reader is truly repulsive. On pages 429 and 435 he speaks of two dogs rendered imbecile by loss of a part of the brain : " The awkward movements of one gave the impression of a jack-pudding," and so on.]

Now, then, I ask you finally, is this sort of thing to go on, or will you try to stop it wholly in England, rendering it first infamous in public estimation, and then illegal by Act of Parliament ? Do not fancy it will *ever* stop of itself. On the contrary, it will extend and extend year after year, till the world is full of it. There is no use hoping for any compromise. It is War to the Knife—Science (or rather that which falsely claims to be Science) against Humanity, and Humanity against Science. This Society in its earlier years strove to effect a compromise, desiring to leave to science all the liberty which could be accorded, and the chance of fulfilling its eternal promises, never yet performed, of making discoveries useful to mankind. But all hopes of such compromise have passed away. The Returns to Parliament, year after year, show that the existing Act, which ought to have protected the animals, is so worked as to be only a protection to the vivisector. Nothing remains but to demand that Vivisection be prohibited altogether —prohibited not only for the sake of the poor brutes, but in the higher interests of the human race, and for the sake of averting a Reign of Cruelty such as the world has never seen, and which will by no means stop short at the torture of the lower animals.

It rests with you, men and women of England, to say whether Vivisection shall, or shall not, go on here in England and throughout Europe and America; for where England leads the march of Humanity, the nations follow. If England hold back there is no hope that from any other country will arise the cry: "In the name of the God of Mercy, and as we hope for His mercy on our own sinful souls, let this torture of His innocent creatures cease".

III.

THE HIGHER EXPEDIENCY.

THE sad subject of Vivisection, to which you are good enough to lend me an ear to-night, resembles an invaded country wherein the attacking party march up by one road and the defending army swarm down another, and a fair pitched battle scarcely ever takes place. We, who attack Vivisection, keep chiefly on the moral line, and denounce the cruelty and consequent immorality of the practice. Those who defend Vivisection (beyond the occasional use of the *tu quoque* argument by reference to field sports and Strasburg pies) mostly confine themselves to flourishing the standard of Science and proclaiming the utility of physiological experiments. I hope presently to lead your thoughts along a third line of argument, which has scarcely, I think, yet received adequate attention; but, before doing so, I will, with your kind permission, outline in as few words as possible what I consider to be the whole *carte du pays* of the controversy.

Much confusion has arisen in this, as in other ethical controversies, by neglect on both sides to define the system of morals on which the speakers proceed. I shall say at once that such study as in my long life I have been able to give to ethics has made me a firm disciple of what has been called the school of Independent Moralists—that is, of those who think that moral Right and Wrong are not dependent on Utility, but exist in the nature of things and in the supreme Will of the universe. This is the school of Plato, Zeno, Butler, Leibnitz, and Kant, while the opposite school, or that which makes right dependent on utility, is that of Epicurus, Grotius, Puffendorf, Bentham, and Mill. Now, believing that Right is independent of Utility, you will notice that I and those who think with me are relieved from any necessity to prove that a practice which we hold to be wrong is also useless. You will see at once the bearing of this on Vivisection. Our contention is—that Vivisection is a wrong practice; not, indeed, because every individual experiment is, *per se*, cruel—that is a mistake of some of our friends—but because the practice is inseparable from cruelty, and has never been and never can be long carried on without cruelty. By this word "cruelty" (which has been so much disputed in this connection) I mean not necessarily "wanton cruelty"—*i.e.*, cruelty without any end or purpose at all, cruelty for cruelty's sake—but I mean the infliction on any innocent and sentient creature of intense suffering for some end other than the benefit of that creature; suffering of which it may be said that it has converted its existence from a blessing into a curse. I consider such cruelty as this to be an enormous moral offence, a greater and more devilish offence than drunkenness or lying or theft. I therefore view Vivisection (as involving such offence) as being morally unlawful and forbidden. Here, then, and on these grounds, the plea of Utility is altogether beside the question and out of court.

But now I turn to those who belong to the school of Dependent Moralists, who hold that Utility constitutes rightfulness, and that the "greatest happiness of the greatest number" is the only test we can apply to the morality of actions. Utterly disagreeing with this moral system (if it were true, I think we ought to smother all our sickly children offhand), I am yet quite ready to argue the Vivisection question on utilitarian principles, only they must be the nobler kind of utilitarianism, such as my honoured friend John Stuart Mill supported. You ask—"Is Vivisection useful?" "Is the practice conducive to the welfare of the community?" "Is it, in short, expedient?" I ask further—"Useful for what purpose? Conducive to what order of welfare? Expedient in what sense?"

It seems to me there are two kinds of utility, and two orders of human welfare, and two kinds of expediencies. As man individually is a twofold being, so the community has a twofold life, a higher life of which the welfare consists in justice, freedom, faith, chastity, sobriety, sympathy, tenderness of the strong for the rights of the weak ; and a lower life of which the welfare consists in physical health and commercial prosperity. We are materialistic enough in these days, Heaven knows ! but I do not suppose anyone will deliberately say that the welfare of the higher life of the nation is not more important than the welfare of the lower ; or maintain that it would profit a nation much to gain a whole world of gold and corn and cotton, and add ten years to the average length of mortal life, if, at the same time, it had lost its soul of honour, its courage, justice, and humanity.

Now it is with this question of the utility of Vivisection to the *higher life* of the community that I propose to occupy you this evening ; and I hope you will agree at starting that this is the main and chief utility to be weighed, and that, if it appear that the practice be detrimental to the higher interests of the community, the question of whether it be useful to the lower interests scarcely deserves serious consideration. I do not forget—and I hope no one will charge me with undervaluing—the vast blessings of bodily health, and even the beneficial influences of health on morality ; but I do maintain that health is not the *summum bonum*, and that if, instead of valuing health as an aid to virtue, we sacrifice the great virtue of compassion to obtain health, then even health and life will be purchased at too dear a price. Into the further controversy of the use of Vivisection to the Healing Art I shall not enter at all to-night. I think I have sufficiently indicated its entirely subordinate place in the general argument, and I need only repeat my adhesion (so far as I may presume to have an opinion on the matter) to the dictum of our excellent American advocate, Dr. Leffingwell, "that, at the best, Vivisection is *prospecting in such barren regions*, that, if pain could be measured by money, no mining company in the world would sanction the outlay". This, then, is our topic for to-night—the MORAL EXPEDIENCY of Vivisection ; the effects to be anticipated from the extension of the practice as regards the higher interests of the community.

To study this question we must begin by inquiring what are the effects of the practice on the vivisector himself? Who and what manner of men are vivisectors? What is the character evolved by a life devoted to such experiments? I will say at once that I think some of our anti-vivisection friends have a little misused the term "demoralising," as applied to the work of Vivisection. They have supposed that a man who does things so cruel to animals must necessarily become thoroughly heartless, altogether inhuman towards men and women; base and brutal in every sense. I suppose some such idea as this was in our noble Poet-Laureate's mind when he described his vivisector in the "Children's Hospital" as coarse and red-faced, and with "big merciless hands". But there is some mistake here. The nature of a man is not often homogeneous; not even logically harmonious. Even the leaven of religion scarcely succeeds, save in the perfect saint, in leavening the whole lump and leaving no lingering besetting sins. Still less often, fortunately, does the leaven of any evil so thoroughly permeate a man's whole character as to exclude every kind of good. The drunkard may be a generous friend; the thief a kind father; the profligate a hero of courage. All history is full of such paradoxes. The only woman to whom the discernment of men has given the title of "Great" is Catherine II. of Russia; and "broad-browed Verulam," while founding modern science, took bribes to corrupt justice. To him, I think, we may fairly point with a slight modification of Pope's famous line—

> "If *science* lure thee—see how Bacon shined.
> The brightest, wisest, meanest of mankind".

To come to still nearer analogies with our subject. The most savage excesses of cruelty towards men and women have proved insufficient altogether to ossify the human heart, and we find the same Nero who murdered his mother and made pitch-torches of living Christians round his gardens, so kind a master to his favourite slaves that they mourned him with breaking hearts, and would no doubt have testified loudly to anybody who accused him of cruelty that he was the very best and gentlest of men.

Cruelty to animals, then, *a fortiori*, however extreme and deliberate it may be, does not necessarily and inevitably extend its corroding influence over every part of a man's character. Some two or three generations ago, indeed, when the notion of any kind of duty to the lower creatures was yet undeveloped in the common conscience (it is so even now among some classes of sportsmen, seal-hunters, trappers, and the like), we have no reason to doubt that every other moral obligation may have been respected by men who on this point were unawakened. You will remember that one of the greatest lights of the religious world of the last century was Newton of Olney, the friend of the gentle-hearted poet Cowper. Newton had been the master of a slave-ship for years, and during the horrible "Middle Passage" must have done and authorised things of which we shudder to read. Yet, after his conversion to the devoutest type of Christianity, we do not find any trace of self-reproach and self-abhorrence for that supreme iniquity—the "sum of all villainy"—as we have learned to recognise the slave-trade. Let us in justice, then, reject the application to Vivisection of the term "demoralising" *in the sense that the practice would demoralise a man all round.* We are not authorised to assume it does so, for example, as regards his family relations or his honesty in a commercial point of view,* though, like other persons who do things which they know to be abhorrent to the feelings of their neighbours, vivisectors are under an ever-present temptation to hypocrisy and equivocation which, I think, the records of the Royal Commission and several later events prove to have not seldom prevailed over their candour and veracity.

* An Italian advocate of Vivisection last year made a grand defence of a Neapolitan vivisector, urging that he could not be cruel to animals, *because* he was very fond of his little girl, and he (the speaker), had seen him caress her on his return from his laboratory. One of the audience remarked, that even the bandits of the Abruzzi were fond of their children, and after the massacre of a party of travellers were wont to return home and embrace their *brigantes-sini.*

The point, however, to which I beg your attention is not de-moralisation *extrinsic* to their pursuit, but demoralisation *intrinsic* in it. What is the moral condition of an habitual vivisector? While he is engaged in his chosen task day after day, is his state one of moral health or of moral disease? It is beyond our province to sift the motives which may lead a man to adopt experimental physiology as a profession. I am told that the most common is the very natural wish for young men to push themselves forward into that notice which is the path to pros-perity. Probably there are other cases wherein the science of physiology itself, without ulterior aims, exercises a strong fascina-tion as that of chemistry does to many disinterested chemists ; the only difference being that the chemists' acids and alkalies have no feeling, while the physiologist must ignore the feelings of his dogs and rabbits. I do not suppose—(I wish to do the worst vivisectors this justice)—I do not suppose that any of them under-take their work originally moved by sentiments of pleasure in the pain they inflict. For the moment I think we may start with the assumption that a vivisector begins usually with simple indifference to, or even some degree of pity for, animal suffering, and much zeal for science ; either science *pur et simple*, or science for the sake of his own (legitimate) ambition. In short, as has been said, he is simply prepared to "cut his way to knowledge and notoriety ". He is also undoubtedly—as the works of the foreign vivisectors show at every page—strongly moved by the desire to disprove what has been supposed to be discovered by rivals. There is a third motive which the advocates of Vivisection are very fond of putting forward as if it were the actual spring of their choice, viz., the motive of pure philanthropy. They sometimes tell us, in language so moving that it ought to draw tears from our eyes, that they see so much of the misery of disease that they would do anything (anything, that is, to a beast) to find out how to cure it. They are each, in fact, a Prometheus ready to steal the fire of heaven for the good of men ; and for that end—not exactly to be nailed themselves, but—to nail any number of dogs or monkeys to that dreadful Caucasus where Professor Rutherford may play the vulture on their livers, or Professor Ferrier on their brains. I find it, I confess, impossible to stretch my credulity quite so far as this, and for several reasons. First, the men who see most of the actual sufferings of humanity and labour night and day (all honour to them!) to relieve them are very seldom addicted to experimental physiology. Not one out of a dozen of the great vivisectors of Europe is a practical physician or surgeon, and some of the most eminent among the latter (notably Nélaton, Sir William Fergusson, and Mr. Lawson Tait) have given their emphatic opinion that nothing is to be gained for their humane purpose by Vivisection. In the second place, I cannot imagine so strangely constituted a being as a man, who should be enthusiastically anxious to relieve the sufferings of unseen men and women (that is, of humanity in the abstract), and yet care nothing at all for the intensest agonies of creatures immediately under his own eye and hand, which, moreover, he generally believes (on Darwin's authority) to be in nearly all respects like in power of suffering, and like in future destination, to the human beings for whom he would sacrifice them. Lastly, I do not believe the Promethean theory (as I beg leave to call it), for the best of reasons—because those who must know most about it, and are most likely to speak the truth about it, emphatically deny and deride it, and treat it as a piece of English hypocrisy to pretend to put it forward.

Adopted from whatever motive, the practice of experimental physiology when constituted into a profession may be regarded with some sad kind of interest. We, poor mortals, have each of us at the best—excluding the periods of youthful training and of declining age —about thirty or forty years to take our part in the things done under the sun. To the great majority of us that part must be a humble one : we must earn our bread in the sweat of our brow, and have not, perhaps, much choice as to the mode in which we do so. Still, we may usually hope that the labour of our brains or of our hands will tend to good and happiness, and that when our work is done at last, we may lay down the spade or the pen and go peacefully home to the eternal rest. But how does the vivisector's choice of a profession seem in this aspect ?

His vocation is to detect the secrets of organic life under the covering of skin beneath which nature has hidden them. He at least hopes to find out something (to use his favourite term) "interesting"—if not useful—to show how this or that nerve or muscle acts on the other; how certain poisons destroy the tissues; how long a dog or a rabbit takes to die in a stove at such a heat; and how long to be frozen in a tub of ice; and (very particularly) where Professor A's previous experiments have failed, and Professor B's experiments required to be repeated by Professor C. To do all this he will need to spend the best of his days in his laboratory among his instruments for cutting, sawing, picking out, burning, keeping up artificial breathing on curarised creatures; and so on.

Here is a description of such a laboratory (no doubt an exceptionally well-appointed one), as it was seen in vacation time by an eye-witness, our honoured friend Baron Weber.

"On the 22nd of August, 1878, I paid a visit to the physiological laboratory in the University of ——* It is in a large, palace-like building. Owing to the holidays and the absence of professors and students, the work of Vivisection was suspended. I was therefore only able to see the different machines and apparatuses, the cages, the empty stables, and the operating rooms. My guide, a regular servant of the institution, first of all led me to a large saloon and a small room on the ground floor, in which several tables and complicated instruments for Vivisection attracted my attention. The blood-stains still remaining on the long table clearly showed the purposes for which it had been used. I observed, too, a large machine worked by gas, having affixed to it an ingenious apparatus and bellows for pumping air incessantly, when required, into the lungs of the animals after they had been treated with curare. On asking whether the animals were rendered unconscious before being experimented on, the answer I received from my attendant was, 'All of them are poisoned with *curate*'. I was then shown the large iron cages, on the grated lids of which the dogs doomed to a painful death are laid, then

---

* Believed to be in Leizpig.

an iron cover is placed over them, having bars in it likewise, so as to allow of their death agonies being well observed. The last dog which had died in this way had been honoured with a *memento mori*, for on one of the sides of the box a student had drawn in chalk the head of a pretty little dog having angel's wings attached to his shoulders, and underneath had written, *Requiescat in pace!* My conductor afterwards led me into the cellars, where iron boxes are kept for securing the dogs till wanted for vivisection. In two small dimly-lighted chambers I saw twenty or thirty of these iron boxes, of different sizes, capable of holding nearly half a hundred dogs. 'And how may dogs are wanted here every year?' I asked. 'Oh, many, very many,' my conductor replied. 'But where do they all come from?' I again inquired. 'From the dealers and so on,' he answered with a grin on his face. What did this long-drawn 'and so on' mean? I need not trouble my readers with my suspicions on this head. An intelligent dog, which probably had had forebodings of the fate awaiting him, with wonderful perseverance had gnawed a considerable hole in one of the oaken doors, in the hope of making his escape. 'But it did not help the blackguard,' sneered my attendant, 'for he could not have got away.' The small windows are high up under the ceiling, and protected with iron bars, and the principal entrance to the cellars is always kept firmly closed. When these gloomy chambers are well filled with the poor intelligent friends and companions of man, awaiting their hours of torture, their whinings and howlings must be most painful to hear.

"My guide now led me into another small very cold room, in which were two large freezing-boxes : one for preserving the limbs and other parts of an animal; the other, a large round tub, my guide said, was 'for freezing a live dog till he becomes quite stiff'. A cold shudder creeps over one when one thinks of the poor terrified and whining animals, after being kept for weeks in these gloomy cellars, being thrown at last into the tub to be 'frozen stiff'. It has been shown that dogs frozen in this way, at intervals only, may live to the sixth day. (See Reports of the Imperial Rudolph Institution for 1869, p. 112.)

"After having been shown all the places set apart for the dogs, my guide took me to see the little pond for frogs; the bird house; the rabbit house, in which one of the four rabbits was lying dead, as it seemed to me from want of food; and lastly I was taken to the place where vivisection is practised on horses. What a miserable ending for those poor old steeds who have passed their lives in the service of man!

"In the most melancholy frame of mind I took leave of these chambers of horrors in this palace of scientific cruelty." *

If you care to finish more elaborately the picture in your mind's eye, you will read the chapter in Claude Bernard's *Physiologie Opératoire*, where he gives minute instructions how to seize and grasp the animals, mad with terror. They are, he complains, "*indocile*" on these occasions; and he "trembles" (physiologists are not very brave) when he sees an inexperienced colleague endeavour to seize a cat! There are machines by which the animals should be seized, long pincers which catch them round the neck, or a noose thrown over their heads, and then the cord is cleverly swung over a door. After this follows another interesting chapter on anæsthetics, narcotics, and curare used *as means of restraint* (the point of view in which genuine physiologists appear principally to regard them). Morphia, for example, which he greatly recommends, "plunges dogs," he says, "into a state of immobility which permits us to place them on an experimenting table without tying or muzzling them; but at the same time *sensibility remains*" (*Revue des Cours Scientifique*, vol. vi., p. 263). And elsewhere he says, "The animal *suffers pain, but has lost the faculty of resistance*". Of curare and all its horrors you probably know enough. Claude Bernard says its effects are "accompanied by *the most atrocious sufferings which the imagination of man can conceive*" (*Revue des Deux Mondes*, Sept., 1864), but nevertheless he mentions quite calmly (*Physiologie Opératoire*, p. 168): "It is now employed in *a vast number of experiments* as a means of restraining the animals. There are but few observations of which the

* *The Torture Chamber of Science*, by Ernst v. Weber.

narration does not commence by notifying that they were made on a curarised dog."

We may therefore take it unhappily for granted that our physiologists, English or foreign, will use curare (which is not *forbidden* by English law, only not accounted an anæsthetic), and that the majority of his victims at all events will undergo this doubled torture.

By-and-by his laboratory will have many creatures in it going through various stages of experiments according to the line of his research. There may be dogs whose eyes have suppurated away, the nutritive nerves at the back of the neck having been severed; others with the spinal marrow cut across, and the hinder limbs paralysed. Cats (perhaps, as in one case in St. Bartholomew's Hospital, ninety together enduring one series of experiments on their bile ducts, creating agony analogous to that of gall stones)—half lying dead about the floor and the rest dying. Beside these there may be a few rabbits and guinea-pigs fed on poisons, or diseased tissues, or inoculated with fetid matter; and two or three dogs which have been compelled for weeks to swallow alcohol till their condition is that of a drunkard expiring in delirium. An old ass crouches in the corner with the backbone, which bore so many burdens for man, sawn across at last; and here and there pigeons are fluttering senselessly, half their brains sliced away and only the ghastly semblance of a bird remaining. Lastly, two or three monkeys with their brains "like a lately-hoed potato field," as one physiologist has described it, becoming gradually idiotic, and exchanging their playfulness and affectionate ways for mournful misery, as they perish slowly of meningitis.

Before I leave these last poor creatures—the favourite subjects of some experiments of an English physiologist who has obtained no little notoriety thereby—I may be allowed to mention that the old heathen Galen, otherwise a merciless vivisector, is said to have found himself unable to bear the human-like semblance of a monkey's agony. After mentioning that he had for some time experimented on them, Claude Bernard states (*Phys. Opér.*, p. 67): " Par la suite, revolté par la ressemblance douleureuse des gestes du singe et de l'homme qui se débat, il se contenta d'agir sur des animaux qui ne presentait aucune ressemblance extérieure avec l'homme ". The great French vivisector himself seems to have received some similar impression, for he dissuades his students from vivisecting the ape, and adds : " Ses mains, ses gestes, ses régards douleureux inspirent toujours une certaine répugnance à le torturer ". Such squeamishness of old pagan and modern Frenchmen has, it seems, been entirely overcome by certain physiologists nearer home.

Do not let me be supposed to affirm that all these miserable creatures are likely to be found together at any one time or in one laboratory. They are specimens of the sort of work going on in various laboratories; and beside them we should expect to find one or more animals actually undergoing vivisection and tied down, or curarised on the torture-trough. The operations in some cases last eight or ten hours, till the wearied vivisector goes home to bed, leaving his victim on the trough to live through the night or be released by death, as may happen. I do not want, however, to dwell on the condition of these animals now, but only on the mental and moral state of the man to whom such a place as I have described is the chosen workshop of life ; what the studio is to the painter, the library to the student, the garden to the florist. In this bright world, among its million interests, *that* is his choice ! In old times when the " Question " was in use all over Europe, and breaking on the wheel was a frequent mode of execution on the Continent, it was a regular business to inflict these horrible punishments; and the executioners in the case of the " Question " were trained to the work and called " Sworn Tormentors ". Of course they were chosen from a very low order of men, and were looked on with horror by their fellow citizens. In Paris there was a family which for generations supplied executioners to the State, and lived wholly apart, the poorest of their neighbours refusing to have anything to do with them, or to intermarry with them. I suppose these unhappy men, who used to be called, one after another, in ridicule, " M. de Paris," must have become (on principles of heredity) as unfeeling about the performance of their dreadful office and the infliction of pain as it is possible for natural constituted human beings to be. But it is recorded that when one of them who was at work when Damiens was condemned received his directions for tearing that wretched assassin with pincers, he replied with a shudder, "No ! he could not do *that*," and resigned his office sooner than obey. Yet these *ténaillements* were absolutely and exactly the same things as an Italian vivisector recently described himself as having done to dozens of harmless animals "*con molto amore e pazienza*". Other of the operations performed by vivisectors more commonly are of a less dreadful nature : some of them, I rejoice to believe, are scarcely painful at all.   Again, others are incredibly odious and revolting, such as the searing with a red-hot iron of a half paralysed animal, or burning its muzzle, or whipping it, to try the amount of its remaining consciousness when half its brain has been taken out ; or adding to the agonies of its condition under mutilation by sewing up or clamping its mouth and eyes or other natural orifices.   Scarcely a rough village farrier in a farm-yard would condescend to the incredible nastiness of some of these gentlemen's operations, which I cannot describe.   You say no doubt, "This physiologist must have very remarkable tastes". True, but in what way?   Both Dr. Rolleston and Dr. Haughton had observed something in human nature which throws on this morbid taste a very lurid light.   Here is what Professor Rolleston told the Commission :

"Kingsley speaks of 'the sleeping devil that is in the heart of every man,' but you may say it is the lower nature which we possess in common with the carnivora.   It is just this—that the sight of a living, bleeding, and quivering organism most un-doubtedly does act in a particular way upon what Dr. Carpenter calls the emotiono-motor nature in us.   I know that many men are superior to it ; but I beg to say that, if we are talking of legis-lation, we are not to legislate for the few, but for the mass, who, I submit, are not always good. . . .   When men are massed together the emotiono-motor is more responsive, it becomes more sensitive to impressions than it is at other times.   That of course bears very greatly on the question of interference with vivisections as employed before masses. I know that I am likely to be exceedingly abused for what I have said."

Dr. Anthony gave his testimony to the same purpose.

"There is a morbid curiosity which is well known to medical men, with reference to operations of all kinds. There are a certain number of persons who are very fond of coming to see the different operations at the hospitals. I look upon that, and particularly on the desire of seeing these operations on animals, as something very, very morbid indeed."

The truth is that the man who has no natural abhorrence and disgust (*ribrezzo*, as the Italians say) at the sight of wounds and agony from which no benefit to the suffering creature is even dreamed of as a relief, or who, having once felt such *ribrezzo*, gets over it entirely, reaches a condition to which the word "callous" scarcely applies. I am afraid that an element of a certain kind of dreadful satisfaction, greediness of sight of horrors, comes over him. I fear he feels as did the women who sat gloating as they watched the guillotine at work in the old French Revolution. Do you charge me with slander in comparing a vivisector (say he who tortured 14,000 dogs in ten years) with the *tricoteuses* of Paris? Alas! the grounds on which I found my belief are very strong, for they are the words of two of the greatest vivisectors of the age, deliberately in their own books describing their ideal of a vivisector as they think he ought to be. Here is what Claude Bernard says—the man to whom Sir James Paget, Dr. Burdon-Sanderson, Professor Foster, and four other English advocates of Vivisection solicited subscriptions to raise the statue now erected in Paris. This is how Claude Bernard describes a vivisector:

"He is no ordinary man. He is a learned man, a man possessed and absorbed by a scientific idea. He does not hear the animals' cries of pain. He is blind to the blood that flows. He sees nothing but his idea, and organisms which conceal from him the secrets he is resolved to discover."

That is taken from the *Introduction à l'Étude de la Médécine Expérimentale*, p. 180, and it is, to my thinking, an awful picture of a man besotted with lust of knowledge, just as murderers are sometimes besotted with lust of gold: the one as pitiless and as regardless of all law, divine or human, as the other. But there is a still darker picture drawn at full length by Cyon, the author of the great standard work which I hold in my hand, the *Methodik*. If anyone doubts the accuracy of the translation which I shall read, I will read out the original. Before doing so, however, it may perhaps interest you to know that the author has recently referred to his book in a long article in the *Gaulois* newspaper, and mentioned as an excellent joke that, when the book was coming out four years ago, his English colleagues implored him not to allow it to be advertised in England. They feared, he said, lest public opinion in England should be alarmed. Here, then, finally, is the perfect picture of a vivisector by Cyon :

"The true vivisector must approach a difficult vivisection with the same joyful excitement and the same delight wherewith a surgeon undertakes a difficult operation from which he expects extraordinary consequences. He who shrinks from cutting into a living animal, he who approaches a vivisection as a disagreeable necessity, may very likely be able to repeat one or two vivisections, but will never become an artist in Vivisection. He who cannot follow some fine nerve-thread, scarcely visible to the naked eye, into the depths, if possible sometimes tracing it to a new branching, with joyful alertness for hours at a time ; he who feels no enjoyment when at last, parted from its surroundings and isolated, he can subject that nerve to electrical stimulation ; or when, in some deep cavity, guided only by the sense of touch of his finger-ends, he ligatures and divides an invisible vessel,—to such a one there is wanting that which is most necessary for a successful vivisector. The pleasure of triumphing over difficulties held hitherto insuperable is always one of the highest delights of the vivisector. And the sensation of the physiologist, when from a gruesome wound, full of blood and mangled tissue, he draws forth some delicate nerve-branch, and calls back to life a function which was already extinguished—this sensation has much in common with that which inspires a sculptor when he shapes forth fair living forms from a shapeless mass of marble."

I said at starting that cruelty to animals does not demoralise a man in *all* ways, but I ask you now, does it not demoralise him *enough ?* The old monks used to think there was a special Devil for gluttony, another for pride, another for sensual vice, and so on ; each demon possessing the soul which yielded to its temptations. If we could believe in a new Fiend of Scientific Cruelty come forth from the Pit, and entering into the souls of physiologists, could we have more lurid light cast into the depths of a possessed man's soul than that of this description? If higher intelligences look down on the things of earth, if—as I believe—the awful Lord of All beholds them, then, it seems to me, the hideous sight of those bared and quivering nerves of the mangled brute must be less frightful in His holy eyes than the human heart wherein every chord of compassion is thus dead beyond revival. Remember, I do not wish you to suppose that all vivisectors have realised the type described by Cyon—Heaven forbid that it should yet be so! But this is what is before them, this is the full-blown flower, of which the English vivisector is perhaps but a bud. Nay, rather, to borrow their own more appropriate language, this is the fever at its normal height. What we have as yet are only the germs of the disease, finding their appropriate nidus in some callous hearts, and breeding in darkness the pestilence which shall hereafter walk at noonday through the land.

Judge now I beg of you, as to the Higher Expediency, the utility as regards all the nobler interests of the community, of allowing this practice to continue, and this type of character to be fixed and multiplied. Good men have been labouring in England for sixty years since the days of Richard Martin to humanise the masses, to suppress brutal sport, to lead the working classes and their children to feel a kindly interest in cattle and horses and asses, dogs and cats and birds ; and the success of their efforts has been wonderful. But what a backwater and ebb of the tide of humanity is in store for us if Vivisection is to become an English institution, sanctioned by law and practised freely all over the country ! How must the poor costermongers feel when they see learned gentleman permitted to do, and even honoured for doing, things a thousand times more cruel than the rough usage of their beasts for which they have been fined and sent to jail ? How must the children in the Bands of Mercy feel when they are told that the dogs and cats and pigeons they have been taught to love and treat tenderly are to be sold to the dealer in the next street that he may send them to the laboratory to be cut up alive? What must the young gentlemen, ay, and the young ladies, who are studying physiology at their colleges and universities become, when they have been subjected for a time to the moral blight of the instruction of such a professor as Cyon has depicted?

A few years since many elaborate experiments were made by the medical officer of the Privy Council to find a cure for cattle-plague. At the end of all, the only advice which could be given to the Government and the farmers was the very simple one, which might have been offered without any experiment—"Stamp it out!" We have now, my friends, to deal with another kind of epidemic, a pestilence affecting—*not* our cattle or even our own bodies, but—the very hearts and souls of men. We have made the "experiment" of a restrictive law (tried a "cultivated virus," in short), and it has proved, as other such boasted nostrums are sure to prove by-and-by, utterly futile. There remains only one course to be adopted as regards this plague of Scientific Cruelty, and I implore you to take it—" STAMP IT OUT ".

IV

THE RIGHT OF TORMENTING.

Mr. Lecky observes that "only during the present century have
the relations of man to brute been brought within the scope of
ethics". It is no wonder that such should be the case, for the
sense of moral obligations towards alien races of men has only
been developed in modern times. The old Jew had scanty mercy
for the Gentile, the Greek for the Barbarian; and all the wild
tribes of Africa and America still regard their neighbours much as
dogs regard cats. The Red Indian will travel hundreds of miles
merely to destroy the villages of the inoffensive Esquimaux. By
degrees, however, the blessed lessons of sympathy and mutual
obligation have extended among civilised mankind, though very
imperfectly still between races distinguished by difference of
colour. How many white men in America, for example, recognise
without reluctance the rights of negroes? What wonder is it, then,
that the idea of owing any duty or forbearance towards non-human
creatures has only quite recently developed itself, and among the
highest nations only? In the memory of men now alive, the pen
of Sidney Smith occupied the pages of the *Edinburgh Review*
with scoffs and sneers at Richard Martin and Erskine for introducing the first Act of any legislation in the world against cruelty

4

to animals. That the state of things at that time needed such legislation, we have only to read one of the novels or tour books of the period to satisfy ourselves. Horses were ridden and driven to death by every young "spark" who could afford to hire one; dogs were used cruelly for draught, and tormented in the streets by brutal boys; cats were skinned alive; and the pious Alleyne recorded in his journal that he paid thirteen pence to afford his friends the pleasure of "Whipping the Blind Bear"!

Now it is my contention that the physiologists, immersed in their studies, have just *stopped at this point.* They are not *before* the age, as they would have us think, and in the "foremost files of time"; but they are *behind* it, and still at the same moral level as the working classes were generally in England eighty or a hundred years ago.

Meanwhile the rest of mankind have morally advanced, and in no direction more markedly than in that of a newly awakened sense of the duty of kindness to animals. But this sense is as yet vague and scarcely formulated; and we all feel when we reflect on the subject, that the nature of that duty and the limits of our rights are exceedingly difficult to define. Bishop Butler's great axiom (which cannot be too often called to mind)—that on the simple fact of a creature being *sentient, i.e.,* conscious of pain, arises our duty to spare it pain—forms the broad basis for all we have to build. But I confess I heartily wish that that noble thinker—the greatest name in the great Church of England—the man, be it remembered in this connection, who said he found no reason why animals should not be immortal,—I wish that this man had gone further, and helped us to define better where to draw the line between cruelty on the one hand, and on the other such impracticable tenderness as that which would spare noxious insects and parasites.

Pondering over these things for years, a method has suggested itself to me of testing the justice of our conduct in any particular towards the brutes. Let me venture to lay it before you, and if it approve itself, we may then take it with us and apply it to this grievous question of Vivisection. Let us suppose that there is an *Umpire* between man and brute—a disinterested and just Spectator, who can alike understand the man's wants and needs, and the inarticulate cries of the humble brute. Such an Umpire, my friends, I believe, actually exists, and I name Him, GOD; but for sake of argument with the physiologist it may be better to speak simply of a hypothetical Umpire and Referee. What sentence, I ask, would such a dispassionate Arbiter pass on our general conduct towards the lower creatures?

Let us suppose the man to say: "I wish to rear sheep, cows, swine, fowls. I will take pains that the species be multiplied; and each individual, so far as I can do it, shall be comfortably fed and sheltered, and supplied with the necessaries of a happy animal's existence for a certain number of months or years—on condition that at the end of that time I am at liberty to take its life in the quickest and least painful way possible—a way far preferable to natural death by old age." Would the Umpire, on behalf of the animal, accept of this bargain? There can be no question he would freely sanction it.

Or suppose the man to say: "I wish to rear horses to drag my plough or carry me on their backs, and dogs and cats to guard my property and be my own fireside companions. I will give them amply sufficient food and water, and I will not overwork my horses, or cause my dog's life to be miserable by chaining it constantly like a criminal. They shall be mercifully killed if at any time their lives become burdensome." Again the Umpire would surely say: "So be it".

Here, then, all our relations to the domestic animals are sufficiently covered and sanctioned. We have only to fulfil our side of the implied contract of careful provision for them while they live and a quick death at the end, to feel that our use of them is morally right, and such as cannot offend their Maker and ours.

Then we have to consider the case of wild animals; and, regarding some of them, the man may say: "They and I are natural enemies, and must always be in a state of war. I must kill them in defence of my life if they be lions or wolves, or in defence of my property or health if they be vermin or parasites."

Again the Arbiter says: "It is well: these creatures would prey on you if you did not prey on them. You are within your rights in destroying them."

The last case is more difficult. It is that of wild animals, such as really wild game and fish (I am not speaking of deer and pheasants, whose case is the same as that of cattle), creatures on which we have conferred no benefit and which threaten us with no hurt if we leave them alone, but which we kill for food. The man pleads: "I need food, and in devouring these animals I only take my place among the carnivora of the world. Nearly all of them live upon other and smaller creatures. Why should my life, the most valuable of all, not be sustained at the cost of theirs? I engage to kill them as quickly as possible."

The answer to this, I believe, would still be acquiescent, though, perhaps, less completely so than in the former cases. Man is here not the lord of the world, but merely a link in the chain of animal life. A clear limitation, however, exists in the terms of the authorisation. It must be *bonâ fide* for use that the harmless wild creature is deprived of life, not killed for the pleasure of killing— as people shoot seagulls by the shore, or pigeons in the disgusting matches at Hurlingham.

Lastly, we come to quite another problem. The man says: "I wish to vivisect an animal. Up to this hour its life has been well cared for, and it has, on its part, served and loved mankind as its powers permitted. Now I wish to tie it down on a vivisecting table, and ascertain, by cutting it open, various interesting facts of science likely to be more or less useful by-and-by. Its death will not occur for several hours, and in the interval it will suffer excruciating agony. Nothing can comfort it, for it knows nothing of the hopes and faith which have sustained human martyrs on the rack. It will feel only that the men whom it loved as if they were gods, have turned to become its tormentors. Utterly helpless, bound, and gagged, and, perhaps, paralysed with curare, it will lie for hours on its torture-trough till my mangling work on its flesh, and bones, and nerves, and brain is fully and slowly accomplished ; and then it may be suffered to expire."

What does the Arbiter say now? The lives of the animals in all the other cases we have supposed were on the whole a joy and blessing, and their deaths were not more painful (generally much less so) than the natural deaths of old age or disease. But the vivisected creature's whole existence has been turned into a misfortune and a curse. The hours of its keen and excessive agony outweigh immeasurably all its poor little harmless joys of food and sunshine, and the love of its master and its offspring. It were well for that creature had it never been born. Does the Supreme Umpire then view such things and sanction them? Can we for a moment suppose Him to pass sentence justifying the vivisector? Nay, my friends, it seems to me that a heavy, heavy condemnation must fall on such tyrannous misuse of human power, and that the voice of every unbiased conscience must pronounce such vivisection a moral offence in the forum of ethics, and a heinous sin before the judgment-seat of God.

This is one view of the case. In another way we may look at it, and note that one of two things must hold. Either our fundamental axiom is false, and a creature, although sentient, has *no* right to be spared pain, and the whole brute creation has absolutely *no* claims at all upon man, who may act to it the part of a devil without offence ; or else, at the very least, man is forbidden to inflict on any animal a torture worse than death. That is the very *minimum* to which we can reduce their claims, if they have any claims at all. Taking their lives is the last stretch of human rights ; making their lives such a curse as that they had better have perished at their birth, is a step far beyond killing them, and one which stands condemned on any principle which we can formulate, except the repudiation of all duty towards them. That vivisectors and their supporters do practically regard animals as having no rights as against man, and that they think *la loi du plus fort* all that is needed for the justification of their cruelties, is unhappily too evidently the real state of the case, albeit not a few of these tormentors are actually members of societies (and in one notorious case, a vice-president of a society) for the prevention of cruelty to animals !*

You will observe that all these arguments concern the question only of *excessively painful* Vivisection. It is the infliction of *torture* which stands condemned by what we have said. That is the first thing. Now I shall tell you why I think that Vivisection, even when it does not inflict torture or severe pain, ought to be forbidden by law, and why the whole practice ought to be totally prohibited.

Assuming that we have proved that the infliction of torture is a moral offence, the corollary follows that, if Vivisection cannot be sanctioned without opening a door to that offence—if no line can be drawn between experiments *per se* almost harmless, and those which involve gross cruelty—if no protection can be given to an animal once it is laid on the vivisecting table in a laboratory, and no guarantee can be obtained of a vivisector's mercy—then the whole practice ought to be stopped. If it be found impossible to separate the use of a thing from the abuse, and that abuse amount to a great moral offence, then it becomes needful to prohibit the use. The Scottish Society and several English societies stepped before us in Victoria Street, in demanding, from the outset the *total* prohibition of Vivisection ; while we only asked for " the utmost possible protection to animals liable to Vivisection ". But I think we may all rejoice that the Victoria Street Society tried the more moderate demand in the first place ; and that thus, without fear of being deemed hasty, or hot-headed, or *doctrinaire*, it has exhibited the spectacle of a band of men of high political and social importance, *des hommes sérieux*, in short, driven on by the logic of facts and the lessons of experience, taught by infructuous legislation and delusive Returns, to quit their original standing ground, and raise their demands to the absolute suppression of a practice which cannot be curbed within the bounds of humanity. The speeches which have been made at our meetings will show you why men so little likely to be borne

* Prof. Ludwig of Leipzig.

away by impulse, and differing so widely from each other politically and religiously as the late Lord Shaftesbury, the Cardinal Archbishop of Westminster, and the Lord Chief Justice of England, yet have one and all come round to the same unhesitating conclusion—*that Vivisection ought to be totally abolished.*

The practical fact is, that Vivisection is a *Method* of research, a useful method, we must presume, in the opinion of those who employ it, though a misleading one in our opinion and in that of many better competent than we to judge the matter. Now, a *method* like this cannot be pursued half-and-half; employed to a certain extent and then dropped or exchanged for another. It must either be maintained *as a method*, or stopped *as a method* and the labours of physiologists turned into the other and, as we think, more truly scientific channels of clinical and microscopic observation. There is no compromise really possible. The idea entertained by the Royal Commission of the "reconciliation of the claims of science and humanity" was wholly delusive. Science ignores humanity, and will be "reconciled" with nothing which stops her invasions by an inch.

And, after all, is not this just what might have been expected? How should it be otherwise? How should such a monstrous notion of our relations to the animals as lies at the root of Vivisection be reconcilable in any way with the laws of sympathy and humanity?

Hitherto I have been discussing the question from the barest and coldest ground of pure ethics. But if I saw a little blue-eyed, fair-haired baby crowing in the sunshine, and holding up its little arms for my embrace, and a wretch of a nurse were to come and deliberately knock its head on the stones, I should not, I think, require to appeal to ethical arguments to satisfy myself that the nurse was doing wrong or to induce me to rush forward and save the baby and pitch the nurse to Jericho—or further. In a similar way we who have made pets of our dogs, or horses, or cats, or even our poor little guinea-pigs and rabbits and doves, when we think of them as kept for days in a vivisector's cellar, then brought out into the daylight of the laboratory, trembling and terrified; piteously, perchance, begging for mercy, but thrown on the torture-trough, tied down, gagged—only the speaking eye still pleading; then slowly carved alive, the nerves dissected out, and all the horrible apparatus of science brought to bear on the poor little quivering frame, which used to respond so lovingly to the caress of our hand,—when we think of this, I say, we do not need to go over all the moral reasons which prove that such deeds stand condemned by God's eternal law. We feel,—well, it is better not to say what I, for one, feel towards the smooth, cool man of science who stands by that torture-trough. Is it wrong to feel so? Nay; but I should be utterly heartless if I failed to feel for a creature who has loved me, and on whom I have bestowed affection.

If Vivisection is to be tolerated at all—if we are to regard the Dog (for example) as the two thousand doctors expressed in their Memorial to the Home Office in 1875, as "*a carnivorous creature specially valuable for the purposes of research*" (*i.e.,* to be carved alive to satisfy scientific curiosity),—then we must, for very shame's sake, and to prevent our children from becoming cynical hypocrites, stop at once all talking and teaching of sympathy and love to animals. If we are going to give up the poor brute to be dissected alive, then, in Heaven's name, let us try to think of it as a mere automaton, a senseless bit of animated matter, which can have no feeling, no intelligence, no faithful affection. To admire its intelligence and fidelity, and lead our children to caress it and to note all its beautiful instincts, and *then* to deliver it to the tormentors,—that is something baser and more odious than the perfidy of an Eastern tyrant. It is only because of our stolid ignoring of the claims of the brutes which prevents us from feeling sick with disgust at such cold-blooded hypocrisy. Let us fancy superior beings—angels, or God Himself—treating *us* in like manner; accepting our humble services, drawing forth our adoring love and fidelity, and then coldly consigning us to the torture chambers whence we shall never escape! Truly when we think of these things the awful words seem to sound in our ears: " With what measure ye mete, it shall be measured to you again ".

I have, I hope, said enough of the reasons why we ask for the total prohibition of Vivisection, on grounds of morality, and of natural, honest human feeling. As I said at starting, if we prove the practice to involve a great moral offence (perhaps I ought to say more exactly, to be so inextricably connected with a great moral offence as that it is practically impossible to sanction it and yet avert the offence), then the exhibition of the fortunate results which might be expected from the practice is irrelevant. If we have no right to invade a defenceless country which lies at our mercy, it would be deemed cynically immoral to write leading articles and make parliamentary speeches, to show how much plunder we might obtain by ravishing it.

But our opponents, who are almost to a man Utilitarians, if not Agnostics, are by no means willing to settle the question on the grounds of simple deductive morals. For a large benefit to the human race, they will generally contend that almost anything is justifiable : and certainly such a small thing as is, in their account, the torture of animals. In short, not a few of them talk grandilo-quently of their *duty* to vivisect, in the "sacred cause of humanity"; and bid us stand by and admire their deep sympathy with human suffering, which makes them sacrifice all their own tender senti-ments of compassion to animals in the hope of bringing some relief to the sick bed from the laboratory. Thus, then, we are brought up short out of what, I suppose, they would call the high *priori* road of discussion, and challenged to say whether Vivisection, even if it be a wrong to the brutes, is not such a service to man as amply to justify its professors in disregarding the lesser obligation? As this line of appeal reaches many good and conscientious hearts, and has been fortified by Dr. Darwin's solemn denunciation of anti-vivisectors as persons who would sacrifice the great interest of the human race to mistaken sentiment, I feel bound to confront it straightforwardly and carefully.

My friends, do not fear that you will sacrifice the interests of mankind by stopping the torture of animals. Those interests never can, and never will, while God reigns on high, be furthered by cruelty and wrong. We need never fear that we relinquish any real good for our race by following out the dictates of justice and mercy.   It is an *impious* doctrine—I say it deliberately, an *impious* doctrine—that God has made it any man's duty to commit the great sin of cruelty by way of obtaining a benefit for suffering humanity ; or that it is the duty of the community to sanction such cruelty for its own benefit.   After all, what are the boasted benefits to be obtained by Vivisection ?   I do not deny that a remedy for any of the diseases of our fleshy tabernacles would be a great benefit ; but, I say, that even for *that*, the price of hardened hearts, and blunted sympathies, and intellects trained to the passionless registration of agony, would be too heavy a price.   I do not believe in the cures said to be effected by help of Vivisection. When we sift any of these stories so often dinned in our ears, we usually find, that if the physiologists have really found a cure or an improved mode of treatment of disease, it has been by methods which (as Dr. Clay says of his most famous operation) " have no more to do with Vivisection than the Pope of Rome ".*

But even *if* I be mistaken—if vivisectors have already made or shall hereafter make discoveries, tending directly and importantly to relieve our bodily pains, even *then* would Vivisection, I ask, stand justified ?   Not so, my friends, assuredly.   Bodily health, relief from pain, prolongation of life, are not the only or the greatest good to be sought by man.   The arguments which these doctors—and, alas ! several bishops also—adopt, all rest on the crude, stupid, *heathenish* assumption that the moral interests of mankind are not worth considering, and the physical interests are all in all.   The unexpressed major term of the whole argument of the Bishop of Peterborough, as I heard him in the House of Lords, was this : " That a practice which, in the opinion of experts, conduces to the bodily health of one or more persons, becomes, *ipso facto*, morally lawful and right ".   I leave you to reflect on the consequences of the adoption of this principle in the present state of medical opinion, and of the sort of practices

* Referring to the operation claimed by the Bishop of Peterborough in the House of Lords as the great triumph of Vivisection, and of which Dr. Clay was the originator.   (See *Brit. Med. Journal*, July 17, 1880.)

which would be lifted accordingly from the rank of Vices to Virtues !

Yet, if this major term be unsound, the whole argument of the lawfulness of Vivisection deduced from its supposed beneficent results falls entirely to the ground. The Inquisitors of old took really higher ground when they professed to burn a few heretics in *the immortal* interests of mankind, and to save, not merely this life, but the life hereafter from destruction.

I often think, however, that we are very "soft" as regards these vivisectors, when we listen to their pretensions to zeal for the benefit of humanity as justifying their disgusting pursuit. These English *augurs*, like those of ancient Rome, must smile when they find one another practising on the gullibility of the public. Foreign physiologists do not think it worth their while to make pretensions to such a sublime enthusiasm of humanity. Dr. Herman, of Zurich, frankly wrote in his famous pamphlet (*Die Vivisections-frage*) : "The advancement of our knowledge and not practical utility to medicine is the true and straightforward object of all Vivisection" (p. 16). I do not deny that there may have been here and there a vivisector who loathed his work (as any man with a heart in his bosom must loathe it), and yet occasionally performed painful experiments in the ardour of scientific research. Such a man, I believe, was Sir Charles Bell. But few and rare are the experiments such a man would, or did, perform ; and often, like your own great Dr. Syme, they would end by repenting all they had done, and denouncing the practice. But if any doctor tells me that Claude Bernard baked his seventeen dogs in a stove, and Mantegazza larded his forty animals with nails, and Schiff tormented his fourteen thousand dogs, all with compunction and regret, and such pain as anyone with natural unperverted feelings would experience, then I say simply, " I don't believe it ". I consider the pretence that they did so as one more of the tolerably numerous (shall we say ?) *illusions* of which a certain " noble profession " will some day be ashamed.

So much for the supposed *motive* of vivisectors, which (I have heard it argued) may nullify the deadly moral consequence of a life spent in the work of torture. We anti-vivisectors are sad sceptics. It is true that we almost to a man believe in God, and in such a thing as duty ; but then we somehow do not believe quite implicitly in physiologists ! We think a man who will bake, and burn, and lard with nails, and dissect alive harmless and helpless creatures is possibly capable of cloaking his hateful proceedings under a mantle of philanthropy when he is talking to the mere Philistine lay public. We think that a man who freely chooses for himself the life-work of a Familiar of this modern Inquisition, a sworn Tormentor of the new Question Chamber ; a man who devotes his few years under the sun, in God's bright world, to the task which the imagination of Dante has given to the fiends in the pit of darkness—we think, I say, that that man's soul suffers under more deadly disease than the palsies and cancers for which he vainly pretends to seek the cure. For my own part, I say, and I think you will all say with me, Let me bear the burdens which God may lay on me, and die when to Him seems good. But let me go out of this life of shadows into the eternal world, able to think it would not be an implied *curse* I should invoke on my soul were I to desire, like Theodore Parker, that over my grave should be read the words : " Blessed are the merciful, for they shall obtain mercy ".

V.

WHAT IS CRUELTY?

FROM THE "ZOOPHILIST".

THIS question recurs so often in the anti-vivisection controversy, and such vague and conflicting replies are commonly given
to it, that we believe it may be serviceable to our readers if we
present them with the definition of Cruelty which, on careful reflection, appears to us most accurate. It will be borne in mind
that we deal only with that most serious kind of Cruelty which
constitutes a great Moral Offence—namely, the infliction of very
severe Pain (or torture) of body or mind. There are minor forms
of Cruelty (more properly, perhaps, to be described as *Unkindness*),
consisting in the infliction of small Pains or annoyances, or the
deprivation of Pleasures, in either case without adequate reason.
With these unkindnesses we shall not here concern ourselves. It
may be noted, however, that, while the sanctity of human life places
unjustified homicide in the first rank of crime, in the case of the
lower animals on the contrary, killing them in a painless or quasi-
painless manner, may best be considered, ethically, as *depriving
them of the sum of the Pleasures* which prolonged life might give
them. Thus, to kill an animal painlessly may be perfectly justifiable on many grounds, and even be merciful if the creature's
sufferings necessarily outbalance its pleasures; or it may be an
act of Unkindness (minor cruelty), as the case may happen. But
it is, under no circumstances, equivalent to the infliction of extreme
Pain (torture) whereby the creature is not merely deprived of the
Pleasure of existence, but existence is converted into an evil.

The reasons, therefore, which may justify killing animals do not justify torturing them.

CRUELTY may be objectively defined as *the voluntary infliction by a Moral Free Agent on a Sentient Being of severe Pain, not beneficent to the sufferer and not authorised by Justice.*

The infliction of Pain is beneficent to the sufferer :

> *a.* When, in the case of a Moral and Intelligent being, it is calculated to obtain for him overbalancing Moral or Mental advantages (*e.g.*, corrective Punishments).
>
> *b.* When, in the case of any Sentient being, it is calculated to obtain for him overbalancing physical advantages (*e.g.*, Surgical operations).

The infliction of severe pain is authorised by Justice :

> *a.* When it is the proportionate Retribution for trespass (*e.g.*, Judicial punishments).
>
> *b.* When it is the Repression of invasion of rights (*e.g.*, wounds given in War or in self-defence).
>
> *c.* When compensation is made for it, presumably acceptable to the sufferer.

CRUELTY, subjectively defined, may be of any of the following classes :

> *a. Ignorant Cruelty ;* the cruel person being unaware of the pain which he causes.
>
> *b. Careless Cruelty ;* the cruel person being indifferent to the pain which he causes.
>
> *c. Wanton Cruelty ;* the cruel person causing pain for the sake of the emotional excitement which he derives from the spectacle.
>
> *d. Malignant Cruelty ;* the cruel person causing pain from hatred of his victim, and taking direct pleasure in his pain.
>
> *e. Interested Cruelty ;* the cruel person causing pain, with or without reluctance, for ulterior purposes of his own or the benefit of third parties.

It will be perceived that, of all the above classes of cruelty, that which is most dangerous is the *Interested Cruelty*, which inflicts severe pain for ulterior purposes. *Ignorant Cruelty* can be in-structed, *Careless Cruelty* may be admonished and corrected, *Wanton Cruelty* and *Malignant Cruelty* are condemned alike by law and public opinion, and are already in process of suppression in all civilised countries. But the *Interested Cruelty* which justifies the torture it inflicts by pointing to profits to be obtained thereby, cannot be instructed or admonished, nor, in the present state of law and public opinion, can it always be punished or reprehended. Yet this is the precise kind of cruelty from which all the worst crimes recorded in history have sprung. Rarely, indeed, has it happened that some ulterior purpose of public benefit has not formed the alleged justification of tortures, whenever and by whomsoever inflicted. It was in the interests of Order and the tranquillity of the Roman State that the Ten Persecutions of the early Christians took place. It was for the preservation of the souls of men from eternal perdition that Catholics made *autos da fé* of Jews and heretics, and that Protestants burned a hundred thousand witches. It was for the safeguard of the Crown and nation that innumerable suspected persons were, in the fifteenth and sixteenth centuries, subjected to the Question by the rack. Even as regards animals, cruelties on a large and systematic scale, such as producing *foie gras,* and flaying living goats and seals, are uniformly committed in the interests of dealers and their customers. In short, were we able to eliminate all *Interested Cruelties* from the wrongs of the human race and of the lower animals, we should find but a small and evanescent residue. On this point, therefore, of *Interested Cruelty,* the whole question of one of the greatest of moral offences practically hinges ; and it is to the last degree important that the obscurity which, in cuttle-fish fashion, the advocates of Vivisection have created around it, should be cleared away. Once for all, let it be understood : *Cruelty does not cease to be cruel because the person who inflicts unjustified and, to the sufferer, useless pain, has in view the interests of other parties ;* any more than theft ceases to be theft because the thief intends to apply the stolen property to the use of his friends.

Many of the advocates of Vivisection have been clear-sighted enough to perceive that their case cannot rest safely on the mere allegation of interests to be subserved by the torture of animals, and have endeavoured to buttress it by the introduction of a doctrine which, in such a connection, is absurdly out of place, namely, that of Vicarious Sacrifice. The divine idea of *the voluntary and conscious self-sacrifice of A for the welfare of B, C, and D* is, by one of those feats of logical legerdemain for which physiologists are famous, made to appear the same thing as the *enforced and unintelligent sacrifice of A, by B, for C's sake !* In other words, we are called on to acquiesce, as if in a sacred and transcendental kind of justice, in the very proceeding which we have always recognised as the essence of *in*justice, namely, "Robbing Peter to pay Paul". If Alice Ayres, instead of heroically sacrificing herself to save her sister's children, had killed one of them to form an easy cushion for the fall of herself and the others, she would precisely have exemplified the vivisector's idea of Vicarious Sacrifice.

VI.

THE NEW MORALITY.

"Blessed are the merciless, for they shall obtain useful knowledge."—New Gospel of Science, Chapter First.

WHEN Mr. Darwin published his greatest work, *The Descent of Man*, he included in it a sketch of the origin and nature of the Moral Sense, such as he supposed he had discovered them to be. In returning him thanks for the great favour he had done to the present writer, in giving her a copy of the book before its publication, she sorrowfully wrote that, in her humble judgment, his views on Morals, if ever generally adopted, would "sound the knell of the virtue of mankind".

It was not then, nor for some time afterwards, quite clear in which direction the new theories would affect practical morality, but it was obvious to anyone who had studied the philosophy of morals that a blow had been struck at the very root of the tree. Unfortunately, while thousands of divines and laymen are always ready to fling themselves with ardour into every controversy which touches ecclesiastical concerns, scarcely one can be found at any time to tackle seriously even the most dangerous of the moral heresies which are broached on all sides in these days. An adequate exposure of the narrow limitations within which any degree of validity ought to be conceded to the Darwinian doctrine of Hereditary Conscience yet waits to be made ; while that pestilent theory, together with the practical application to human affairs of the example supposed to be set by Nature in the "Struggle for Existence," are very rapidly, it is to be feared, undermining the ethics of our generation.

The point on which this vast and portentous controversy here

5

concerns us is the deduction now drawn from Darwinian morality in favour of Vivisection. To put it briefly, the argument amounts to this : " Nature is extremely cruel, but we cannot do better than follow Nature. The law of the Survival of the Fittest, applied to human agency, implies the absolute right of the Strong (*i.e.*, of those who can prove themselves Fittest) to sacrifice the Weak and Unfit, *ad libitum*." Sometimes, and by their most candid and honest adherents, these views are upheld simply as a corollary from the new natural philosophy. This is Nature's plan, they say, in effect; and Man, as merely a part of Nature, can do nothing more proper or sagacious than to fall in with it. Others (and these, we confess, shock us infinitely more) proceed to argue that in following Nature's apparent recklessness in inflicting suffering, man will be *obeying God ;* and that they possess, in short, a new view of religious duty much more extensive and well founded than the old. This view is—that we should each on our small scale carry out those tremendous and pitiless laws which govern the hurricane and the earthquake, and which are ex- emplified in the instincts of the vulture and the tiger. As an instance of the latter style of argument we may refer to Dr. Gore, *On the Utility and Morality of Vivisection* (London, Kolckman, 1884). He says, among other striking things: " The complete disregard of human and animal life by the operations of Nature, as in the recent earthquakes at Ischia and Java, *ought to teach us* that in cases where objects of greater importance and magnitude are involved, pain and death, even of countless numbers of men and animals, is a secondary matter. The necessity of new know- ledge, and of pain and toil to obtain it, are unavoidable conditions of life, and to find fault with this, or object to take the means necessary for gaining such knowledge, *is disobedience of divine commands.*" *

Mr. Girdlestone goes further, and, after rehearsing some re- cently discovered facts in natural historyconcerning the paralysing

* Dr. Gore goes on here to say : " As pain is the unavoidable condition of life, it is our duty to bear it with the least complaint " (p. 25). Quite true— but to *inflict* it ?

of prey intended for their young by wasps and polecats, he says that the inference plainly deducible is that, "so far as Nature's teaching extends, some animals are *meant* to be at the service, even to the point of Vivisection, of other animals, and that Vivisection practised in the service of a higher species is neither unnatural nor impious, unless, at least, we mean to accuse the Author of Nature of impiety" (*Vivisection in its Scientific, Religious, and Moral Aspects*, by G. D. Girdlestone, p. 58).

Similar arguments have been very frequently used by other advocates of scientific cruelty,* and it is becoming clear that the opponents of the practice will, for the future, be frequently called on to reply to the question, "Why should we be more merciful than Nature? Is not the will of God—if we are to believe in God at all—revealed in the laws of Nature? And if so, can we do better than imitate them?"

We think that our friends will do well to face this solemn problem seriously and quietly for themselves before entering on any controversy with pro-vivisectors, and be prepared with such answers as on deliberation they see fit. By no means should they attempt to dispute the facts of the mysterious evil and apparent cruelty in Nature, for on this head the student of Science will make good his ground; but they should (we respectfully recommend) clearly repudiate from first to last this new doctrine—that human Duty is to be learned from external Nature, animate or inanimate; or that God has intended His rational creatures to imitate wild beasts and earthquakes. The final cause of the treacherous and seemingly cruel instincts of many tribes of

* Some go further, and hint pretty plainly that they consider the *involuntary* agony of the poor dog on the torture-trough to be a perfect parallel to the "vicarious sacrifice" of Calvary—a parallel (if it were one) which would place the vivisectors in the same category as Judas and Pilate. Mr. Girdlestone says: "It evidently never occurred to him (St. Paul), or to any writer in the Bible from end to end, that any brute had any right to balance against man's convenience" (p. 40). "Vivisection pain, even prolonged and acute pain inflicted on any brute for the sake of a brother man, for whom Christ died, I should be ashamed of myself indeed if I found fault with anyone for inflicting it" (p. 42).

animals has been pondered with awe-stricken and aching hearts by
thousands of religious-minded men, and will doubtless be sought
in vain by thousands more, till the scales of mortality drop from
our eyes, and the faltering faith of earth is changed for the
rapturous insight of heaven.   But it was reserved for the advocates of Vivisection to treat these dark instincts of unreasoning
creatures, *not* as difficulties in the way of Faith, but as examples
expressly planned by the Creator for the instruction of mankind,
whereon He intends the morality of His rational creatures to be
founded.   We need only here remark that if this were, indeed, the
Divine intention (as Dr. Gore and his allies would seem to assume),
then that purpose has hitherto been strangely frustrated, since the
entire progress of our race from prehistoric times till now has been
in a diametrically opposite direction, and Civilisation itself has
consisted in the advancing conquest by each successive generation
over the bestial, cruel, and predacious instincts.

The truth seems to be that these modern Men of (merely
physical) Science are so absorbed in their material researches that
they have actually dropped out of sight all the moral and spiritual
sciences together ; and they go about in the footsteps of Mr.
Darwin, endeavouring to gather the grapes of Morality off the
thorns of Physics and Zoology.   No such fruit grows on such
trees.   Spiritual truths are spiritually discerned, and moral truths
are morally discerned, and neither the one nor the other are to be
got at through researches into things which are not spiritual and
not moral.   Is it any marvel that so it should be ?   If God be
Himself the holy, all-pervading SPIRIT of the universe, the im-
personated Law of Righteousness ruling in all worlds for ever,
must it not be in the *spirits* of His rational children that He
chiefly reveals Himself and His holy will ?   To imagine that He,
our God and Father, never speaks in the "still small voice" of
conscience, but *does* speak in the earthquake and the thunder-
storm, this is the Baal-worship of modern days.   That He leaves
us to follow an "hereditary conscience," a "set of the brain,"
derived from generations of forefathers as blind and forlorn as
ourselves, and that He intends us to go forth over the face of the

earth studying earthquakes and cyclones and the habits of insects and vermin, that so we may deduce therefrom some rule of duty for daily use—this is the childishness of science.*

If we are to admit such a source for our morality, then we must take it as a whole, and apply it not merely to our treatment of animals, but also to our treatment of men. The dynamite assassin and the Nihilist have, as Dr. Gore says of the earthquake, objects in view of "greater importance and magnitude" than the pain and death of a few men, and they do right, therefore, to be as indifferent to them as was the earthquake of Ischia to the desolation it wrought. Truly the "Humility of Science"—of which we hear much, but see perhaps less than might be desired—can be no better exemplified than by the choice of teachers made by these modest advocates of Vivisection, who relinquish Plato and Kant, Moses, and a greater than Moses, and makes themselves the disciples of the wasp and the polecat.

---

* "It is not so much by means of unenlightened sentiments that men hold communion with the Creator, as by a knowledge of the great laws and principles by which Almighty Power governs all things, and which, largely by means of experiments, scientific men have discovered. And the men who know most about the powers which regulate the universe and determine human actions are the most likely to know about a Cause of all things" (Dr. Gore, p. 22). On this showing, all the prophets and saints of old knew less of God, and had less "communion" with Him, than, *e.g.*, M. Paul Bert.

VII

COMMENTS ON THE DEBATE IN THE HOUSE OF COMMONS (APRIL 4, 1883),

ON MR. REID'S BILL FOR THE TOTAL PROHIBITION OF VIVISECTION.

THE first observation which must occur to every well-informed reader of this discussion, after the recognition of the sound judgment and high feeling of the advocates of the measure, is the extraordinary recklessness wherewith its opponents permitted themselves to make easily checked misstatements concerning plain matters of fact. Either utterly ignorant of the subject on which they presumed to correct Mr. Reid and Mr. Russell, or else relying on the ignorance of the House and on their successful tactics in leaving no time for response and exposure, these gentlemen contrived in the three hours which they monopolised out of the four and a-half of the debate, to make just twenty-eight assertions, everyone of which we shall presently show to be erroneous and misleading.

1. Mr. Cartwright, early in his speech, referred, as evidence of the spontaneous humanity of physiologists, to the Resolutions in favour of the use of anæsthetics in Vivisection, passed by the British Association (which, with characteristic inaccuracy, he styled the British *Medical* Association) in 1871.

The practical value of that humanity so publicly exhibited *on paper*, may be estimated by the fact that within four years the cruelty of Vivisection had risen so far, and the notorious *Handbook* by the most eminent English physiologists had created so much scandal, that Dr. Lyon Playfair himself, on the 12th May, 1875, introduced a Bill whereby the provisions of the paper resolutions might have had a chance of realisation ; a similar Bill being simultaneously introduced by Lord Henniker into the House of Lords. Had the British Association Resolutions of 1871 been anything better than a delusive *brutum fulmen*, no such Bills, no subsequent Royal Commission, no eventual legislation, would ever have been heard of.

2. Mr. Cartwright next spoke of the "eminent gentleman" who deposed before the Royal Commission that he " knew of no case of wanton cruelty in Vivisection by an English experimenter ". This very "eminent gentleman"—Mr. Colam—must be flattered at the lofty importance given to himself and his words by the advocates of Vivisection ; but, as he has himself explained, by "wanton cruelty" he means " suffering caused without any object except to gratify a cruel mind ".   Such cruelty *having no scientific purpose*, the absence of it in English experimentation in no way affects the arguments of those who attack cruelty committed *for scientific purposes*.   It may be added that Mr. Colam furnished the Royal Commission with 800 foolscap pages of records of experiments, some of which he affirmed (1539) were instances of "protracted agony ".

3. Mr. Cartwright then twitted Mr. Reid for not alluding to the prosecution of Professor Ferrier.   He said that that prosecution "lamentably broke down.   The charge brought against Dr. Ferrier was that he operated without a licence and infringed the law by doing those things to which the hon. and learned member referred, but the charge was not supported by one tittle of evidence."
The " tittle of evidence " on which the charge of the Victoria Street Society against Professor Ferrier was supported was simply the direct and repeated statements of the two leading medical papers in London, the *Lancet* and the *British Medical Journal* ; viz., that Dr. Ferrier had exhibited in King's College, and in the

presence of one hundred members of the Medical Congress, certain monkeys on which he had performed his well-known experiments. As the Home Office replied to the Society's inquiries that Professor Ferrier had no licence authorising him to perform those experiments, the legal advisers of the Victoria Street Society naturally thought that they had a clear case of infraction of the law. But what was the " break-down " of the case wherein Mr. Cartwright triumphed, and on whom did it throw discredit ? Both the medical papers, as we have said, attributed the experiments in question to Professor Ferrier. They stated that " the animals were monkeys on which Professor Ferrier had operated some months previously," and which " Professor Ferrier was willing to exhibit"; that they were "exhibited by Professor Ferrier". These statements had remained for four months without any modification or correction. Yet, when the prosecution took place, the editor of the *British Medical Journal* brought his reporter, Dr. Roy, into Court to swear point-blank that he had made a mistake in attributing the experiments to Professor Ferrier, who had nothing to do with the experiments, and that from first to last they had been to his knowledge the work of somebody else— to wit, Professor Yeo. The reporter of the *Lancet* was not in Court ; but when the prosecution proposed an adjournment for his examination, Professor Ferrier's counsel stated, in the presence of the editor of the *Lancet*, that he had communicated with that reporter, and that he was prepared to swear the same as Dr. Roy.

Now, assuming, as we are bound to do, that this was not perjury on the part of the medical journals' staff and of Professor Michael Foster (who swore likewise that the experiments were performed by Professor Yeo), there are only two hypotheses open—

Either, *first*, Dr. Roy, in his draft report of the experiments he had just witnessed, attributed them rightly to " Professor Yeo," and then the editor, for some occult reason, substituted throughout the name of " Ferrier " for " Yeo ".

Or, *second*, Dr. Roy wrote " Ferrier," by mistake, all through a long report, when he meant " Yeo "; and (wonderful to relate)

Professor Gamgee, in reporting for the *Lancet*, underwent precisely the same very remarkable hallucination ! *

We should have imagined—our legal advisers imagined—that the harmonious elaborate reports of experiments by the two great organs of the medical profession, afforded something more than a "tittle of evidence" on the matter ; but the upshot certainly justified Mr. Cartwright's denial that there *was* a "tittle of evidence" against Professor Ferrier. Only it may be questioned whether the "break down" of a case, under such circumstances, ought to be felt most "lamentable" by the prosecutors, who believed in the substantial veracity of the medical organs ; or by the defendants, who escaped by a process more nearly resembling thimble-rigging than is commonly witnessed in English courts of justice. "Who do you think, gentlemen, we have got under this cup?" "Why,

---

* Since the above was first printed the secret has been blurted out by the inculpated parties themselves, in the *Philosophical Transactions of the Royal Society* for 1884. In this imposing publication we find a "*Record of Experiments on the Effect of Lesion of Different Regions of the Cerebral Hemispheres*," by DAVID FERRIER, M.D., and GERALD F. YEO, M.D. The paper was read January 24, 1884. In the "Prefatory Note" we read : "The facts recorded in this paper are partly the results of a research *made conjointly by* Drs. Ferrier and Yeo, *aided by a grant from the British Medical Association*, and partly by a research made by Dr. Ferrier alone, aided by a grant from the Royal Society" : and further, "the *conjoint experiments* are distinguished by an asterisk". Among those so distinguished we find those on the two monkeys which formed the subject of the celebrated trial. So now we have it confessed in words for which Professor Ferrier is responsible, if they are not his own—that he had the leading share (Professor Ferrier's name always appears first), in the experiments the authorship of which he denied at the trial; and that he, conjointly with Professor Gerald Yeo, received a grant of money from the British Medical Association for the purpose of performing the same ! When we reflect that Prof. Michael Foster of Cambridge, Prof. Burdon-Sanderson of Oxford, and Mr. Ernest Hart, Editor of the *British Medical Journal*, were all present in Bow Street Police Court while the trial in question was going on, and (to all appearance) keenly enjoying and approving the defence of Prof. Ferrier, a certain measure is afforded to the British public of the straightforwardness and reliability of the vivisecting clique. If these things were done *under oath*, what may we expect to find in their books and reports?

Professor Ferrior, to be sure! We saw him put there by the *Lancet* and the *British Medical Journal*." "I think you are mistaken, gentlemen," says the *Prestidigitateur*, as he raises the cup, and lo! there, in sooth, is Professor Yeo!

4. The most important of Mr. Cartwright's distinct misstatements is that concerning the Cat and Dog Clause in the Vivisection Act. According to the verbatim report, taken for the *Zoophilist*, Mr. Cartwright said: "No cat, dog, horse, ass, or mule can be operated upon without a specific certificate for the purpose, and then only on the approval of the Home Secretary".

According to the *Times* report, he said to the same purpose: "It was further provided that no cat, dog, horse, mule, or ass could be operated upon".

I cannot but wonder whether any statement as distinctly false as this, respecting an existing law under immediate debate, was ever imposed upon Parliament. When we reflect that Sir William Harcourt sat close by Mr. Cartwright during his speech, and witnessed this misleading of the House, and yet neither then nor when he himself rose to speak on the same side attempted to correct it, our confidence in the candour of the administrator of the law, or else in his acquaintance with the law which he administers, must one or other be rudely shaken.

Here is what the Act really says, clause 5: "Notwithstanding anything in this Act contained, an experiment calculated to give pain shall not be performed *without anæsthetics* on a dog or cat, except on such certificate being given as in this Act mentioned . . . and an experiment calculated to give pain shall not be performed on any horse, ass, or mule except on such certificate being given".

The two words marked in italics were inserted into the original Bill (which had placed all the five animals under like special protection) under the pressure of the 2000 doctors who memorialised Sir Richard Cross on the 10th July, 1876. So hastily was this done that the margin stills bears the original note, "*Special restrictions on painful experiments on dogs, cats, &c.,*" although, by means of this insidious interpolation, all special restrictions on experiments on dogs and cats were removed, while they were still left on experiments on horses, asses, and mules. As *no* vertebrate animal can, under the Act, be vivisected at all without the use (real or pretended) of anæsthetics, unless under special certificate for such purpose, dogs and cats are left by this clause as it now stands, precisely in the same position as snakes, rats, and toads. The *British Medical Journal* of August 12th, 1876, triumphed in the success of the memorialists in leaving the most sensitive, affectionate, and intelligent of animals in the same unprotected state as that of the poor vermin of our cellars and ponds. It remarked, p. 211: "Then as to the Cat and Dog Clause, *all that is objectionable* is removed by the introduction of the words 'without anæsthetics,' which, in fact, relegates cats and dogs to the same place as other animals ".

It is ground for just indignation that seven years after this transaction an advocate of Vivisection should rise in Parliament and assure the House that "no cat or dog can be operated upon without a special certificate," while the administrator of the Act sat by complacently and allowed the House to accept the statement as true! The *Times*, next day, reproduced this false statement of Mr. Cartwright, on the faith, no doubt, of his authority and that of Sir William Harcourt, and thus sent it to the four winds to deceive the friends of tortured animals throughout the world.

The importance of this matter cannot be overrated, for dogs are at once, as M. Richet lately confessed in the *Revue des Deux Mondes*, the favourite victims of physiologists (from their size, habits, and cheapness), and at the same time the very animals which, from their sensitiveness, intelligence, and attachment to mankind, we feel it to be most cruel and treacherous to torture. The whole race of these loving creatures, and of the almost equally affectionate and quite equally sensitive cats, were made over, by this insidious interpolation of two words into Lord Carnarvon's Bill, to the "uncovenanted mercies" of every licensee who would profess to use an anæsthetic (even combined with curare) in his operations. To the judgment of the majority of anti-vivisectors more than half the value of Lord Carnarvon's Bill was lost by this wretched concession to the clamour of the 2000 doctors crying after the poor dogs: "Give them up for Vivisection! They are *carnivorous creatures, specially valuable for the purposes of research!*" Yet this whole transaction was ignored or denied by the Parliamentary advocate of Vivisection, and the Home Secretary allowed him to deny it, and uttered no word to remove the false impression so given to the House!

5. Mr. Cartwright asserts that the "settlement of 1876 has been loyally acquiesced in by the medical profession".

I should hardly call it a "loyal acquiescence" in a measure of restriction to proclaim on the housetops that no restriction ought to exist; but this is what the medical profession did by a unanimous vote at its great International Congress of 1881. After asserting that experiments on animals were indispensable to all future progress, it added: "*It is not desirable to restrict competent persons in the performance of such experiments*".

6. Mr. Cartwright said that he "had been at the trouble to put down the number of licences, and that he found that the highest number that were ever granted in any one year was 32, in the year 1879 to 1880".

There were, as it happens, 36 licences registered in that year according to the returns for England and Scotland, beside 8 for Ireland. But this was *not* the year in which the largest number of licences were in force. In the Report of 1879 the Inspector says, p. 2: "The total number of licences in force during any part of the year 1878 was 45".

7. Mr. Cartwright said: "In the case of those animals to experiment upon which a specific licence is necessary" (he meant a certificate), "the number of licences issued was, in the first year, none; the second, 4; the third, 6; the fourth and fifth none; the last year only 1".

Having begun by declaring erroneously that dogs and cats could
not be vivisected without a special certificate, he proceeded to
count the numbers of special certificates, and left his hearers to
suppose that no dogs and cats were vivisected except with such
certificates.   But, as I have above shown that dogs and cats may
be vivisected without a certificate (and, of course, no certificate is
ever asked for, or given, for vivisecting them), it follows that these
certificates, though delusively registered in the column " Permitting Experiments on Cats, Dogs, Horses, Mules, and Asses,"
must one and all have been given for those (always rare) experiments of physiologists performed on the more expensive animals—
horses, mules, and asses.

That dogs have been actually vivisected in large numbers by
simple licences (without special certificates) under the Act is a
fact which was brought to light by a recent correspondence
between the President of the Victoria Street Society and the
Home Secretary, whose attention was drawn to the fact that Dr.
Roy had published in Professor Foster's *Journal of Physiology*
records of his numerous experiments on dogs in Cambridge in
1881, and that no record of a special certificate for such purpose
appeared in the Returns of 1882.   The answer of the Home
Office was to the effect that Dr. Roy was perfectly within the law
in what he had done.   He had performed experiments on dogs
(they were among the most awful ones which can well be conceived), but he exhibited (or said he exhibited) some anæsthetic
along with curare, and his licence perfectly covered all that he
had done, nor was it needful that any record of the circumstances
should appear in the Returns.

8. Mr. Cartwright said : " Dr. Rutherford is a man of high
honour, and he has stated that so far from having practised upon
forty dogs, or anything like it, the whole of his experiments have
been confined to twelve dogs in one year.   This was necessarily
the case, because he was restricted by his licence, and he abided by
his licence strictly and loyally."

If, indeed, Dr. Rutherford be a man of " high honour," it is distressing to think how afflicted he must be at this statement of his friend in Parliament, contrasting, as it does, with his own signed report of his own experiments published in the *British Medical Journal* in 1877-8-9.

The report of these experiments extends through twelve separate numbers, the last two of which are taken up by a general summary of what he is pleased to term "results". Of the remaining ten numbers I possess nine, containing a detailed statement of the number of experiments reported at full length. Each Report concludes with the examination, *after death*, of its victim.

The figures are: 11, 20, 2, 6, 3, 3, 3, 8, 6—total, 62 dogs.

9. Mr. Cartwright said that "a large amount of benefit is acquired by the medical profession from these experiments, and it is a noteworthy fact that there is *never any need to renew an experiment when once made*".

The following is some of the evidence which the Royal Commission received on this subject:

Professor Humphry said (635): "Experiments have to be repeated and confirmed many times before a fact is really established," and (740) agreed with Dr. Ray Lankester that "the number of experiments must increase very rapidly if the progress of science is to be kept up". Dr. Rutherford told the Commission (2993): "Last year, for purposes of research, I think I used about forty dogs". He has since, in other series of exactly similar experiments "used" sixty-two (*vide* above). Dr. Lauder Brunton told the Commission (5721) he had used ninety cats in one series of experiments, and (5747) "that he had "used a much larger number". Dr. Crichton Brown said (3164) that "forty-six animals" were sacrificed in trying if chloral was antagonistic to picrotoxine, and (3178) that twenty-nine animals were used in Dr. Ferrier's series. These are the small and modest figures of English Vivisection, as admitted before the Royal Commission.*

* I say nothing of the myriads of victims of foreign recklessness, as when Majendie, according to Flourens, sacrificed 4000 dogs to prove one hypothesis true, and another 4000 to prove it false, and when Orfila poisoned 6000 dogs

10. To show that the restrictions of the Act produce injurious consequences, Mr. Cartwright said he would take the case of Professor Lister. "It is," he said, "in the knowledge of everyone that that gentleman's discoveries have really revolutionised surgical science, and, in the opinion of those best acquainted with the subject, he has reduced the mortality of man by seven or eight per cent."

This is a rather "large order" on our credulity. According to the Registrar-General's Returns the death-rate for England in the last thirty years has only declined altogether a fraction less than three per cent; and I have not heard that any much greater decline has been noticed in any other country, whether Listerism prevail therein, or the population still remain in ignorance of that great discovery. It appears also that there is not only some doubt about the "reduction in the mortality of man" through the "carbolic craze," but even a question whether a certain additional mortality be not directly due to it. Dr. Keith, of Edinburgh, will probably be generally considered one of those "well acquainted with the subject," and he says of the carbolic treatment of Lister, after mentioning that some patients had died of it, "I have given it up, believing that on the whole it did more harm than good" (*Trans. Intern. Med. Congress*, 1881, vol. ii. p. 236). Mr. Lawson Tait also may be supposed to be "acquainted with the subject," and after an immense number of carefully graduated experiments he came to the conclusion that "carbolic acid has done much more harm than good, and that it would perhaps have been better if we had never heard of it". Dr. Dudgeon remarks : "Some surgeons have had to give up carbolic acid, because it poisoned not only their patients, which might be borne with equanimity, but even their illustrious selves, which

in the course of his researches in toxicology. M. Blatin, quoting the Viennese *Lumière*, says that "it is calculated that the number of animals carried off at Vienna by physiology in 1850, 1851, and 1852 reached 56,000—to wit, dogs, 26,000 ; cats and rabbits, 25,000; horses and asses, 5000. Dr. de Cyon has just told us (*Contemporary Review*, April, 1883, p. 505) that he has performed ' an incalculable number of vivisections ".

was intolerable. A recent attempt in the Paris hospitals to apply the carbolic acid treatment to the cure of typhoid fever was followed by disastrous consequences, the mortality having been shocking" (Hahnemann, &c., p. 95).

11. Mr. Cartwright said that "the provisions of the Act made it impossible to operate except in a public place".

The "provisions of the Act" do no such thing. There is nothing concerning public places in them. All the laboratories in the kingdom are sufficiently private for anything Professor Lister could reasonably desire to do in them; and in several cases private residences have been licensed for Vivisection, *e.g.*, one in Queen Anne Street, and another at 35 Park Road South, Birkenhead. The desire for still further and closer privacy on the part of Dr. Lister is somewhat ominous. What experiments *can* they be which he desires to make and dare not, under the same shelter as that of which Dr. Rutherford and Dr. Roy have availed themselves?

12. Mr. Cartwright said that "the evidence brought forward for Lamson's conviction was based on an experiment upon a living animal".

In point of fact the mice experiments proved nothing, and could prove nothing, as regards aconite; and the experts were so well aware of the fact that they did not press them at the trial. They were discarded by judge and jury alike. From a larger point of view we recognise that, as numerous substances poisonous to man are innoxious to various animals, all such experiments on animals in poison cases are liable to conduce, *not* to the ends of justice, but to the most fatal mistakes.*

13. Mr. Cartwright (and after him Dr. Playfair) told several wonderful stories of patients at death's door, all saved, as by

*See Dr. Berdoe's pamphlet on *Drugs*, published by the Victoria Street Society, 1889.

miracle, by their medical attendants, who instantly there and then experimented on some animal and solved the problem of life and death on the spot.　These are the sort of anecdotes which, we fear, pro-vivisecting doctors are in the habit of narrating to tearful old ladies, who confess to them their intention of sending five pounds to the Anti-Vivisection Society, and who must be rescued from such infatuation by the most lively efforts of the medical imagination.　But to find these "fairy tales of science" solemnly told in the House of Commons to confiding legislators is somewhat surprising.　It is difficult to believe that the narrators are not aware that such problems as they presuppose are insoluble in any such way; and that practical physicians and surgeons are hardly ever vivisectors at all, much less disposed suddenly to have recourse to Vivisection to elucidate single cases whereon the practice could scarcely throw light under any conceivable contingency.　We have heard a gentleman remark that "if his leg were to be cut off, he should like his doctor first to cut off the leg of a dog to see how it was done".　Some such crude idea of the *modus* of surgery, and of the objects of physiological research, seems to have prevailed in the House of Commons, when it listened to such histories as that, told by Mr. Cartwright, of a patient in lockjaw for whom his doctor prepared a drug.　It was difficult, Mr. Cartwright said, to ascertain the strength of the preparation without testing it, and so, according to Mr. Cartwright's account, the doctor heroically broke the law and applied the test.

What this mysterious drug may be, of which the preparations are unmarked in the pharmacopœia, we cannot guess.　But if, *because* his preparation of it did not happen to kill a dog or a mouse, the heroic doctor ventured to administer it to a man, we can safely say he risked breaking something more than the Vivisection Act—to wit, the Sixth Commandment.　Another wonderful story about an oculist is even more vague and silly.

14.　Dr. Playfair, after Mr. Cartwright, "took up the wondrous tale," and gave a remarkable illustration of the mischief of restricting Vivisection.

"If a patient," he said, "was constipated, and it was supposed to be necessary to employ so drastic a remedy as croton oil, but the medical man wished to see, in the first instance, if castor oil would serve his purpose, he could not do so if this Bill (Mr. Reid's) passed into law."

Truly it is surprising how the medical men in the House of Commons could sit by with grave faces and listen to this kind of thing. Had Mr. Reid been allowed time to cross-examine Dr. Playfair as to how he proposed to test the croton oil and castor oil on healthy dogs, cats, guinea-pigs, or rabbits, so as to obtain an insight into their probable action on a human patient labouring under a specific attack, it would have been instructive, and perhaps diverting to the solemn labours of the British Senate.

15. Dr. Playfair remarked "that the operation of the law is examined by two inspectors—one appointed for Great Britain, Dr. Busk, whose medical capacity is well known, and the other, Professor Stokes, for Ireland".

Mr. George Busk, F.R.C.S., the inspector for Great Britain, has, I understand, never been a practising physician, and consequently his "medical capacity" can scarcely be "well known". As to "Professor Stokes," I am much interested to identify his personality. There is indeed a celebrated physician in Dublin named Dr. William Stokes; but then he is not "Professor Stokes," and is not inspector under the Vivisection Act. And there is a "Professor Stokes" who gives lectures on Memory at the Aquarium; but he has, so far as I am aware, nothing to do with Vivisection. And finally, there is a Dr. Thornly Stoker, of Dublin, whose signature is attached to the Parliamentary Returns under the Vivisection Act, and who may therefore reasonably be supposed to be the Irish inspector. Dr. Playfair apparently composed, for the use of Ireland, a sort of human shamrock of the real inspector, Mr. Stoker; the Dublin physician, Dr. Stoker; and the lecturer on Mnemonics at the Aquarium.

16. Dr. Playfair said that "Dr. Ferrier made a distinct

declaration to the Royal Commission that his experiments were made under anæsthetics, and when the animals were not suffering pain ".

This is no doubt literally true. But *after* the actual cutting and cautery, the poor monkeys are recorded by Dr. Ferrier in his *Croonian Lecture* (published by Trübner & Co.), mostly to have perished through weeks of misery; dying at last of that very painful disease—purulent meningitis. The assertion of the painlessness of the *actual experiment* of removing part of the skull and mutilating the brain is therefore delusive; I might almost venture to say wilfully misleading.

17. Dr. Playfair admitted that the "literature of the subject abounded with shocking examples of cruelty, but the instances are all, except in one or two cases, taken from foreign sources. Unluckily, there has been a very great indifference to suffering abroad, but we are not asked to legislate for abroad."

Certainly we are not asked to legislate for abroad. But when we find our English physiologists working in foreign laboratories, bringing foreign physiologists to assist them here, and welcoming the most eminent vivisectors to their Congress with open arms, and finally subscribing to raise a statue to the very prince of tormentors —Claude Bernard—it is time we should legislate so as to keep for ever from our shores this "very great indifference to suffering" which Dr. Playfair thinks simply "*unlucky*," but which we think criminal. There is already a " Channel Tunnel " between English and continental laboratories. We desire to maintain our "silver-strip ".

18. Dr. Playfair cited the killing of wolves and snakes in India as if it had a direct bearing on the question of vivisecting domestic animals in England.

Probably most readers will agree with Mr. George Russell, who " failed to see the connection " between the two things. Perhaps this is what is called in sporting parlance " drawing a red herring across the scent ".

19. Dr. Playfair makes a great display of ethical philosophy in laying down the canon—

" Man's duty to man is greater than his duty to beasts ".

I entirely concur in the principle, but I consider that it requires those who hold it to prohibit Vivisection. Man's paramount duty to man is founded on the fact of the moral nature of man, and, consequently, regards, primarily and before all others, the interests of that moral nature. We are required by the highest ethics to seek the moral benefit of our brother before his physical welfare ; his *Virtue* before his *Happiness.* This being the case, we must endeavour to stop every practice injurious to the moral interests of humanity. Vivisection is unquestionably thus injurious to the moral interests of humanity, irrespective of the contention whether it be or be not conducive to any physical advantage.

20. Dr. Playfair spoke of the time when Galvani "put a copper hook through the spine of *live* frogs and hung them on the iron rails of his balcony in Bologna ".

"The lover sees the beloved object everywhere." Dr. Playfair sees Vivisection even where it does not exist. The marvel of Galvani's (or rather, I believe, the Signora Galvani's) discovery was, that it was possible to stimulate the muscles of *dead* frogs. Over that same balcony in Bologna now hangs the inscription commemorating that it was

DALLE *MORTE* RANE

that Galvani "*scoperse la Ellettricita animale*".

21. Again, we have a wonderful story of two German students engaged with a poison of which the properties are "so terrible" that Dr. Playfair would not even "name" it to the House, lest, (as it would seem) the British Parliament might be suddenly seized with the passion of a Brinvilliers or a Locusta.

"It is postponed in its action and then produces idiotcy or death. An experiment on a mouse or a rabbit would have taught them the danger."

How would it have taught them the danger, supposing the "terrible" poison, for example, had been belladonna, of which rabbits can eat large quantities without hurt? Or how, if they had tried the "terrible" drug on a mouse, would the "postponed" idiotcy of that small rodent have inspired these unfortunate Germans with proper caution?

22. Dr. Playfair said: "There are only thirty or forty laboratories in the whole world engaged in studying the laws of life," &c.

It is to be presumed that before Dr. Playfair undertook to share this discussion, he at least glanced over the Parliamentary Returns of Licences for the past year; or that, if he failed to look at them, Sir William Harcourt must certainly have done so. Yet Dr. Playfair stated—and Sir William Harcourt did not correct him in stating—that there are "only in the whole world thirty or forty laboratories".

It happens that according to the latest Return there are now (so far as its clumsy arrangement permits of calculation) just thirty-two licensed laboratories *in the United Kingdom alone.* There are thirty-nine more in France, duly registered by Government, thirty-two in Italy, twenty in Germany, five in the Netherlands, five in Switzerland, four in Austria, four in Sweden, one in Denmark, and one in Norway—total, one hundred and forty-three laboratories in Europe alone, with two hundred and forty-one physiologists officially attached to them.

23. Sir William Harcourt attacked Mr. Reid's Bill because it would stop scientific cruelty and leave other cruelty untouched. The sneer came somewhat inopportunely when the House has just refused to admit the clause of the second Bill promoted by the Victoria Street Society (Mr. Anderson's), whereby all animals held in captivity would have been placed under protection.

24. Sir William Harcourt told Mr. Reid that though he had "listened most attentively" to his speech he "never heard one cruel experiment".

It is well that the opponents of Vivisection should once for all know what experiments they are which the Home Secretary does not think cruel. We therefore reproduce here the exact words of Mr. Reid to which Sir W. Harcourt had "just listened most attentively".

"I will take one instance from certain experiments performed by Professor Rutherford, and reported in the *British Medical Journal*. I refer to the series of experiments commenced December the 14th, 1878. These experiments were thirty-one in number. No doubt there were hundreds of dogs sacrificed upon other series of experiments, but now I am only referring to one particular set, beginning, as I say, on the 14th of December, 1878. There were in this set thirty-one experiments, but no doubt many more than thirty-one dogs were sacrificed. All were performed on dogs, and the nature of them was this: The dogs were starved for many hours. They were then fastened down; the abdomen was cut open; the bile duct was dissected out and cut; a glass tube was tied into the bile duct and brought outside the body. The duct leading to the gall-bladder was then closed by a clamp and various drugs were placed into the intestines at its upper part. These experiments were performed without anæsthetics—the animals were experimented upon under the influence of a drug called curare."

Here is a second: "Let me refer to what has been done by Dr. Roy in 1880, partly in the physiological laboratory at Cambridge, and partly in the Leipsic Institute, the experiments being carried out on rabbits, cats, and dogs. The animal was placed under curare; artificial respiration was used; that is to say, a tube was pushed down the animal's windpipe, and worked by an engine in regular puffs in order to keep the blood oxygenated. Then the back, skull, chest, and abdomen were opened. I don't suppose these were always opened in one animal, as in many cases the animal would have died. No doubt sometimes part of the experiment took place on one, and sometimes on another. The various organs were dissected out. The principle nerves, such as the sciatic nerve and so on, were tied in two places and cut. This lasted for many hours. It is stated the animal was under the influence of anæsthetics, but the use of curare is admitted. In the most scientific opinion, when curare is used, it neutralises the use of the anæsthetic. I feel myself at a great disadvantage in treating of these matters as compared with the gentlemen beside me; but if I am making a mistake, I trust I may be corrected. In this instance, however, I believe I am right. Curare creates paralysis: it paralyses the muscles and prevents the animal resisting or showing the symptoms by which alone the existence of anæsthesia can be tested."

These experiments—let it never be forgotten—the present Secretary of State for the Home Dapartment, in whose hands rests the executive of the Vivisection Act, does *not* consider "cruel". I should very much like to hear Sir William Harcourt's definition of a "cruel experiment".

27. Perhaps the most important thing in this debate is the frank avowal of the Home Secretary that he has "accepted the assistance" of the Association for the Advancement of Medicine by Research—a Society avowedly formed for the encouragement of Vivisection—in working the Act of 1876. Here is a *Kilmainham Treaty* again! But to apply to the Land League to keep the Fenians in order would, in comparison, be a statesmanlike proceeding on the part of the Executive. The Act was professedly aimed to *restrict* Vivisection, and thus "to reconcile the claims of Science and Humanity," according to the recommendation of the Royal Commission. The working of it was entrusted to one of her Majesty's Secretaries of State, no doubt expressly to afford the public a guarantee that the restriction should be a *bonâ fide* one, and that the balance between Science and Humanity should be held fairly. Now we find that the gentleman whom we are called to trust for the carrying out of this compromise has "obtained the assistance" of the persons who have founded an Association to promote Vivisection !

28. Finally, Sir William Harcourt interrupted Mr. George

Russell when speaking of vivisectional demonstrations to students, by this astounding assertion : " Under the Act these demonstrations are prohibited," or (as he was reported by the *Times*) " Under the Act demonstrations were forbidden ".

Now in the Act in question (39 and 40 Vict., c. 77, clause 3, section 1) are these words : " Experiments *may be performed* under the foregoing provisions as to the use of anæsthetics *by a person giving illustrations of lectures* in medical schools, hospitals, or colleges, or elsewhere, on such certificate being given as in this Act mentioned, that the proposed experiments are absolutely necessary for the due instruction of persons to whom such lectures were given . . . ".

The permission for demonstrations to students thus accorded by the Act has been used, according to the Returns, every year since the Act was passed ; and, in the last of these Returns, issued from Sir William Harcourt's own office in 1882, for 1881, no less than sixteen persons are registered as holding such certificates, "*permitting experiments in illustration of lectures*". In 1878 there were 8 such certificates registered, in 1879 there were 15, and in 1880 also 15. The inspector himself, in his Report for 1878, mentions that there were in that year 47 experiments performed under such certificates in illustration of lectures.

It seemed sufficiently unaccountable that Sir William Harcourt should sit by silently while Mr. Cartwright misled the House respecting the bearing of the Act of 1876 on the Vivisection of cats and dogs. But that he should himself interrupt a speaker for the purpose of telling the House *that demonstrations are "prohibited under the Act," when they are NOT prohibited, and when he has himself, in the past year, GIVEN TO SIXTEEN PERSONS permission to use such demonstrations*, is a fact which I forbear to qualify, since I cannot do so in terms which it would become me to use.

It is consolatory to reflect that, even with the help of the twenty-eight misstatements above signalised, the advocates of

Vivisection dreaded a Division, and had recourse to Sir J. M'Kenna's inane remarks to "talk out" Mr. Reid's Bill. We may speculate hopefully as to the result when the facts become sufficiently public to compel vivisectors and their supporters to rely on *truth* only to defend their practice, and then allow a well-informed Parliament to decide on the issue.

VIII.

A REPLY TO SIR JAMES PAGET ON VIVISECTION.

THE trilogy of articles devoted to the praise of Vivisection in the number of the *Nineteenth Century* for January, 1882, opens by observations from Sir James Paget, which promise to carry on the controversy upon the broad ground of the rights of man over the lower animals. This ground has only been brought within the domain of ethics during the last century, and is as yet imperfectly mapped out. Large allowance must therefore be made for those who fail to recognise where their favourite practice transgresses the border-line of offence, while the practices of other men lie within the frontier. Persistent obtuseness, however, of this kind, if generally exhibited by a class of educated persons, must assuredly mark that class as behind the age in moral perception, howsoever exalted may be their intellectual claims.

The sequel of Sir James Paget's discussion unfortunately fails to bear out the anticipations which its opening had raised, of a fair and broadly-based debate. He disclaims any intention of discriminating the ethical character of different uses and misuses of animals, and simply throws together a heap of cruelties as a sort of earthwork behind which to shelter Vivisection. They are all condoned, he says, by custom, and Vivisection may well be condoned also, along with the least objectionable of them. Its "pains" are less, its "uses" greater.

At this point, of course, I must prepare to explain my reasons for parting company with Sir James Paget, and I do so with no small difficulty, *not* because those reasons are few or weak, but because they are so overwhelming that it is hard to state them plainly, reserving the respect claimed for my opponent. Answering a less esteemed person, I confess I should mark off the steps of his argument as almost alternately a *suppressio veri* and a *suggestio falsi.* Replying to a man of high mental, moral, and religious pretensions, I can merely marshal the facts to be weighed against his assertions and implications, and leave my readers to judge how far mistaken zeal and *esprit de corps* can produce a veritable moral colour-blindness, disabling a man from perceiving that the thing which he describes as green like grass is in truth crimson as blood.

1. Finding public sentiment on the subject of animal suffering in a state which he would diagnose as one of *hyperæsthesia*, Sir James begins by administering a sedative. The lower animals, he assures us, almost certainly feel pain less acutely than even the hardiest men. Would that I could believe it ! But how is this pleasing theory to be reconciled with the testimony of Professor Pritchard (Professor of Anatomy, Royal Veterinary College), whose acquaintance with animals must be tenfold greater than that of Sir James, and who told the Royal Commissioners (Minutes, 846) : "I have performed some thousands of operations on them (dogs and horses), and I have never yet been able to detect any difference in sensation between the skin of either one or the other and the human subject beyond this, that the cuticle or external covering of the skin is thicker in some animals than in others, and of course the knife has to penetrate deeper to reach the sensitive structure ; but when once it has reached it I think it is as sensitive in one animal as in the other ".

And again (847) : "He had never seen anything to make him think differently than that, as regards the physical sensation of pain, it would be equal to that in a human being ".

It is true, as Sir James says, that savages undoubtedly feel pain less than civilised men ; but in the same degree we must conclude that wild animals feel it less than domesticated ones ; and it is generally these latter on which vivisections are performed. The very fact that physiologists use horses, dogs and cats, for numberless experiments on the nervous system, and select delicate and petted dogs to exhibit "reactions" (*anglicè*, spasms of agony) under their operations, is proof, at all events, that they believe that the sensitiveness of these creatures bears a terribly close analogy to that of man.   This particular line of Sir James's argument will scarcely, then, lead the reader very far in the direction he desires.*

2. After arguing generally that animals feel pain less than men, Sir James proceeds to suggest the notion that vivisections are, after all, only like surgical operations on human beings, under another name.   "Of course," he says, "the pains given in experiments on animals not under anæsthetics were as various as were those which, before 1846, were given in surgical operations." "*As various?*"   Surely yes! and a little more so.   Did surgeons ever open up the backbones of men and irritate the spinal

* It is, however, the persistent habit of vivisectors to deny both the general sensitiveness of animals and their particular sense of the worst injuries.   Professor Pavy told the Royal Commission (2159) that a frog would not find being put into boiling water very painful, and that its efforts to escape were only " physical action in the muscles ".   Dr. Sibson (4745) was "not of opinion that raising the temperature of animals till they died would produce great suffering," though he thought (4750) Goltz' experiment of boiling a frog to death " a horrible idea ".   He also thought (4751) that very little suffering was produced by Chossat's of starving animals to death, with which he was " very familiar," and which Dr. Sharpey denounced (420) as " very severe," and " causing great suffering ".   After this it is natural to find Professor Humphry holding (616) that disease in an animal is not so painful as in man ; and various witnesses, speaking of artificially induced erysipelas, scarlet fever, diphtheria, small-pox, jaundice, and tuberculosis, as not painful diseases but (in the case of tuberculosis) " the very reverse ".   In short, if the victim writhes, moans, and shrieks, it is all " unconscious action in the muscles ".   If it lies still, paralysed by the intensity of agony, then, as Dr. Wickham Legg said of his sixteenth cat—which had first had its bile duct tied and then the " diabetic puncture " made through its skull with a chisel (5281)—"we may doubt whether it (the operation) be painful, because as soon as the cat comes out of the chloroform it lies in a hopeless state, and does not move at all or give any signs of feeling ".

marrow, as Chauveau, Brown-Séquard, and others have done to thousands of dogs, horses, and other animals? Or roast them alive, like Professor Wertheim's thirty dogs? Or "lard" them with nails after Mantegazza's fashion with guinea-pigs and rabbits? Unless surgeons before 1846 were wont to treat their human patients in some such ways as these I am afraid we must set down Sir James's parallel between the varieties of vivisection and those of surgery as distinctly misleading.

3. Continuing the same paragraph above quoted, Sir James says : " But for the worst I think it probable that the pain inflicted in such experiments as I saw done by Majendie was greater than that caused by any generally permitted sport ; it was as bad as that which I saw given to horses in a bull-fight, or which I suppose to have been given in dog-fighting or bear-baiting. I never saw anything in his or any other experiments more horrible than is shown in any of Snyder's boar-hunts, or in Landseer's 'Death of the Otter'. "

Majendie, being long dead, is the great scapegoat of physiologists, and even Dr. Sharpey (who was by no means a squeamish person) told the Royal Commission (444) that when he was a young man he went to the first of a series of Majendie's lectures, but was so utterly repelled by what he witnessed that he never returned. We are not told how many of these lectures Sir James Paget found it possible to attend, but, as he compares the experiments therein exhibited to the sufferings of the horses killed in the bull-fights which he also frequented, it becomes a matter of interest to inquire what he saw, and so enable ourselves to use those weights and measures he has offered us—the bull-fight, the dog-fight, and Landseer's pictures—to estimate the pain of Vivisection. Does he seriously think those brutal sports, or the chase of the wild boar or the otter, really cause as much agony as the single experiment, for example, of Majendie, when he removed a dog's stomach and substituted a pig's bladder?

In comparing the agonies of vivisected animals with the pangs of creatures killed in the chase or the arena, we must remember that the former are endured in cold blood by animals fasting, thirsting, tied down on the torture-trough, and, possibly, curarised. The latter are borne by creatures so excited that, like soldiers in battle, they are comparatively unconscious of them till they are ended by death.

4. Sir James continues his estimate of the pains of Vivisection as follows : " I have never seen or read of an experiment on a fish so painful as ligger fishing ". (By some fatality, I have never read of any vivisectional experiments on fishes, and they are certainly very rare.)   "I doubt whether any experiment on fish or reptile can in an equal time give more pain than is given in long-playing a deeply-hooked salmon.   Probably a thoroughly heartless vivisector (if one could be found) might inflict in a day more pain than a heartless sportman, but in the ordinary practice of experiments on animals it is not possible. . . . I believe therefore, that with these few exceptions which I have mentioned (all quoted above), there are no physiological experiments which are not matched or far surpassed in painfulness by common practices permitted or encouraged by the most sensitive and humane persons of the time " (p. 923).

It is true that Sir James six years ago told the Royal Commission (379) that he knew " nothing " of the experiments at Florence, Leipzig, Vienna, or Paris, and (481) that he " was not conversant with all that goes on abroad," and (354) did not know the *English Handbook* "well".   Nevertheless, I must believe that, before undertaking to instruct the readers of the *Nineteenth Century* on the Vivisection controversy, this eminent gentleman at least dipped into the leading works on the subject ; let us say the *Handbook* and Pfluger's *Archiv*, and the treatises of Béclard and Cyon, Schiff and Paul Bert.   I must believe that, before placing his respectable name at the head of a committee to receive contributions for a monument to Claude Bernard, he had acquainted himself with that great vivisector's principal works—his *Leçons sur le Diabète, Leçons sur la Chaleur Animale, Physiologie Opératoire*, &c.   And with these books in his hand, and their blood-freezing illustrations in his memory, he writes such a paragraph as this !

I hold Sir James Paget to his words, and call on him to repeat to the public his assurance that the victims of the experiments which I shall now cite did not suffer more than animals killed as usual in the chase or the arena.

We will take, first, the numerous rabbits and the seventeen dogs baked to death in his friend Claude Bernard's stove. These animals, Bernard tells us (*Leçons sur la Chaleur Animale*, p. 347), survived respectively eight minutes, ten minutes, twenty-four minutes, and so on, according to the heat of the stove, and according to the position of their heads within it, or outside of it. It became impossible, he says, of each case, "to count the pantings. At last the creature falls into convulsions and dies—uttering a cry". Let Sir James Paget think of that death-cry of the dog, baked to death, and then tell us again that the sensitive, intelligent, faithful brute, so vilely used, suffered no more pain than a deeply-hooked salmon in the river, or a partridge shot in the turnip field! He will find it rather difficult, I think, to bring English gentlemen to acquiesce in such comparison between field sports and "chamber sports"! Or let us measure the pain of another French experiment. Here is one performed by M. Bert (late Minister of Education and Public Worship in France), described in the *Archives de Physiologie*, vol. ii., p. 650, and thus explained to the Royal Commission : "In this experiment a dog was first rendered helpless and incapable of any movement, even of breathing, which function was performed by a machine blowing through a hole in its windpipe". All this time, however, "its intelligence, its sensitiveness, and its will, remained intact," "a condition accompanied by the most atrocious sufferings that the imagination of man can conceive" (*vide* Claude Bernard in *Revue des Deux Mondes*, 1st September, 1864, pp. 173, 182, 183, &c.). In this condition the side of the face, the side of the neck, the side of the fore-leg, interior of the belly and the hip, were dissected out in order to lay bare respectively the sciatic, the splanchnics, the median, the pneumo-gastric and sympathetic, and the infra-orbital nerves. These were excited by electricity for ten consecutive hours, during which time the animal must have suffered unutterable torment, unrelieved even by a cry. The inquisitors then left for their homes, leaving the tortured victim alone with the clanking engine working upon it, till death came in the silence of the night and set the sufferer free (Minutes, 4111).

Or, turning to Germany, and keeping ourselves within the last ten years, let us cull a few specimens of torture work from Pfluger's *Archiv.* In vol. ix., p. 183, after speaking of eighty dogs with their spinal nerves cut, here is a single example: "The spinal cord of a strong grey poodle dog was cut in two places, February 27 and March 13. The second injury made fearful ravages." (The description cannot be quoted.) "As it might be expected from the miserable appearance of the animal that it would not live long, it was *about to undergo another operation* on the 8th April, but died during the preparations" (p. 14). "Fifty-one dogs had portions of their brains washed out of the head, which had been pierced in several places. Most of the animals died of inflammation of the brain." Then follows an "interesting" experiment on a delicately-formed little bitch. The left side of the brain was extracted, wire pincers were applied to the hind feet. The creature whined, howled piteously, and foamed at the mouth. At last it became blind. The dissected brain "resembled a lately-hoed potato field".*

Or shall we go to Italy for evidence of the character of Vivisection? Here is a *résumé* of Professor Mantegazza's account of his own researches *Del Dolore (Fisiologia del Dolore*, Florence, Felice Paggi, 1880, 1 vol., 12mo). On devoting himself to this particular study the Professor congratulates himself: "I had therefore before me a little-explored region of pathology; it had all the allurements (*le seduzioni*) and all the difficulties of the unknown" (p. 93). The problem was to create intense pain, and at the same

---

* Most of these experiments were performed by Professor Goltz, whose friendly rivalry with Professor Ferrier (or should we say Professor Yeo?) at the London Congress is described in the *Lancet* and *British Medical Journal.* Such were the "honoured guests" of the memorable Congress whose Resolutions in favour of Vivisection we are called on to accept as a final settlement of the question!

time to keep the creature motionless in an attitude which would not (like lying on its back) interfere with respiration. The ingenious Professor hit on two ways to accomplish this double purpose, "either by exasperating the pain so that its influence overcame the action of the muscles of motion; or by planting sharp and numerous nails through the soles of the feet in such a way as to render the animal nearly motionless, because in every movement it would have felt more acutely its torment" (p. 95). Then follow the details of twenty-eight experiments. Many of them, he says, occupied two days, all of them one day at least. The Professor prefaces what is to follow by this remark (p. 101): "These my experiments were conducted with much DELIGHT AND EXTREME PATIENCE for the space of a year". (*Queste mie esperienze furono condotte con molto amore e pazienza moltissima per lo spazio di un anno.*)

One experiment is on a guinea-pig nursing its young; another on a dove enclosed in the machine and tormented for nearly two hours, then taken out, and after some respite put back again for another hour and fifty-five minutes, with "many nails in its feet and wings," and again subjected to the action of the *tormentatore*, which leaves it often *accasciata* (prostrated) with pain (p. 106). Two white rats, after two hours of the machine, are "larded with long thin nails in their limbs". They "suffer horribly, and, shut up in the machine for two hours more, they rush against each other, and, not having the strength to bite, remain interlaced with mouths open, screaming and groaning" (p. 107). A rabbit was placed for six hours in the machine, and next day larded with nails and shut in the machine for six hours more. Another rabbit was "*imbottito di chiodi*" (quilted with nails). The result of the whole twenty-eight experiments is a synoptical table of the water and carbonic acid produced under the various degrees of "little pain," "much pain," "cruel pain," and "atrocious pain," respectively. It appears that the average of all the observations differs only by two centesimi from the average of normal respiration (p. 115).

Or shall we turn to America, where Dr. Austin Flint (another honoured guest of the British public at the recent Congress) boasts, in his *Human Physiology*, that he has frequently removed the kidneys from dogs, the animals lingering for three or four days in extreme torture (p. 403)?   He likewise advises students in copying the agonising operation of cutting the fifth nerves not to use an anæsthetic, as the experiment is more "satisfactory" with the evidence of pain.

Or, to come nearer home, here is what has been done in Edinburgh to at least fifty dogs under the express sanction of the law as it now stands.   The explanation is by Dr. Walker: "The first part of the performance consists in making the animal fast from seventeen to nineteen hours.   At about 9 A.M. it is brought into the laboratory. . . . Curare is injected to prevent struggles and cries. . . . Another operation is now necessary to keep up respiration.   This is done with a pair of bellows through an aperture made in the windpipe.   An incision is made in the middle line of the stomach and a tube inserted into the bile duct into which an opening has been made.   The cystic duct is now occluded by a clamp; an opening is made into the part of the intestinal canal called the duodenum, and a cholagogue or some other substance to be tested is inserted in it.   The experiment is now said to begin, and to those whose feelings and conscience have not been seared with a hot iron the sight of the miserable and helpless victim would be intolerable. . . ."

And, finally, here is the "last thing out" in Vivisection: "The *Lancet* of 17th September, 1881, contains an account, headed 'Electrical Tetanus,' of some experiments by M. Richet.

"Repeated electrical stimulation," it appears, produces on rabbits a state of tetanus (cramp) arresting respiration, which may be kept up artificially.   In respect of dogs, the following is the account given of those experimented on by M. Richet, and detailed (we may add) without one word of condemnation in the *Lancet*.

"In the dogs the electricity employed was not sufficiently powerful to arrest respiration, and death was due to the elevation of temperature.   The ascent of the thermometer was extremely rapid, so that *after the tetanus had lasted for half an hour* the lethal temperature of 111 or 112° F. was reached. . . . The proof that the increased body-heat is the cause of death was furnished by the fact that if the animal is *kept cool by artificial means* it may bear *for more than two hours extremely strong currents, which cause severe tetanus, without dying for some days*. . . . Usually death occurs when a temperature of 112° is attained, but in some cases it reached 112°·5 and even 113°·3. . . . At 111° the breathing is so frequent that it is hardly possible to count it, and so feeble that scarcely any air enters the thorax" (*Lancet*, 17th September, 1881, p. 515).

"Thus these most miserable animals were subjected for two hours at a time to currents of electricity, causing such intense agony of cramp and heat together that they either expired, with their blood 14 degrees above the normal temperature (simmered, in short, in their own blood), or lingered for a day or two, having been 'kept cool by artificial means' during their hideous torture. M. Richet may safely challenge the world—perhaps the inhabitants of even a worse world than this—to rival him in the ingenuity of his torture " (*Zoophilist*, No. 6).

This, as I have called it, is the last thing accessible to the lay reader in the way of experiment, but I hereby call on any man of candour and honour out of the hundred scientific gentlemen who heard Dr. Roy (to whose tender mercies the animals in the Brown Institution are entrusted) give his account of his own experiments on the innervation of the kidney, in the Physiological Section at the late Congress, to tell us what those experiments were.   Perhaps they will prove a ghastly counterpart to Sir James Paget's ideal picture of the dogs who were "happier" after Vivisection than before.

Physiologists must not be surprised if to the natural indignation excited by records of the sufferings of harmless brutes be added among anti-vivisectors some exasperation, due to the sense that they tread on a quagmire whenever they approach this enchanted ground, whereon honest Englishmen seem to lose all our national characteristics of humanity and straightforwardness.* We talk

* A remarkable instance of this bogginess of the physiological territory was recently experienced by the Committee of the Victoria Street Society, on the occasion of the prosecution of Professor Ferrier. Here are the articles in the two leading medical journals, on which the Society based its proceedings, and also the notes of the shorthand writer in Court at the trial :

British Medical Journal.

Public Report.
20th August, 1881.

"The members were shown two of the monkeys, a portion of whose cortex had been removed by Professor Ferrier."

Reporter—(Dr. Roy's)—Sworn Evidence.
17th November, 1881.

Q. Did Professor Ferrier offer to exhibit two of the monkeys upon which he had so operated ?

A. At the Congress, no.

Q. Did he subsequently?

A. No; he showed certain of the members of the Congress two monkeys at King's College.

Q. What two monkeys?

A. Two monkeys upon which an operation had been performed.

Q. By whom ?

A. By Professor Yeo.

Lancet.

Public Report.
8th October, 1881.

The interest attaching to the discussion was greatly enhanced by the fact that Professor Ferrier was willing to exhibit two monkeys which he had operated upon some months previously. . . . "

"In startling contrast to the dog were two monkeys exhibited by Professor Ferrier."

Counsel's Statement.
17th November, 1881.

Dr. WAKELEY, *sworn, examined by* Mr. Waddy :

Q. Are you the Editor of the *Lancet*?

A. I am.

Q. Can you tell me who it was furnished this report ?

A. I have the permission of the gentleman to give his name. Professor Gamgee, of Owens College, Manchester.

Mr. WADDY: What I should ask is that one might have an opportunity of calling Professor Gamgee.

Mr. GULLY : We have communicated with Professor Gamgee, and I know very well that he will say precisely what was said by Dr. Roy.

contemptuously of the pious frauds of the elder priesthood ; but that the Priesthood of Science, which ought to be the very service of Truth, should lie open to the charge of persistent prevarication, is a humiliating spectacle indeed.

Sir James concludes with the usual boast of the great improvements of modern surgery and medicine due to Vivisection. I can only say that when our medical advisers find cures for cholera, consumption, cancer, leprosy, or even the cattle plague, or are more successful than the despised bone-setter in curing simple sprains and dislocations, it will be time for us to recognise their vast achievements. Just now the sad story of President Garfield affords but a poor confirmation to the lay intellect of Sir James Paget's position. Seven eminent surgeons and physicians, receiving 100 and 1000 dollars a day, issued all through Mr. Garfield's lingering sufferings incessant bulletins, which in the light of the subsequent autopsy are proved to have been if not deliberate falsehoods, then a series of blunders and mistakes from beginning to end.

I submit that in this reply to Sir James I have shown—

1st. That his *suggestions*—(*a*) of the lesser sensibility of animals, (*b*) of the comparison of surgical operations with Vivisection, and (*c*) of the latter with cruel sports—are in each case "SUGGESTIONS OF THE FALSE".

2nd. That his *suppressions* of the worst facts of contemporary physiological investigations are "SUPPRESSIONS OF THE TRUTH ".

IX.

DARWIN AND VIVISECTION.

[THE following letters—not inserted in the *Life of Charles Darwin*—appeared in the *Times* of the 19th and the 23rd of April, 1881.]

MR. DARWIN AND VIVISECTION.

(TO THE EDITOR OF THE "TIMES".)

SIR,—May I, as President of the Society for the Protection of Animals Liable to Vivisection, request you to insert in your paper a letter from Miss Cobbe, our able honorary secretary, in answer to one from Professor Darwin, which appeared this morning ?

I am myself among those who, in the language of the learned Professor, "are deeply ungrateful to these benefactors of mankind ". It is, on the contrary, an honour and a joy to be deeply grateful to such distinguished men as the late Sir Charles Bell and others still living, who have confessed their experiments to have been unnecessary, cruel, and without results.

I am, Sir, your obedient servant,

SHAFTESBURY.

Liverpool, April 18.

(TO THE EDITOR OF THE "TIMES".)

SIR,—Mr. Darwin, in the letter which you publish to-day, has fallen into some errors, which, in the case of a man of his celebrated accuracy, are not a little remarkable. Apparently, Blue-

books are less in this great philosopher's line of study than pigeons
or carnivorous plants.   Mr. Darwin says that he "took an active
part in trying to get an Act passed such as would have removed
all just cause of complaint (on the subject of Vivisection), and at
the same time have left physiologists free to pursue their researches,"
a Bill very different from that which has since been passed.   This
Bill, which Mr. Darwin promoted, was brought into the House of
Commons by Dr. Lyon Playfair, Mr. Spencer Walpole, and Mr.
Evelyn Ashley, and ordered to be printed, May 12, 1875.   If Mr.
Darwin will be at the trouble to compare this Bill (which is printed
in the appendix to the Report of the Royal Commission on Vivisection) with the existing Act of 1876, and point out in what
respect the former is "very different" from the latter, he will con-
fer a favour on many of your readers who find both the principles
and details of the two Bills almost identical.

Secondly, Mr. Darwin repeats the assertion, which has been
boldly made again and again by the advocates of Vivisection (as it
would seem with sublime confidence in the inability of the general
public to consult Parliamentary Papers), that "the investigation of
the matter by a Royal Commission proved that the accusations
made against the English physiologists were false".

Now, Sir, the Report of the same Royal Commission (page 17),
which lies before me as I write, contains the following carefully-
drawn and well-weighed phrases : "It is manifest that the practice
(of Vivisection) is from its very nature liable to great abuse. . . .
It is not to be doubted that inhumanity may be found in persons
of very high position as physiologists. . . . That very severe experiments are constantly performed cannot be doubted. . . .
Besides the cases in which inhumanity exists, we are satisfied that
there are others in which carelessness and indifference prevail to
an extent sufficient to form a ground for legislative interference."
These phrases which, as referring to reasons for "legislative interference," can necessarily concern English physiologists alone and
not foreigners, afford, I venture to think, a direct contradiction to
Mr. Darwin's assertion.   Instead of the investigations before the
Commission proving, as he says they did, "that the accusations

against English physiologists were false," they proved to the conviction even of Mr. Huxley and Mr. Erichsen, that in the main they were true. Considering that the Report goes on to say, " Evidence of this nature is not easily obtained," this result was a remarkable vindication of the principle of " *magna est veritas*," and that such a man as Mr. Darwin should write to Sweden to misinform his correspondent, and through him all Europe, respecting the registered result of a great public inquiry, appears to me exceedingly to be regretted. As to Mr. Darwin's concluding observations respecting the benefits already derived from Vivisection, I am of course not competent to argue with so great an authority. It sometimes would appear, however, that men of science mistake the discovery of the cause of a disease, and the means of its transmission, for the very different discovery of an available remedy. Professor Virchow's experiments in conveying trichinosis to rabbits were announced with a flourish of trumpets five years ago. Surely we ought not to have heard of the recent outbreak of that dreadful malady had those experiments been so immensely beneficial as Mr Darwin would have us believe ? We seem to be always condemned to listen to a repetition of the story of the old Egyptian magicians who succeeded in reproducing the Plagues, but failed to cure them.

But lastly, Sir, I beg to ask whether the principles of the evolution philosophy require us to believe that the advancement of the "noble science" of physiology is so supreme an object of human effort that the corresponding retreat and disappearance of the sentiments of compassion and sympathy must be accounted as of no consequence in the balance ? Ought we to rejoice if a human being has spent a lifetime in the work (or, as some of us deem it, in the heinous sin) of deliberate torture of God's harmless creatures, if, at the end of all, he can boast that he has added a detail or two to the store of physiological facts ? A living professor of this noble science concludes his report on his own systematic tormenting of scores of animals ("larding" them with nails and other devices) by the remark that he has pursued his investigations *con molto amore e pazienza* (*Del Dolore*, p. 25). If only one human soul had descended to such a moral abyss as this confession reveals, I should, for my part, consider that the pursuit which had led him thither, instead of being an "incalculable benefit to. humanity," had done our race more injury than physical science, were her proudest boasts verified, could repay. What shall it profit a man if he gain the whole world of knowledge and lose his own heart and his own conscience?

I am, Sir, yours truly,

FRANCES POWER COBBE,

Hon. Secretary, Society for the Protection of Animals from Vivisection.

1 Victoria Street, S.W., April 18.

(EXTRACTED FROM THE "TIMES" OF 23RD APRIL, 1881.)

MR. DARWIN ON VIVISECTION.

(TO THE EDITOR OF THE "TIMES".)

SIR,—Mr. Darwin adduces the fact that the report of the Royal Commission includes a reference to Majendie as if it were thereby proved that foreign physiologists were the only, or chief, objects of the condemnation of the Commission. My contention, in the letter which you did me the honour to publish on the 19th inst., was—that the Commissioners must have had the English physiologists primarily in view in all their remarks, which otherwise were totally irrelevant to their purpose—namely, that of reporting on the necessity of legislative interference with English physiologists. Doubtless the interchange of extreme politeness which took place between the Commissioners and the "eminent men" on whose doings they sat as judges, preventing them from citing by name the evidence which had been brought before them respecting vivisectors at home, and caused them to refer, rather illogically, to that grand scapegoat of the physiologists, Majendie.

The outcome of the whole elaborate inquiry—viz., that the Commission ended by reporting distinctly in favour of the " enactment of a law by which experiments should be placed under the control of the Home Secretary" (p. xx.)—is assuredly evidence sufficient that the Royal Commissioners did not acquit English physiologists of the charges made against them.   Would Mr. Darwin have us believe that they desired to see experiments in England placed under the control of the Home Secretary because Majendie had performed cruel experiments in France?

With regard to the assurances of the Secretary of the Royal Society for the Prevention of Cruelty—of which so much capital has been made by the advocates of Vivisection—that " he believes the humanity of English vivisectors to be very different from that of foreign physiologists," it would be satisfactory to know on how intimate an acquaintance with the proceedings of either one or the other he founded his opinion, and whether it extended beyond two or three forewarned visits to certain laboratories at the request of his own committee.   A gentleman, who had certainly much larger opportunities for forming a sound judgment of the matter— Dr. Klein, the assistant of the most eminent physiologist in England, Dr. Burdon-Sanderson—gave a very different verdict. Having honestly stated that he (a foreigner) had "no regard at all " to the sufferings of animals (Minutes, 3539), and mentioned that there "is no such thing abroad" as the outcry which had been made concerning Vivisection by certain English journals (3549), he was asked, "Did you believe that, generally speaking, there is a very different feeling in England?"   Dr. Klein's answer was concise, and, I think, with all deference to Mr. Darwin, conclusive: "Not among the physiologists; I do not think there is " (Minutes, 3553).

The obvious truth to which it is vain to close our eyes is, that Vivisection always has been, and must be, the same thing all the world over; and that it is impossible for a man to devote his life to such a practice without experiencing a great ardour for scientific curiosity and a corresponding recklessness and callousness respecting the sufferings which the gratification of that curiosity may involve.

I am, Sir, truly yours,

FRANCES POWER COBBE,
Hon. Secretary S.P.A.V.

1 Victoria Street, April 22.

X.

THE JANUS OF SCIENCE.

THE position in which we, the opponents of Vivisection, find ourselves at present is this:

We seek to stop certain practices which appear to us to involve gross cruelty, and to be contrary to the spirit of English law. Our knowledge of them is derived almost exclusively from the published reports and treatises prepared and issued by the actual individuals who carry out those practices; and our arguments are grounded upon *verbatim* citations from those published reports and treatises.*

The persons whose practices we desire to stop, and their immediate associates, now meet our charges of cruelty by articles in the leading periodicals, wherein the proceedings in question are invested with a character not only diverse from, but opposite to, that which they wear in the scientific treatises and reports above-mentioned.

I shall, in this paper, endeavour to indicate the outlines of these

---

* *E.g.*, the *Handbook of the Physiological Laboratory*, by Drs. Burdon Sanderson, Lauder-Brunton, Klein, and Foster, London, 1873; Béclard's *Traité Elementaire*, Paris, 1880; Claude Bernard's *Physiologie Opératoire*, *Traité sur le Diabéte*, and *Sur la Chaleur Animale;* Cyon's *Methodik*, Giessen; Paul Bert's *La Pression Barométrique*, Paris, 1878; Mantegazza's *Del Dolore*, Florence, 1880; Livon's *Manuel de Vivisections*, 1882; *Archives de Physiologie*, edited by Brown-Séquard, Charcot, and Vulpian; Schiff's *Fisiologia Esperimentale*, 1866; *Pharmacology and Therapeutics*, by Dr. Lauder-Brunton, 1880; *Transactions of the Royal Society*, 1875; *Journal of Physiology*, Michael Foster, 1882; Goltz' *Verrichtungen des Grosshirns*, 1881.

diversities and contradictions, premising that, from the nature of the case, the argument is a cumulative one, of which the full force can only be felt by those who have actually perused the treatises and experienced the impression which they are calculated to produce.   Afterwards, I shall deal with some subordinate matters respecting which my statements in a previous article (in the *Fortnightly Review*) have been called in question.

1. In the first place, the PURPOSE of the great majority of experiments is differently described in the scientific treatises and in the popular articles.   In the former, the *raison d'être* of most experiments appears to be the elucidation of points of purely scientific interest.   It is only occasionally that we meet with allusions to diseases or their remedies, and the experiments are generally described as showing that one organ acts in one way and another in another; that such a lesion or such an irritation produces such and such results and reactions; and (especially) that Professor A.'s theory has been disproved and that of Professor B. (temporarily) established.   In short, every page of these books corroborates the honest statement of Professor Hermann of Zurich: "The advancement of science, and not practical utility to medicine, is the true and straightforward object of all Vivisection. No true investigator in his researches thinks of the practical utilisation.   Science can afford to despise this justification with which Vivisection has been defended in England."—*Die Vivisectionsfrage*, p. 16.

We now turn to such articles as the six which have appeared in the *Nineteenth Century* and the two in the *Fortnightly Review* in defence of Vivisection, and, *mirabile dictu !* not a solitary vivisection is mentioned of which the direct advancement of the Healing Art does not appear as the single-minded object.

2. Again, the SEVERITY of the experiments in common use appears from the Treatises and Reports (always including the English *Handbook*, *Transactions*, and *Journal of Physiology*) to be truly frightful.   Sawing across the back-bone, dissecting out

and irritating all the great nerves, driving catheters along the veins and arteries, inoculating with the most dreadful diseases, cutting out pieces of the intestine, baking, stewing, pouring boiling water into the stomach, freezing to death, reducing the brain to the condition of a "lately-hoed potato field"; these and similarly terrible experiments form the staple of some of them, and a significant feature in all.

But turning now to the popular articles, we find Professor Gerald Yeo assuring the readers of the *Nineteenth Century* that "he has calculated that about twenty-four out of every hundred of the experiments (in the Parliamentary Returns) might have given pain. But of these twenty-four, four-fifths are like vaccination, the pain of which is of no great moment. In about one-seventh of the cases the animal only suffered from the healing of a wound." Sir James Paget afforded us a still more *couleur de rose* view of the subject. He said: "I believe that, with these few exceptions, there are no physiological experiments which are not matched or far surpassed in painfulness by common practices permitted or encouraged by the most humane persons".

3. Again, as regards the FEELINGS of the vivisectors. In reading these terrible treatises we do not meet with one solitary appeal against the repetition of painful experiments, one caution to the student to forbear from the extremity of torture, one expression of pity or regret—even when the keenest suffering had been inflicted. On the contrary, we find frequent repetitions of such phrases as "interesting experiments," "very interesting experiments," "beautiful" (*schöne*) cerebral inflammation, and so on. In short, the writers, frankly, seem pleased with their work, and exemplify Claude Bernard's description of the ideal Vivisector—the man who "does not hear the animal's cries of pain, and is blind to the blood that flows, and who sees nothing but his idea and organisms which conceal from him the secrets he is resolved to discover".*
Or, still more advanced, they realised Cyon's yet stronger picture

* *Introduction à l'Etude de la Médecine Expérimentale*, p. 180.

in his great book of the *Methodik*, of which, by the way, he has lately told us in the *Gaulois*, that when the book was coming out his English colleagues implored him not to allow it to be advertised in England.

In this most important treatise M. Cyon tells us :

"The true vivisector must approach a difficult vivisection with *joyful excitement.* . . . He who shrinks from cutting into a living animal, he who approaches a vivisection as a disagreeable necessity, may be able to repeat one or two vivisections, but he will never be an artist in Vivisection. . . . The sensation of the physiologist when, from a gruesome wound, full of blood and mangled tissue, he draws forth some delicate nerve thread . . has much in common with that of a sculptor."—*Methodik*, p. 15.

This is the somewhat startling self-revelation of the vivisector, made by himself to his colleagues. The picture of him in the *Nineteenth Century* and *Fortnightly Review* is almost as different as one face of Janus from the other. We find him talking of the power of "controlling one's emotions," "disregarding one's own feelings at the sight of suffering," "subordinating feeling to judgment," and much more in the same strain, whereby the vivisector is made to appear a tender-hearted martyr to the Enthusiasm of Humanity.

4. Again, as to the NUMBER of animals dissected alive, the treatises make us suppose it to be enormous. M. Paul Bert gives cases of terrible experiments on dogs placed under the compression of eight atmospheres and coming out stiffened, " so that the animal may be carried by one paw just as a piece of wood " ; and on cats which, when dissected after death, showed a "marrow which flowed like cream " ; and of these experiments he gives the public instances up to No. 286. Schiff is calculated to have " used " 14,000 dogs and nearly 50,000 other animals during his ten years' work in Florence. Flourens told Blatin that Majendie had sacrificed 4000 dogs to prove Bell's theory of the nerves, and 4000 more to disprove the same ; and that he, Flourens, had proved Bell was right by sacrificing some thousand

more. Dr. Lauder-Brunton himself told the Royal Commission (Q. 5721) that in one series—out of three on one subject—he had sacrificed (without result) ninety cats in an experiment during which they lingered four or five hours after the chloroform (Q. 5724), with their intestines " operated upon ". He also carried on another series of 150 experiments on various animals, very painful, and notoriously without results (Q. 5748). This is the scale on which vivisections abroad and at home are carried on, if we are to be guided by the treatises.

Turn we now to the popular articles ; and we find mention only of the very smallest numbers. Sir William Gull minimises Bernard's stove-baked dogs to six (concerning the correction of which statement, see further, p. 118), and Professor Yeo brings down those of Professor Rutherford's victims to twelve (for which also see p. 140). Every reference to numbers by physiologists is apparently, like those of the Fuegians, limited to their digits.

5. Again, as regards *Anæsthetics*, throughout the treatises I cannot recall having once seen them mentioned as *means of allaying the sufferings of the animals*, but very often as convenient applications for *keeping them quiet.* Claude Bernard in his *Physiologie Opératoire*, and Cyon in his great *Methodik*, each devote a section to them as MEANS OF RESTRAINT ("*contention*"), and describe their merits from that point of view. Morphia, for example, Bernard recommends because it keeps the animal still, though "*il souffre la douleur*" ; and of curare (which, he says, causes "the most atrocious sufferings which the imagination can conceive"), he remarks, without an expression of regret, that its use in Vivisection is so universal that it may always be assumed to have been used in experiments not otherwise described. Nor can haste explain this omission to treat anæsthetics from the humanitarian point of view, for the treatises contain long chapters of advice to the neophyte in Vivisection, how he may ingeniously avoid being bitten by the dogs, or scratched by the yet more "*terrible*" cats, which are, Bernard pathetically complains, "*indocile*" when lifted on the torture-trough.

Turning to our *Nineteenth Century* essayists, we find chloroform is everywhere, and curare nowhere.

6. Lastly, there is not a trace in the treatises—even in the English *Handbook*—of the supposed Wall of China which guards the Flowery Land of English Vivisection from the hordes of outer barbarians who practise in Paris, Leipsic, Florence, Strasburg, and Vienna. We find, on the contrary, a frequent and cordial interchange of experiments and compliments. Our English vivisectors study in the schools of the Continent, and in several cases have brought over foreigners to be their assistants at home. When Claude Bernard died, so little did English physiologists think of repudiating him, that a letter appeared in the *Times* of March 20, 1878, inviting subscriptions to raise a monument to his honour, signed by Sir James Paget, Dr. Burdon-Sanderson, Professor Humphry, Professor Gerald Yeo, Mr. Ernest Hart, Mr. Romanes, and Dr. Michael Foster. Even in 1881, when Professors Goltz, Flint, Brown-Séquard, Béclard, and Chauveau joined the International Congress in London, they were received with the warmest welcome from their English colleagues, one hundred of whom accompanied Professors Goltz and Ferrier to inspect the dogs of the former and the monkeys of the latter (I beg pardon, of Professor Yeo); and when Professor Goltz returned to Germany, he published a volume containing beautiful coloured pictures of the mutilated brains of his dogs, and dedicated it—to whom does the reader think? To—

"HIS ENGLISH FRIENDS!"*

All this does not look exactly like hearty disgust and repudiation of the foreign system.

But turn we to the *Nineteenth Century* and *Fortnightly Review*, and lo! the garments of our English physiologists are drawn closely around them, and we are assured they have "no connection whatever with the establishment over the way". I am even rebuked for placing on the same page (in the article "*Four*

* *Verrichtungen des Grosshirns*, 1881.

Replies") certain English experiments and "the disgusting details of foreign atrocities, which excite a persistent feeling of repugnance". Professor Yeo says he "regards with pain and loathing such work as that of Mantegazza," and asks me bitterly: "Why repeat the oft-told tale of horrors contained in the works of Claude Bernard, Paul Bert, Brown-Séquard, and Richet in France, of Goltz in Germany, Mantegazza in Italy, and Flint in America?" (p. 361).

Surely this is a cargo of Jonahs thrown overboard together? Claude Bernard—the prince of physiologists, to whom this same Professor Gerald Yeo, four years ago, wished to raise a statue! Brown-Séquard—the honoured of Professor Huxley! Professor Flint—who, six months since, was the favoured guest of every scientific throng in London, and who, I presume, is of Anglo-Saxon race, only corrupted from humane British Vivisection by evil American communications! And lastly, Goltz!—poor Professor Goltz, who had so many cordial hand-shakes on quitting perfidious Albion, while the autumn leaves were falling, and who is now flung down the Gemonian stairs, a sacrifice to the rabble of anti-vivisectors even while the ink is scarcely dry on the touching dedication of his book:

"SEINEN

FREUNDEN IN ENGLAND

GEWIDMET

VON DEM VERFASSER".

May not this new Raleigh fitly cry, *not*, "O the friendship of Princes!" but "O the friendship of Physiologists!"

Thus we see that, as regards, first, the *Purpose* of the majority of vivisections; second, their *Severity;* third, their *Number;* fourth, the *Feelings* of the experimenters; fifth, the use of *Anæsthetics;* sixth, the *Difference* between English and foreign Vivisection,—in short, on every one of the points of importance in the controversy,—there is contradiction on the broadest scale between the scientific treatises and reports which are prepared for "brethren of the craft," and the articles which are written in lay periodicals for the edification of the British public.

It is for the reader to judge which class of statement may, with the greater probability, be held to represent the genuine doings and feelings of the writers.

I now proceed to examine some of the minor points whereon my statements in the *Fortnightly Review* for January have been attacked by the writers in the *Nineteenth Century* and *Fortnightly Review* for March.

Sir William Gull is, no doubt, a great authority on drugs and diseases.*   Perhaps for that reason he has scarcely devoted much leisure to the study of morals and divinity.   Had he done so he would scarcely have asked, "What casuist can doubt the moral duty" (of pressing on the acquisition of knowledge) "with the parable of the Talents before him?"   The casuist is, I think, yet to be found who will maintain that the pursuit of Knowledge is not morally limited, like every other human pursuit, by the lawfulness of the means to be therein employed; and certainly our fashionable physician stands alone in an interpretation of the Gospel parable which would represent the Teacher as recommending the man with five talents to increase them—let us say, by knocking down and robbing—the man with one.   As Sir William Gull has, however, begun the study of the Bible, I may point out to him that in the opening chapters of Genesis he will find the ruin of the whole human race attributed to "the acquisition of knowledge" regardless of lawful limitation.

The experience of six years has convinced most of us that to argue a point of animal suffering with a vivisector is not a very hopeful proceeding.   There is one matter, however, wherein, as he seems to refer to me, I shall try to convict Sir W. Gull.   He ridicules my expression of "baking alive," applied to the dogs in

* Sir William Gull told the Royal Commission, however (Q. 5545), when asked, "As regards remedial drugs, are there many which you can enumerate as having been discovered by those processes?" (vivisections), "I am sorry to say that I am not a great believer in drugs".

Bernard's stove; and through a page and a half he labours to explain that the sufferings of Bernard's victims were only those of a man dying of fever. "The animal—or man," he says, "is under such circumstances (those of fever) baked alive"—and he leaves the impression that in his opinion the pain of the stove and the pain of the fever were equal. Here is what a physiologist of a different school wrote recently in the *Spectator*, respecting similar observations made by Mr. Edmund Gurney in the *Cornhill Magazine:*

"In the baking experiments, of which Mr. Gurney states a great deal has been made, according to him 'the actual mode of death was not exceptionally painful,' in proof of which he states that 'the stages of death were faintness and exhaustion, passing on to coma, and, finally, some convulsive movements'. Now, Mr. Gurney, being a layman, may be excused when, misguided perhaps by some friendly vivisector, he comes to the incredible conclusion that death by baking is not exceptionally painful; but he ought, at the very least, to have taken the opinion or description of the experimenter who performed the experiments, to whom full reference was given. As he has failed to do so, I shall supply the quotation in question from Claude Bernard, in *La Chaleur Animale*, Paris, 1876, page 356: 'When the animal feels the toxic effects of the heat, it presents a series of symptoms which are constant and characteristic. At first, it is somewhat agitated; soon respiration and circulation become accelerated; the animal gasps, it pants, at last it falls into convulsions, and with a scream (*poussant un cri*), it generally dies suddenly.'

"Surely Mr. Gurney does not mean to quibble over the terms 'boiling alive' and 'baking alive'. As far as the experiments are concerned, where the animals were placed till they died in a little oven over a fire (of which a woodcut, reproduced by photography, of the original, in *loc. cit.*, page 347, generally accompanies the textual descriptions), no other term could possibly be applied than 'baking alive'."—*Spectator*, Feb. 11, 1882.

In short, if for "stove" we substitute "oven," we shall be in a position to give an answer to the simple questions—1. Is the pain of fever (such as many of us have endured for three weeks, and recovered afterwards) equivalent to the pain of being put into a machine at such a temperature as that we should die in a few minutes? 2. Ought a living rabbit inside such a machine to be described by a different word from a dead rabbit put into it and taken out after a few minutes longer, *fit to be eaten?*

I am content now to leave this point, which is a sample of the general treatment of our charges by the advocates of Vivisection; but before dismissing Sir W. Gull, I must express my amazement that he should have quitted the safe field of vague denial and suggestion, and committed himself to a matter of definite numbers, whereon his readers need only use their eyes on a visit to the Victoria Street Society's Library, to see that he has made a statement—as an Italian would politely say, *pienamente inesatto.* Sir William says (pp. 460, 461), "Bernard, in these (stove) experiments, sacrificed two pigeons, two guinea-pigs, less than twenty rabbits, and *six* dogs". Where did he find this number "six"? I have before me Claude Bernard's own book, wherein the disputed experiments are detailed, and diagrams of the stoves inserted (pp. 347 *et seq.* to pp. 358, 359); two pages are occupied by a synoptical table of the experiments which were performed in the first and simplest stove or oven, with the diagram of which many of my readers are no doubt familiar. In this table I read in one column the word "*chien*" three times, then eleven times, and then twice. Only one of these dogs is said to have survived, having been withdrawn after thirty-six seconds only of the stove. Another, which was also withdrawn, died in four hours.

If Sir William Gull finds that 3 + 11 + 2 amount to 6, I shall venture to offer him a copy of Colenso's Arithmetic, out of consideration for his patients, to whom his peculiar views of the First Rule might prove of importance in a prescription for physic.

Of the *second* stove or oven, of which Bernard gives a diagram in his next chapter, and in which another series of dogs and other animals were baked, Sir William Gull takes no notice at all. From his triumphant conclusion respecting the results of the martyrdom of the "six" dogs, the unwary reader might suppose that we had quite got to the bottom of the mystery of fever. To those who have lost their nearest and dearest by such disease, there must be something ineffably tantalising in these perpetual boastings—while we are all the time precisely where we were ; and I confess to being, for my own part, just a little sick of these Hopes which (it has been remarked) "spring eternal in the physiological, as in the human, breast". She is, I think, some-what of an impostor this "Hope" of Science—who leans not on an anchor, but against a vivisecting trough ; and whom her traditionary sisters, Faith and Charity, would certainly hasten to repudiate. The references to this Hope in every page of every defence of Vivisection call to mind the story of Sir Boyle Roche in the Dublin Parliament, when he maintained that the Union with England had brought uncounted—but not easily defined—benefits to Ireland. "Honourable gentlemen," said Sir Boyle, with Hibernian eloquence, "may titter, *but when the Day of Judgment comes* they will see the good the Union has done to Ireland." Just so. And when the Day of Judgement comes—scarcely sooner—we shall look for the promised cure of fever and cholera, cancer and consumption, by means of Vivisection.

Sir William does not conclude without again parading his singular ignorance of the rudiments of ethics. Quite calmly he enounces the astounding canon : "Our obligations to the lower creatures *arise out of ourselves*. We owe it *to ourselves* that we should treat them with tenderness." The Catholic doctrine, that we owe it to God to be kind to His creatures, exhibits one side of the truth. The doctrine of the intuitionalist Butler and of the utilitarian Bentham, that we owe to every sentient creature to spare it pain, simply because it is sentient, sets forth the larger truth. But the doctrine of Sir William Gull, that duty to the lower animals is exclusively a *personal* duty (like truth, temperance, and chastity), seems to reveal incomprehension of the very alphabet of morals. There is, however, just one thing which the great teachers of physical science deem beneath their notice. It is that science which deals with the noblest part of the noblest creature. The ganglion of a worm or the egg of a maggot is in their eyes more interesting than the heart of a poet or the conscience of a saint.

In the second essay in the *Nineteenth Century*, the writer, Mr. Fleming, mentions with entire satisfaction (heightened by the usual condiment of Hope) various successful experiments of inoculation of rabies, tuberculosis, glanders (applied to a " *worthless* " horse), and of anthrax.

Into the interminable controversy respecting vaccination in all its forms, and the justice of the pæans over "cultivated virus" (delightful phrase!), which have been ringing in our ears this winter, it would be idle here to speak. I note that already there are signs of a return to a comparatively reasonable frame of the scientific mind, noticeable particularly in a report published in Dr. Lauder-Brunton's journal, the *Practitioner*, for March, of experiments made in Hungary in correction of those of Pasteur. The Commissioners sent by the Minister of Agriculture say that they "cannot overlook the fact that after the protective inoculations, *the deaths from other diseases*, or more correctly those in which the post-mortem appearances were those of catarrh, pneumonia, distoma, strongylus, and pericarditis, and not those of anthrax, occurred exclusively among the inoculated animals" (p. 233). They add that "there are still several doubts about the method from a public health point of view," and that "of great importance is the question whether the meat, milk, &c., of inoculated animals can convey anthrax". After referring to the inconceivable multiplication of disease germs in living and dead animals, which would follow the extensive use of inoculation— germs which "might regain their original virulence, and in this roundabout way affect men and other animals"—the committee conclude that the "immediate general application of Pasteur's method in the form demonstrated to us here would be precipitate, that it should least of all be recommended by the State ; and that . . . the performance of protective inoculation by private individuals should be completely forbidden . . ." (p. 235).

The men of science will no doubt wrangle over this matter for some time to come. Meanwhile the lay public may exercise its own humble common sense on a problem nearly connected therewith. Whither is Pasteurism to lead us? Vaccination as a protection from one special epidemic is a thing which the majority of Englishmen have accepted as a wise measure, though the anti-vaccinators have shown cause both to doubt the extent of its preservative power, and to credit it with certain "ghastly risks" more terrible than those from which it should shield us.*

Accepting vaccination, however, as a preservative from one disease, how will it be when we and our cattle employ twenty similar preservatives for twenty other diseases? Is it really to be believed that the order of things has been so perversely constituted as that the health of men and beasts is to be sought, *not* as we fondly believed by pure and sober living and cleanliness, but by the pollution of the very fountains of life with the confluent streams of a dozen filthy diseases? Mr. Fleming indites a psalm of triumph over the prospect of a boundless field of inoculations just opening to the activity of medical men and veterinary surgeons, who will go forth like so many sowers to scratch the people and cattle, instead of the ground ; and drop "cultivated virus" by way of seed,—or, possibly, tares, as the case may prove. Are we then, our oxen, our sheep, our pigs, our fowls (that is to say, our own bodies and the food which nourishes them), all to be vaccinated, porcinated, equinated, caninised, felinised, and bovinated, once, twice, twenty times in our lives, or in a year? Are we to be converted into so many living nests for the comfortable incubation of disease germs? Is our meat to be saturated with "virus," our milk drawn from inoculated cows, our eggs laid by diseased hens—in short, are we to breakfast, dine, and sup upon disease by way of securing the perfection of health?

Surely, when this last medical bubble has burst, it will be deemed the emptiest and the ugliest of the long series of which potable gold and the Elixir of Life formed the beginning.

* See (1889) article on Vaccination in *Encyclopædia Britannica.*

The third article in the *Nineteenth Century* is by Dr. Lauder-Brunton, one of the authors of the *Handbook*. The gist of it consists in the attribution to Vivisection of certain alleged advances in our knowledge of digitalis, strychnia, Calabar bean, pepsin, chloral, and nitrate of amyl. One would conjecture at first sight that, with all these new weapons wherewith to combat the Destroyer, the doctors would by this time have sensibly reduced the rates of mortality, and that at least four or five diseases should have been definitely conquered. A few figures to such effect from the Registrar-General's Report (which I fear somehow records quite an opposite state of things) would certainly be more satisfactory than to find all these new remedies paraded before us without any means of checking the boasted results. The unsatisfactory nature of these large statements may be noted even by one who, like myself, cannot pretend to get to the bottom of the matter—for example, in two instances out of Dr. Lauder-Brunton's list:

"The experiments of Luchsinger," Dr. Brunton says, "and of Rokitansky prove"—so and so. "If, then, we should give strychnia at bedtime to the consumptive patient, we should prevent the sweats. We try it accordingly, and the result shows that the practical deductions from these apparently useless experiments on animals are correct, for the sweats cease and the prostration disappears" (p. 485).

This kind of thing addressed to the public who read the *Nineteenth Century* sounds delightfully clear and conclusive. But, by chance, I compare it with another report, written by Dr. Brunton for his scientific brethren, and reprinted from *St. Bartholomew's Hospital Reports*, vol. xv. In this latter honest report there are cited only four cases wherein the beneficent effects of strychnia were tested. In Case 1 the patient died, having had no "night-sweats until a few days before death". In Case 2 the remedy for the sweats caused the patient to think it increased her cough every time it was administered. In Case 3 the remedy seems to have made little difference. In Case 4 it seems to have stopped the sweats, but we are not told whether the patient recovered. These results scarcely bear out, I think, the unlimited assertion in the *Nineteenth Century*, that on the application of the remedy "the sweats cease and the prostration disappears".

Again, Dr. Lauder-Brunton tells us—as if the matter were beyond doubt:

"The action of carbolic acid was first systematically investigated by Lemaire, and its application by Lister to surgery is one of the greatest boons to humanity of modern times. Of its importance in antiseptic surgery no one can be ignorant" (p. 485).

Who that reads the above in the *Nineteenth Century* would suppose that at the recent Congress one of the most eminent surgeons and vivisectors in Scotland, Dr. Keith, stated that he had abandoned the system of carbolic acid, because he found it to poison both himself and his patient? Another no less eminent English surgeon, Mr. Lawson Tait, wrote publicly two months ago of Mr. Lister's boasted ligature: "If the carbolic ligature had never been tried on animals, where it seems to answer admirably, it never would have been tried on human patients, where it fails miserably and has cost many lives."—Letter to *Birmingham Daily Mail*, July 21, 1882.

I now reach the essay of Professor Yeo in the *Fortnightly Review*. It chiefly consists of contradictions of my statements in the January number of the same *Review*, together with some remarks on the lucid article of the Lord Chief Justice, which had perhaps best be passed in silence.

Professor Yeo refers at great length to the annual Parliamentary Returns of Licences and Certificates granted under the Vivisection Act, to prove the extreme paucity of painful experiments, and adds, "No one will, I think, presume to say that this evidence is not absolutely unimpeachable and without prejudice".—"No one?" Why, who in their senses take the word of accused men for their own secret doings, and of what else do these returns consist? There is not even a pretence of real personal overlooking of the laboratories by the inspector, much less of visits paid unawares. No doubt Mr. Busk has correctly noted the number of licences actually granted by the Home Office—so far is a safe matter of official routine. But respecting the number of experiments performed under each licence, and the degree of pain inflicted in such experiments, it is really crediting us with too much simplicity, "weak-minded humanitarians" though we be, to suppose we shall take the word of the very men whom the returns are intended to check! Did not Dr. Yeo indulge in a smile when he wrote the following: "There are no signs of any attempt to keep back anything on the part of the experimenters; on the contrary, they seem to have been *rather too punctilious*"?

It is not easy to write on such a matter as inspection under the Vivisection Act made by an inspector who has been the elected Vice-President of that Royal Society to which all the leading vivisectors belong; but the following fable will perhaps convey the sense in which not a few of us regard the matter:

FABLE.

"A Farmer once was much troubled by Mice in his Barn. So he went to the Lion and begged for a Cat. The Lion at first promised to send the Cat, but presently up came 3000 Mice to the Lion's Den, and squeaked so loud at the notion, that the Lion, who has a sneaking kindness for Mice, shook his mane and winked at the Mice, and spoke thus: 'I must give the Cat to Mr. Bull; but don't be afraid! Pussy shall not eat you.' So the Cat was turned into the Barn. It was a nice sleek Cat, who went purring up and down with a bell round its neck, and never condescended to look down a Mouse-hole. Indeed, it had enough to do lapping its own cream without thinking of Mice. So whenever anybody asked how things were going on, the Cat said always 'Purr,' and never 'Mew, mew;' and after a few years there were twice as many Mice in the Barn as when the Farmer asked for the Cat."

Professor Yeo next quotes, as of great weight against anti-vivisectors, the resolution of the recent Congress in favour of Vivisection. Considering that among the votes taken in favour of this resolution were no doubt his own and those of Professors Humphry, Rutherford, Ferrier, Bacelli, Hermann, Brown-Séquard, Charcot, Béclard, Chauveau, Virchow, Flint, and Goltz, it is almost quizzical to ask us to be impressed by their solemn approval of their own practice. A general meeting of the Dominican Order under the presidency of Torquemada would assuredly have passed equally unanimously a parallel resolution: " That this assembly records its conviction that *Autos da Fè* have proved of the utmost service to religion in the past, and are indispensable to the immortal interests of the human race ".

Lastly, I come to the portion of Professor Yeo's article which personally concerns me. I take up the glove he has thrown down, and call my readers to witness that I do so without the smallest hesitation.

Professor Yeo disputes three of the cases of English cruelty cited by me in the *Fortnightly Review* for January. He writes :

" In the first the physiologist is quoted as saying : ' As soon as the cat comes out of the chloroform it lies in a helpless state, and does not move or give any signs of feeling '. Commenting on this case, Miss Cobbe—quite ignoring the important word *chloroform*—suggests that the animal is paralysed by the intensity of its agony. Can she really understand the matter so little as to imagine that an animal suffers intense agony when it is completely stupefied by chloroform ? "

Commenting on these remarks of Professor Yeo, I observe that he, quite ignoring the important words " *comes out of* " before " chloroform," rebukes me for not understanding the cat to be " stupefied by chloroform " when the experimenter had expressly described it as having " *come out of the* chloroform ". What does " coming out of chloroform " mean, if not that the anæsthetic effects of the drug had ceased ?

2. Professor Yeo disputes my statements respecting Professor Rutherford's experiments, which he says were " taken from an

inaccurate account of the operations by Dr. Walker," and are introduced by the statement that at least fifty dogs, under the express sanction of the law as it now stands, were used in the experiments. Professor Yeo goes on to say :

"We have seen by the official reports that no such number of animals suffered pain during the year in which Professor Rutherford made these experiments (1878). . . . I happen to know that the exact number of animals used by Professor Rutherford under the certificate in question was twelve, and that they form three-fourths of all the experiments where the pain can be called appreciable that were done during that year."

In my reference to Professor Rutherford's experiments in the *Fortnightly Review*, I gave no date whatever, and I know not by what authority Professor Yeo pleases to fix on that of 1878. According to Dr. Rutherford's own statement in the scientific reports of the *British Medical Journal*, May 5, 1877, and December 14, 1878, I find that altogether no less than sixty-seven dogs (as a minimum) were tortured. "Each experiment," Professor Rutherford says, "lasted the entire day, at the close of which the animal was killed and the alimentary canal examined." In the series for 1878, I find that thirty-one dogs were thus experimented on ; and I now ask Professor Yeo to be good enough to explain how the "twelve dogs" which he "happens to know" was the "EXACT" number used by Professor Rutherford in 1878 managed between them to be killed *thirty-one times over*, and have their alimentary canals thirty-one times examined ? Truly, these conflicting accounts of Professor Rutherford in a scientific report, and of Professor Rutherford's friend in the *Fortnightly Review*, are exceedingly puzzling to the lay intelligence ; but perhaps Professor Yeo's little mistake of twelve dogs for thirty-one still leaves his statement "accurate enough for scientific purposes ".

As to Professor Yeo's reference to the official report, which states that "no such number of animals suffered pain during the year in which Professor Rutherford made these experiments," I can only remark that, with Professor Rutherford's own account of his dogs in our hands, we need no better evidence of the trustworthiness of those official reports on which half Professor Yeo's paper is founded as "unimpeachable evidence".

3. Finally, we arrive at Professor Yeo's last challenge. He says (p. 361):

"The third set of experiments adduced in proof of English cruelty is that performed by Dr. Roy on the innervation of the kidney, which was mentioned in the Physiological Section of the International Medical Congress. Of these experiments, Miss Cobbe admits she knows nothing, yet she suggests that they may prove a ghastly counterpart to some others, and she appeals in a telling manner to Dr. Roy's hearers to tell us what those experiments were. I heard him on that occasion, and have also seen him operate, and I can assure your readers *that the infliction of pain had no part in the investigation,* for the animal was kept under chloroform all the time, and was killed before it recovered from the anæsthetic" (p. 362).

Here, then, we have something definite to go upon. Professor Yeo says he "*has seen*" Dr. Roy "operate," and that the "infliction of pain had no part in the investigation". It would be too miserable a prevarication to offer this assurance concerning one experiment, if others of the same series involved frightful agony under curare alone. I therefore assume that Dr. Yeo has here pledged his honour that the infliction of pain had no part in any of these investigations of Dr. Roy described at the Congress, certainly not in the leading part of them. Now, what are the facts?

Dr. Roy has, I find, published an account of these experiments in two articles: first, on the Mechanism of the Renal Secretion, in the *Proceedings of the Cambridge Philosophical Society,* May 23, 1881; and second, on the Physiology and Pathology of the Spleen, in the *Journal of Physiology,* for January, 1882. In both these articles he states that the animal—rabbit, cat, or dog, in most cases the latter—was kept fully under the influence of ether, chloroform, or morphia, or a combination of two of these, from the commencement to the end of the experiment. These statements will be presently analysed.

I now offer to the reader a summary of the contents of these papers, and a commentary upon them, drawn up by a gentleman perfectly qualified to deal with them scientifically :

" Of the character of these experiments all foreign experimenters would acknowledge that, if they were not performed on animals fully under the influence of some anæsthetic or narcotic, the animals must have suffered atrocious agony, more severe, perhaps, than in any of the so much reprobated experiments performed by Mantegazza ; for that experimenter trusted to the nails with which he larded his victims for causing irritation of any sensory nerves they might touch in their passage, while in Dr. Roy's experiments the most sensitive nerves were first carefully dissected out, then tied, and the cut ends irritated by electricity.   Now, it so happens that the major portion of both series of experiments consisted in watching the effects of reflex action resulting from electrical irritation of the cut ends of a large number of sensory nerves upon the blood-vessels or circulation in either organ.   It is also certain that such reflex actions *could not be obtained from animals rendered insensible by anæsthetics or narcotics.*   On this point the evidence of Dr. Brunton, himself an eminent vivisector, and joint author of the notorious *Handbook,* as given before the Royal Commission (5745, 5811), is very explicit, and it is therefore clear from the results that the animals were made to suffer this, the most agonising part of the experiments.

" The mutilations caused by dissecting out the various structures to be manipulated might fairly be described as something truly awful, as the detailed account presently to be given will demonstrate.   Most of these mutilations could be performed even with advantage to the operator, under anæsthetics, as a means of keeping the animals quiet, but some could only be done well under curare and artificial respiration ; for example, the dissecting out of the roots of the splanchnics on both sides of the thorax, where, but for artificial respiration, the lungs would collapse and the animal at once die of suffocation.   And, as a matter of fact, we are informed in both articles that curare and artificial respiration were used in the experiments to keep the dogs quiet ; and if under this drug stimulation of the sensory nerves took place (and such a condition was, from an experimenter's point of view, the most appropriate), then the animals (to use Claude Bernard's classic expression) 'endured the most atrocious sufferings that the imagination of man can conceive'.

"As regards the first and, from the published details, the most severe of the two series of experiments, that on the kidneys, the use of curare and artificial respiration is referred to without any modifying circumstance or remark; and that there was great cruelty in that series we have upon authority that neither Dr. Roy nor Dr. Yeo would dare to impugn. In the account of the second series of experiments, on the spleen, Dr. Roy speaks (207 and 221) sometimes of the curare being used, ' in addition to an anæsthetic agent,' during electric stimulation of nerves and of the medulla. Now, in the first place, we absolutely deny the possibility of keeping an animal insensible by anæsthetics during curarisation; and in the second place, if it had been possible to do so, the operations now referred to are precisely those which could not be performed, that is to say, they would give no result if so performed; and this we shall prove also from the very clear evidence given before the Commission by Dr. Lauder-Brunton, to whom we have already referred as an accomplished physiologist and part author of the *Handbook.*

" Dr. Brunton's evidence refers specially to that very operation on the medulla, and to the whole class of electrical stimulation of the nerves which we are now considering; and as it is too valuable to be mutilated in any way, we give the evidence exactly as it stands in questions 5472-3-4-5.

"'Mr. Forster asked (5742): Then the purpose for which wourali (curare) is used is in order to keep the animal quiet, to make the experiment an easier one to conduct?—Yes, in frogs and in the higher animals it is to get rid of some of the effects which might be due to irritation of the nerve centres. For example, this is the case in some physiological experiments that have been made in Germany by irritation of various parts of the nervous system of the upper part of the spinal cord (*i.e.,* medulla). You want to

ascertain the influence of that part upon the vascular system generally, the system of blood-vessels, and you want to ascertain that
alone. If you irritate this upper part of the cord after you have
given wourali, you only get the action upon the blood-vessels;
but if you were to irritate this part without giving wourali previously,
you would get the irritation conducted all down the ordinary motor
nerves, and get all the muscles set into violent action; the action
of the muscles would react upon the vessels, and you would get
the whole experiment disturbed.

"'5743. Is there anything to prevent your giving both drugs, or
giving them mixed together, so as to stop the pain by the chloroform and the nervous movement by wourali?—YES, THERE IS, and
it is this: in very many of these experiments you want to ascertain
what is termed the reflex action; that is to say, that an impression is made upon a nerve, and goes up to the cord, and is
transmitted down. Now, chloroform acts upon the reflex centres,
and abolishes their influence completely; so that if you give the
wourali, which paralyses the ends of the motor nerves, and give
chloroform, which paralyses the reflex centres, you deprive yourself of the possibility, in many instances, of making satisfactory
experiments.

"'5744. But are there not many instances in which you give
wourali simply for the purpose of getting the animal perfectly quiet?
—Yes, those instances I have named.

"'5745. But if it is done for the purpose of getting the animal
perfectly quiet, could not chloroform be given also?—No, for that
very reason; if you were to give chloroform, the experiment
would be at an end; you would have abolished the action of the
reflex centres, and thus you might as well not do the experiment
at all.'

"Now, with that exact and lucid explanation of Dr. Brunton
before them, dare either Dr. Roy or Dr. Yeo pretend that an
anæsthetic was used to make the animals insensible, either under
curare or without it, while electrical excitation of those sensory
nerves was being conducted, to obtain reflex reactions on the
blood-vessels of kidney and spleen? And *not* being used, can

they deny that during all these operations the poor mangled cats and dogs suffered atrocious agony?

"There is still another insuperable difficulty in rendering curarised animals insensible by anæsthetics which may occur to many who are not physiologists. Most people are aware of the necessity of touching the cornea, or doing some similar action, while giving chloroform for a surgical operation, by way of testing the presence of sensibility, through inducing some slight reflex action if sensibility persists. On the other hand many persons know by this time of the great difficulty there has been in ascertaining whether or not sensitiveness persists during the motor paralysis produced by curare. Scientific opinion at the present day is almost unanimous in holding that curare leaves sensation and consciousness intact, but that is a question which has only been fully corroborated on human beings who have been operated upon under curare, and 'who remember all that has passed around them, and the sufferings they have experienced' (Bernard, in *La Chaleur Animale*, p. 63). As then the motor nerve to all muscles of expression are paralysed, what possible sign could be taken by Dr. Roy to mean that the animal was insensible? The thing is simply impossible, and this fact, coupled with the equal impossibility of getting any results from experiments of the kind we are considering, will probably lead most people to place another value upon Dr. Roy's statement about anæsthetics than that which he evidently desires.

"Let us now describe the mutilations and the character of the operations which took place in some or other of these experiments upon the kidney alone, probably in most of them; for, thanks to the secrecy guaranteed by the present Act, we cannot tell the number of animals sacrificed, and we are forced to take everything from the vivisector's own story:

"First, the animal would be curarised and artificial respiration established. Then the kidneys on both sides would be arrived at by means of an incision through the loins; they would then be dissected clear of all their surroundings, often with 'the most laborious and minute cleaning of the walls of the artery and vein';

they would then be enclosed in a peculiarly shaped box, whose interior communicated with a clockwork registering instrument (plethysmograph and Ludwig's kymograph).

"Again, the back of the skull would be cut away, and the little brain (*cerebellum*) lifted up to allow the medulla oblongata to be excited by weak induced currents of electricity. Incisions would be also made along each side of the windpipe, and the carotid arteries dissected out and closed at times by applying a clamp. The same instrument would be also applied to the innominate artery, to the renal arteries, to the large branches of the aorta in the abdomen, and to the abdominal aorta itself, below the point where the arteries to the kidneys are given off.

"The chest and abdomen would be opened along their whole length and a glass tube tied in the pipes (ureters) which carry the urine from the kidneys to the bladder.

"The spinal canal would be opened in the region of the neck by cutting through the backbone, and the roots of the whole of the nerves leading to the anterior limbs (branchial plexus of nerves) dissected out.

"The roots of the splanchnics in the thorax and these nerves in their course through the diaphragm would also be dissected out. To do this the anterior surface of the backbone in the chest and belly would have to be cleared on both sides, and the contained organs moved from side to side as required.

"The nerves leading to each kidney (from seven to eleven in number) had also to be dissected out.

"The great nerves of the hip and leg (sciatic nerves) had also to be reached, and also the vagus, the great nerve which supplies all the organs in the chest and abdomen.

"All the nerves mentioned were tied in two places and cut, the tying being for the purpose of lifting up either cut end (central or peripheral end) in order to excite it by electricity. Now, tying a nerve, even although no bigger than a thread, causes extreme agony (Evidence Minutes, 4230), and in these poor animals all the principle sensory nerves in the body were so tied. Then the central and peripheral cut ends of these nerves were stimulated with electricity from time to time, to see what might chance to happen to the circulation in the kidneys.

"Sometimes the artificial respiration was stopped for three or four minutes to see what would happen to the same circulation during suffocation.

"Various solutions of chemicals and drugs—nitrate of soda, urea, acetate of potash, digitalis, and common salt, also defibrinated blood, and serum from other dogs, were injected into the veins, to see what effect these would have on the kidney secretion.

"And what were the results of this horrible series of experiments? Every time a nerve was excited and a pang of agony shot through the animal's frame there was only one result (except when the nerves to the kidney were cut, and therefore telegraphic communication broken) which happened invariably—the kidney contracted.

"Another page might be filled with such details, and we have not even yet reached the experiments on the spleen."

Here then is my answer to Professor Yeo's assertion, as an eye-witness, that "the infliction of pain *had no part in Dr. Roy's investigation*".

And here is also my answer to the charge of having misrepresented British physiologists by comparing them to foreign vivisectors. Dr. Roy, it is stated, is a young Scotchman, trained in Edinburgh. He obtained, through the recommendation of Professor Burdon-Sanderson, the office of Professor-superintendent of the Brown Institute, and, through that of Dr. Michael Foster, the George Henry Lewes Scholarship founded by the late George Eliot. It was doubtless by the help of the latter endowment that he visited the continental laboratories, and in one of them performed some of his experiments in concert with Professor Cohnheim. The remainder of the series, as well as the whole series of experiments on the spleen, were performed in the Physiological Laboratory of Cambridge.

Thus the attempt of the advocates of Vivisection to distinguish modern English Vivisection from the Vivisection practised by

foreigners in Germany, Italy, and France, once for all falls to the
ground.   These experiments of Dr. Roy—among the most
agonising in the records of Vivisection—took place neither far off
nor long ago, nor yet were they the work of any foreigner.   They
were done by our own countrymen, within the last two years,
and the greater part of them on English ground.   Nay (most
significant fact of all), the report of them was publicly read in the
Physiological Section of the London Congress of 1881, and not
one voice among all the English physiologists present was raised
to express disapproval or rebuke.

———

Professor Gerald Yeo, in the May number of the *Contemporary
Review*, inserted the following letter in rejoinder to the above
article :

"To the Editor of the 'Contemporary Review'.

"11 King's College, London, 14th April, 1882.

"Dear Sir,—In an article on ' Vivisection and its Two-faced
Advocates,'* which appears in the current number of the *Contemporary Review*, there are some inaccuracies which should be
noticed, and as Miss Cobbe directly appeals to me to explain
a point where she is in difficulty, I beg you will allow me an
opportunity of gratifying her, and preventing your leaders from
being misled.

"In page 611 Miss Cobbe says: ' We find Dr. Brunton assuring
the readers of the *Nineteenth Century* that "he has calculated
that about 24 out of every 100 of the experiments (in the
Parliamentary Returns) might have given pain.   But of these 24,
four-fifths are like vaccination, the pain of which is of no great
moment.   In about one-seventh of the cases the animal only
suffered from the healing of a wound."'   Nothing resembling this

* The name under which the above article, " The Janus of Science," was originally published.

occurs in Dr. Lauder-Brunton's article in the *Nineteenth Century*. But it is a tolerably accurate quotation of the sentence by which I introduced the following table in the *Fortnightly Review* of last month, which shows the amount of pain inflicted in 100 vivisections :—Absolutely painless, 75 ; as painful as vaccination, 20 ; as painful as the healing of a wound, 4 ; as painful as a surgical operation, 1—total, 100.   This is a perfectly correct statement of fact.   In page 614 Miss Cobbe refers to some remarks of mine about foreign physiologists ; and, completely misinterpreting my meaning, makes it appear as if I had accused a number of my foreign colleagues of perpetrating certain 'horrors'.   I did not admit that the physiologists abroad are cruel, nor did I in the least intend to endorse the truth of the stories which I mentioned as having been 'oft-told' *by Miss Cobbe*.   It never could have occurred to my mind to accuse the gentlemen named of anything like cruelty, because the one amongst them that I know best, and to whom Miss Cobbe refers with ironical pity, is a most kind and humane man, who never omits to give chloroform when it is possible to administer it, and is devotedly attached to the lower animals.   I should be indeed sorry did anyone imagine that I adopted Miss Cobbe's view of Professor Goltz's character, for I know him too well, and am proud to call him my friend.   Perhaps I was premature in judging harshly of Mantegazza's operations— the one foreign experimenter I did 'throw overboard'—because my knowledge of his work was derived solely from Miss Cobbe's writings, and may be quite incorrect.   If she can attribute to Dr. Brunton words which I wrote one month ago, she may have put down to Signor Mantegazza the writings of some author of the old Italian school.   In page 622, Miss Cobbe, a second time, mistakes the total number of experiments done by Professor Rutherford for those done by him 'under the express sanction of the law as it now stands'.   Professor Rutherford's experiments, though published in 1877-78, extended over some ten or eleven years, and possibly were as numerous as is stated.   All but twelve, however, were done without the 'express sanction' of any special law, the Act not being in existence, and therefore Miss Cobbe's assertion, 'that at least fifty dogs under the *express sanction of the law* as it now stands were used in the experiments,' is as far from the truth as when I contradicted it a month ago. There is no want of accord between Professor Rutherford's reports and those of the Home Office such as Miss Cobbe infers. The scientific description does not say when or under what restrictions the experiments were made. If, instead of being absolutely accurate, the Parliamentary Reports be as 'untrustworthy' as Miss Cobbe implies, they surely set forth all the experiments 'done under the express sanction of the law,' and thus must include those in question. It was only in the year 1878 that Professor Rutherford held this special certificate, and in it the number of experiments was limited to *twelve*. If Rutherford did more than this number they were not 'under the express sanction of the law as it now stands,' and he must have acted illegally. That he did not thus contravene the Act, and, further, that Miss Cobbe knows full well that he did not do so, I am thoroughly convinced by the fact that her vigilant Society has not instituted a prosecution. The riddle Miss Cobbe so jocosely puts to me, 'How twelve dogs can be killed thirty-one times over,' now answers itself; and I venture to hope that the 'little mistake of twelve dogs for thirty-one' now obviously appears—even to the meanest 'lay intelligence'—to be of Miss Cobbe's manufacture, not mine. I have received the following letter from Dr. Brunton, whose evidence is quoted by Miss Cobbe in refutation of what I said about the painlessness of Dr. Roy's experiments, and in support of the false assertion she makes (page 624), namely, 'We absolutely deny the possibility of keeping an animal insensible by anæsthetics during curarisation' :

" ' Dear Yeo,—I know of no reason whatever to prevent animals being kept perfectly insensible to pain by chloroform, during curarisation, and I believe that anyone who dogmatically denies the possibility of this is guilty either of gross ignorance or wilful misrepresentation. The sentences from my evidence before the Royal Commission, quoted by Miss Cobbe, do not apply to Dr. Roy's experiments. I there expressly said, "In many instances" the administration of chloroform prevented satisfactory experiments from being made, knowing that this is *not* the case in all instances, but that some reflex actions, especially those connected with the vascular system, occur during the most profound chloroform narcosis.'

" 'Truly yours,

" 'T. LAUDER-BRUNTON.'

"From this, it would appear, that the 'gentleman perfectly qualified to deal scientifically' with the matter (as Miss Cobbe states) knows little or nothing about it. It is a pity she should depend for her skilled information upon a person whose chief discretion seems to lie in his not disclosing his name. For it would be mere waste of time to expose the numerous fallacies of an anonymous authority. But I think it only fair to Miss Cobbe to let her know that, in a few places where this prolix statement bears at all on the point at issue, the opinions it contains are completely wrong, or, to use her own well-worn phrase, not even 'accurate enough for scientfic purposes'. And I must repeat, in a most positive manner, my assertion that 'the infliction of pain had no part in Dr. Roy's experiments'.

"I am, dear Sir, yours obediently,

"GERALD F. YEO."

To the above the following rejoinder was made by Miss Cobbe with assistance.

1. I avow that in my article, "Vivisection and its Two-faced Advocates," I did write "Brunton" for "Yeo"; and that, hitting out against so many antagonists, I erroneously attributed to one what had been said by another.* The matter is not of the smallest consequence to the argument, as Professor Yeo is, as he says, the authority for the statement I controvert; and I may even congratulate myself that in the arduous and sickening task of answering all these "eminent" men of science, an unlearned woman like

---

* This blunder has been of course corrected in the reprint in this volume.

myself has fallen into no real blunders, since, had I done so, they
would infallibly have been pounced upon like this slip, which by
some freak of destiny has once again involved in a cloud the
duplicate personality of Professor Yeo.   In the mystified condition wherein the Bow Street trial of last winter left the members
of the Victoria Street Society, they may even plausibly imagine
that I ought to have written, not "Brunton," but "Ferrier," as
the author of Professor Yeo's experiment—made this time, not on
the brains of monkeys, but on the credulity of the British public.

2. With respect to Professor Yeo's reply to my remarks on the
"cargo of Jonahs" he had thrown overboard in the *Fortnightly
Review*, I think I can do nothing better than to cite the rich
addition he has here made to THE ZOOPHILIST'S pleasant collection of—

PHYSIOLOGISTS—IN PARALLEL COLUMNS.
PROFESSOR GERALD YEO.

"FORTNIGHTLY REVIEW." *March* 1, 1882, pp. 360-1.	"CONTEMPORARY REVIEW." *May* 1, 1882, p. 897.
"Surely those who are so happy in detecting in foreign languages the revolting descriptions of pain-giving experiments have not failed to search carefully into the writings of English physiologists in order to find out their method of work? Why repeat the oft-told tale of horrors contained in the works of Claude Bernard, Paul Bert, Brown-Séquard, and Richet in France, of Goltz in Germany, Mantegazza in Italy, and Flint in America?"	"I did not admit that the physiologists abroad are cruel, nor did I in the least intend to indorse the truth of the stories which I mentioned as having been so oft-told, by *Miss Cobbe*. It never would have occurred to my mind to accuse the gentlemen named of anything like cruelty."

It is beyond my power to say anything which shall add vivacity
to these self-contradictions of Professor Yeo.   The astounded
reader is driven to the hypothesis that it must be Professor Yeo's
"*döppelganger*" who has mischievously written in his name, either
the first paragraph or the last.

As to the observation that Professor Yeo " did not in the least intend to indorse the truth of the stories which he mentioned as having been oft-told by *Miss Cobbe*". I wish to ask (if such a thing can be had from a physiologist) a categorical answer to the following question :

Does Professor Yeo mean to imply that those " stories " (every one of which were quoted *verbatim* from the original works of the vivisectors who recorded their own experiments) were FALSELY quoted by me? Or does he imply that the vivisectors accused themselves in their own works of cruelties which they had never performed?

If Professor Yeo does not intend to convey either of these meanings, I then ask him to say in plain English what he does mean by referring to the " stories," with an italicised sneer, as " oft-told *by Miss Cobbe ?* "

Is it possible that this honourable gentleman intended covertly to convey to his readers a doubt of the veracity of these " stories " which it is absolutely impossible he can himself feel, and which I defy him to express in plain terms?

3. I now pass to a more serious part of Professor Yeo's letter, viz., his statements respecting Professor Rutherford. The complications wherewith he has involved this matter are, at first sight, bewildering, but I trust the reader will presently find himself in possession of some clear information on one of the most important chapters in the history of British Vivisection which Professor Yeo will have been instrumental in dragging into notice.

Professor Yeo began, in the *Fortnightly Review* for March, by attacking my perfectly accurate statement that, according to Professor Rutherford's own published statistics, "at least 50 dogs under the express sanction of the law as it now stands have been used in the experiments " of that ingenious physiologist. And his argument took the form of two distinct assertions: (1) That "the year in which Professor Rutherford made those experiments" was 1878; (2) that "the exact number of animals used " was twelve.

With the first of these assertions it is not necessary now to deal, for the curiously characteristic reason that Dr. Yeo has here set himself to demonstrate its falsehood. " Professor Rutherford's experiments" he now asserts—with as perfect gravity as though he had not declared the precise opposite exactly a month ago— "though published in 1877-78 extended over some ten or eleven years". He is as inaccurate as usual, by the way, in this statement of the dates of publication, a large proportion of the experiments in question having been published in the *British Medical Journal* of neither 1877, nor of 1878, but of 1879. That, however, is a detail of very minor importance and only noteworthy as a fresh instance of that congenital incapacity for accurate statement which seems to be the special "note" of the vivisector. The only point of real importance is that, having "refuted" my calculation by the plain statement that these experiments were made in 1878, he now—forgetting apparently that the statement was his, not mine—quietly gives it the lie direct!

The question thus far is simply between Professor Yeo in the March *Fortnightly* and—Professor Yeo in the May *Contemporary*. It is a question of but little interest, except to those who like myself are pretty well acquainted with the moral atmosphere of the laboratory.

And so we come to his second assertion, that the number of dogs sacrificed was exactly twelve. And here the question becomes one, not between Yeo and Yeo, but between Yeo and Rutherford.

Now what says Professor Rutherford in his own signed report of his own experiments published in the *British Medical Journal* in 1877-8-9?

The report of these experiments extends through twelve separate numbers, the last two of which are taken up by a general summary of what he terms "results". Of the remaining ten numbers we have only been able to procure nine, and here is a detailed statement of the number of experiments reported at full length in them, each report concluding with the autopsy—or examination *after death*—of its victim.

					Dogs.
5th May, 1877,	...	...	...	...	11
7th July, ,,	...	...		...	20
14th Dec., 1878,	...	...	...		2
21st ,, ,,	...	...	...	...	6
28th ,, ,,	...	...	...		3
11th Jan., 1879,	...	...	...		3
18th ,, ,,	...	...		...	3
25th ,, ,,	...	...	...	...	8
1st Feb., ,,	...	...	...	...	6
Total	...	...	...	...	62*

The "law as it now stands" was passed in 1876, the year previous to the earliest of these reports.

And this is not all. If the case stood merely thus there might perhaps be found some simple soul who rather than believe that an Englishman could be guilty of deliberate falsification would accept Dr. Yeo's triumphant figment that these experiments, kept back from the public for no conceivable reason for two years after the publication of the previous "series," had really been performed ten or a dozen years before them. Happily the report itself shows on the face of it the absolute falsehood of such a statement.

In the series of experiments by which Professor Rutherford had demonstrated to his own satisfaction that calomel had no effect upon the liver, the drug had been injected, not into the stomach, but into the duodenum. For some time the profession accepted this brilliant discovery, and perhaps in some cases left off trying to cure overloaded livers by calomel or blue pill. At last one of their number suggested that, in that omitted passage through the stomach, the calomel would have been brought into contact with a considerable amount of hydrochloric acid, undergoing in the contact conversion into corrosive sublimate.

The experiments by which this wonderful result was reached were published, as we have seen, in 1875. It took nearly a year

* See *ante*, *Comments*, p. 128.

before this absurdity was demonstrated. And *some of the very earliest of the sixty-two experiments above detailed are prefaced—in the "British Medical Journal" of 7th July, 1877—by the statement that they were expressly undertaken in consequence of that demonstration.*

These are the experiments which Dr. Yeo now solemnly declares were performed at intervals *during the ten or eleven years before!*

One word more. Dr. Yeo says "that Professor Rutherford did not contravene the Act, and further, that Miss Cobbe knows full well he did not do so, I am fully convinced, by the fact that her vigilant Society has not instituted a prosecution". If Dr. Yeo's audacity were less absolute, he would surely have foreborne to recall to public memory his own share in one of the most disgraceful trials which ever concerned his profession and its organs. When the Victoria Street Society can find a case resting on *lay* evidence, or supported by the honour of the non-scientific English press, Professor Yeo may be sure they will not delay an hour to institute a fresh prosecution under the Vivisection Act.

4. Coming next to Dr. Brunton's letter to Dr. Yeo, wherein he denies to Dr. Roy's experiments the application of the quotation from his evidence before the Commission, I may at once acknowledge the difficulty which I find in dealing with a man who, when the interests of animal-torturers demand it, can thus frankly forswear his previously published opinions.

Anyone who takes the trouble to compare Dr. Brunton's evidence, as quoted by me from the Minutes of the Royal Commission, with the first paragraph in his letter, will at once notice the glaring contradiction between them ; and to make this clearly evident, I again quote

PHYSIOLOGISTS— IN PARALLEL COLUMNS.

DR. BRUNTON'S EVIDENCE BEFORE THE COMMISSION.	DR. BRUNTON'S LETTER TO DR. YEO.
"5748. Mr. FORSTER : Is there anything to prevent your giving both drugs or giving them mixed together,	"I know of no reason whatever to prevent animals being kept perfectly insensible to pain by chloroform

so as to stop the pain by the chloro-form, and the nervous movements by curare?

Yes, there is, and it is this: In very many of these experiments," &c., &c.

during curarisation, and I believe that anyone who dogmatically denies the possibility of this is guilty either of gross ignorance or wilful misrepresen-tation."

In the second paragraph of his letter he further states: "*Some reflex actions, especially those connected with the vascular system, occur during the most profound chloroform narcosis*". This is a flat contradiction to his statement recorded in Minute 5811, where he denies the possibility of acting reflexly on the vascular system of the submaxillary gland when by opium or chloroform the reflex was paralysed. It is not so very long since Dr. Brunton was engaged in a controversy with Dr. Hoggan on this very point, in which he not only did not venture to deny the opinion he gave the Commission, but he actually repeated it in his first letter to the *Spectator* in these words: "*The only part of the experiment which cannot be shown on a deeply anæsthetised animal is the reflex action of the lingual nerve*".

I suppose Dr. Brunton has been educated on the subject of his letter since he appeared before the Commission, for if he knows no reason now to prevent chloroform being given with curare, he was very careful to impress upon the Commission (5740): "*If I use chloroform I do not use wourali; I use one, but not both*". In fact, the only interest attached to Dr. Brunton's letter is the readiness with which he abjures his previously published opinion, for neither he nor Dr. Yeo have ventured to reply to the crucial query stated in my article, or to explain to me "*when the motor nerves to all the muscles of expression are paralysed, what possible sign could be taken to mean that the animal is insensible?*" This, I am informed, has hitherto been proved to be practically impossible; and it appears deplorably like a prevarication, or something worse, on the part of Drs. Lauder-Brunton and Yeo, to make it appear as if it were possible, when they must know that it could not have been done. That the blood pressure in the kidney rose every time that Dr. Roy twanged a sensory nerve was only too true evidence that the animals suffered excessive torture during his frightful experiments. This, however, gave the measure of their *sensibility*, not of their *in*sensibility, during their long martyrdom.

Already our English advocates of Vivisection have earned the ridicule of their foreign brethren by justifying their hateful practices on the plea of seeking advantage for humanity, instead of pursuing abstract knowledge, and Dr. Brunton must now surely present a pitiful figure in the eyes of any of them who read this letter, when they find that, for the sake of giving an equivocal denial to an opponent, he is ready to declare that, during experiments for ascertaining the effect of reflex stimulation of nerves upon the blood-vessels of the kidney, it is possible and advisable during curarisation to keep the animal insensible by chloroform. If, however, there exist any one of them who confides in Dr. Brunton's or Dr. Yeo's scientific opinions, he will no doubt be delighted to learn that means have been discovered of telling when an animal, paralysed by curare, has been at the same time rendered insensible by chloroform !

Surely every tyro in physiology and in medicine recognises the possibility of giving too much or too little chloroform to either man or lower animal, and the physical signs which afford warning in either case ? Perhaps either Dr. Brunton, Dr. Yeo, or Dr. Roy will tell us *how* these signs were given by their curarised victims ? In the event of too much chloroform being administered, does the machine for artificial respiration gasp or breathe stertorously in order to show that death is imminent ? And when, on the other hand, the quantity of chloroform is too small to keep the animal insensible, how is the return to sensibility to be detected when all the muscles of expression are paralysed ? The whole pretence is really monstrous.

As for Dr. Yeo's thrice-repeated statement that "*the infliction of pain had no part in Dr. Roy's experiments,*" he must see from the foregoing reasons that it is impossible that anybody who knows the nature of curare, can accept it. He has come forward to play as usual the dreary game of thimble-rig which seems the special trade of physiologists in the Vanity Fair of Science; and it is almost as difficult for an unlearned person to detect the trick as for honest Hodge to point out the precise position of the pea. Nevertheless I hope that in this letter I have succeeded in clearing up every one of the points on which Professor Yeo has challenged my accuracy.

When——I ask sorrowfully——when will that Medical Profession which claims to itself, and which ought to deserve, the title of "noble," rise up with manly indignation and say : "Vivisection may be good or bad, right or wrong, but whichever it be, it is a disgrace to our order that men who profess to represent us should defend it by shuffling arguments and barefaced misstatements. This controversy is lowering us every day in the eyes of our countrymen ; not solely because we have taken up the hateful position of advocates of animal torture, but because we resort to such base methods of argument to carry on the contest." May I live to see the day when a thousand medical men shall follow Mr. Lawson Tait in such a course of honour and honesty !

XI.

MR. LOWE (NOW LORD SHERBROOKE) AND THE VIVISECTION ACT.*

I⊤ is an injudicious friend who proclaims on the housetops that a gentleman has received a *soufflet,* when the little incident to which he refers might have been described as an amicable tap, or as a blow aimed at a third party. With such ill-advised partisanship we think that the wiser members of the medical profession must just now charge several of their advocates who have discussed the Vivisection Act, and notably the right honourable representative of London University, who in the October number of this *Review* informed the world that the doctors had been "singled out for treatment to which no Government ever before thought of exposing any respectable trade, much less a highly-educated, liberal, and honourable profession". The spectacle is, of course, impressive of an ex-Chancellor of the Exchequer converted, like another Saul, by sudden illumination, to the true faith of Science, and casting in his lot thenceforth with the persecuted vivisector. It may prove also a valuable lesson to London University that a Tory Government has been guilty of deliberately insulting the learned profession which has therein its headquarters. Nevertheless, even these objects may, we should apprehend, be attained at too dear a cost if, when the passions of the hour have had time to cool down, reflection should show that the real dignity of that honourable profession has been needlessly jeopardised, and a hastily-judging public led to think that a majority of both Houses of Parliament has seen good reason for administering to it a rap on the knuckles.

* Reprinted from the *Contemporary Review,* October, 1876.

A year ago the leading physiologists of England, and the medical body which has (with rather superfluous chivalry) identified itself with their affairs, occupied a position which we venture to think was infinitely more respectable than that to which its over-zealous friends have now consigned it. At that time, when general attention had been called to the cruelties practised in foreign laboratories, and to those seemingly recommended to English students in the *Handbook of the Physiological Laboratory*, several physiologists and other scientific men of great eminence were understood to have instructed their Parliamentary champion in ordinary, Dr. Lyon Playfair, to bring into the House of Commons a "Bill to Prevent Abuse in Experiments on Animals made for the purpose of Scientific Discovery". This measure sets forth in the preamble that it is "expedient to prevent cruelty and abuse in the experiments made on living animals," and proceeds to lay down that "any person, for the purpose of new scientific discovery, but for no other purpose, shall be permitted to make an experiment," on conditions very closely resembling those enforced by the present Government Act. In particular it is provided (clause 4) that "any person desirous to obtain a licence under this Act may apply for the same to one of Her Majesty's Principal Secretaries of State". The Secretary of State is at liberty to grant, and subsequently to revoke, the licence, if he sees fit. Offences under this Act are to involve penalties not exceeding £50 or three months' imprisonment, and may be prosecuted and recovered "in manner directed by the Summary Jurisdiction Act". As we have said, this was the legislation which English physiologists themselves promoted, and which the Royal Commissioners in their Report (p. xii.) say "must be accepted (without committing to all its provisions all who were favourable to it generally) as a *proof of the readiness of men of the highest eminence in science to submit to the consideration of the Legislature this difficult question*".*

* Dr. Pavy thinks the passing of Dr. Playfair's Bill would pacify public feeling, without interfering with legitimate vivisection (Minutes of Royal Commission, 2074).

The tone, in short (genuine or assumed), of the representatives of science at that time was—

> " Let the galled jade wince, our withers are unwrung ".

" We are conscious of no cruelty, and we desire to prevent the actual or possible perpetration of it by other people, whether raw students or unauthorised amateurs ; and to forestall any importation of the reckless practice of foreign laboratories into English schools."

This attitude was certainly far from undignified ; and, had the Government Bill been permitted to pass as originally introduced by Lord Carnarvon (or with such slight modifications as the experience of physiologists *working in good faith to make the measure effective* might have advised), the profession would have continued to hold as high a position, possibly a higher one than ever, in public estimation. It would have been understood that its leading members had resolved to make good the well-sounding but hitherto ineffective Resolutions passed by their representatives at Liverpool in 1871 ; and that, at a critical juncture in the advance of physiological investigation, they desired to co-operate with the State in setting up a permanent barrier against the abuses to which, from the nature of the case, their pursuit is liable, and which already accompany it in those foreign schools where it is most ardently followed.

A counter-current of sentiment bearing the strongest marks of professional pique and irritation unhappily arose in 1876, and soon carried the physiologists and their medical and political

---

Dr. Burdon Sanderson has had some conferences with Dr. Playfair, and assents to the general scope of his Bill (2220).

Mr. Charles Darwin cordially approves in the main of Dr. Playfair's Bill (4662).

Dr. Gamgee cannot consider that reasonable regulations would be a slur on the profession, and is of opinion that a properly worked system of licences would be a great advantage (5425).

Dr. Handyside does not object to legislation (5938). Thinks there would be no more " slur " felt under legislation with regard to Vivisection than there is with regard to the Anatomy Act (5962).

adherents in a direction totally opposite to this larger-minded and more worthy policy. It was discovered at the eleventh hour that the legislative interference which the wiser members of the profession had last year invited, and which was recommended to the Royal Commission by such men as Sir Thomas Watson,* Sir George Burrows,† Professor Humphry,‡ Dr. Taylor,§ Professor Rolleston,‖ Dr. Pavy,¶ Dr. Antony,** and Mr. Darwin,†† would (as certain younger and hotter heads had asserted) involve a "slur" on the profession, and place its honourable members on a par with licensed publicans and sinners. A whole band of talkers and writers suddenly broke forth in a sort of Great-is-Diana chorus, glorifying the "noble," "humane," "learned," and thrice "honourable" profession of medicine, till it seemed as if Mr. Cross and Lord Carnarvon had been guilty almost of impiety in touching anything which concerned men possessed of all the virtues and liable to none of the failings of humanity; and that it was, to say the least, totally superfluous, if not outrageously impertinent, for the State to interfere with them and insist on any inspection of their proceedings, as it is authorised to do regarding those of meaner mortals, such as schoolmasters and manufacturers. It was even forgotten that when another great medical scandal arose in the last generation, and the public took alarm at the suspected complicity of some too ardent students of science with the mode adopted by Burke and Hare for supplying their "subjects," the profession had gladly sanctioned the Anatomy Act, involving precisely the same principle of State inspection as the Vivisection Act, with the difference (well pointed out by Professor Rolleston) that, if inspection were needful where only dead matter is concerned, *à fortiori* it is called for where the quivering flesh of living animals is subjected to the scalpel.

In the storm of angry emotion thus aroused a spirit of trades-unionism seems to have silenced the voices of those wiser and calmer men who must needs have regretted that in zeal against wholly imaginary insult their colleagues were losing sight of the

---

* Minutes, 170, *et seq.*   † Ibid. 173.   ‡ Ibid. 753.   § Ibid. 1175.
‖ Ibid. 1340.   ¶ Ibid. 2074.   ** Ibid. 2444.   †† Ibid. 4662.

true dignity which should have been won by the exhibition of a cordial desire to co-operate with Government in relieving their profession from a suspicion of complicity with cruelty, and a readiness to submit, if needful, even to vexatious formalities for such a purpose. The principal medical bodies held a series of excited councils, and the Home Office stood a siege of deputations, till the contest ended in a compromise, of which Mr. Lowe remarks (and in this we agree with him) that it is satisfactory to none of the parties concerned, neither to the physiologists, to the Government, nor to the public. Perhaps it was inevitable that some such lame conclusion should ensue when 3000 representative members of that profession which introduced Dr. Playfair's Bill in 1875, signed, in 1876, a remonstrance to the Home Secretary, in which (as Mr. Lowe describes it) they "repudiated with a just indignation the idea of placing them under inspection, and of requiring that they should take a licence" (p. 719). It is carrying the knight-errantry of a Parliamentary representative far to qualify as "just" the indignation of gentlemen at receiving one year what, in substance, they had asked for the year before. Mr. Lowe, after analysing the Government Bill, observes (p. 716) that "a measure more objectionable can hardly be conceived". We respectfully invite him to compare it afresh with Dr. Playfair's Bill, and to specify in what essential particular (except the fifth clause, granting special protection to horses, &c.) it differs from that measure. Can it possibly happen that a measure seems to Mr. Lowe to be harmless when promoted by Mr. Lowe's constituents, but in the highest degree "objectionable" when introduced by Mr. Lowe's political foes?

Where the sentiments of irritated *amour-propre* on one side, and humane indignation on the other, are exasperated as they have been during this most painful controversy, it is not marvellous that accusations of misstatement and exaggeration should be mutually bandied about. Among the opponents of Vivisection the lavish use of strong adjectives by one cohort of their camp ("our army swore terribly in Flanders") has been confounded with the very different error of voluntary misrepresentation of

facts.   If the latter could be laid in many cases at the door of
even the most hot-headed of humanitarians, we should not find
again and again (even in the recent article in the *Fortnightly
Review*) the hundredth repetition of the taunt respecting the
blunder about the eyes of animals dissected at one of the London
hospitals.   That mistake, it is necessary to repeat once more, was
caused by the bad grammar of the learned hospital authorities in
their prospectus, and was justified by the natural construction of
the sentence ; which, moreover, was simply quoted as it stood.

On the other hand, it is really surprising to see how often on
the side of the physiologists positive assertions are ventured upon
which reference to an easily attainable book must immediately
disprove.   The most common of these (exposed over and over
again in the *Spectator*) is once more reproduced by Mr. Lowe ;
namely, that the Royal Commission "entirely acquitted the
physiologists of any charge or even suspicion of inhumanity," and
that the Commission reported "directly to the contrary" of the
suggestion that "the desire of knowledge has overpowered the
feelings of humanity, and that the great results of research have
been bought at an unnecessary amount of sufferings " (p. 717).
Similarly Mr. Hutchinson, in the *Fortnightly Review* (Sept., 1876,
p. 315), coolly observes that " everyone who has read the valuable
report of evidence collected by the Royal Commission must have
felt relieved at the discovery that neither by the testimony of friend
or foe could it be proved that any excesses or abuses had taken
place in England ".*   To read such passages, and much more to

* Mr. Hutchinson goes on to say : " As regards the vague reports which
reach us respecting the doings in foreign laboratories, it behoves us to receive
them with caution and charity.   For the most part they are capable neither of
proof nor disproof, and in many cases the testimony on which they are at present
based is open to much doubt " (p. 315).   Does Mr. Hutchinson mean by " vague
reports " the extracts which have been printed *verbatim* by the S. P. A. V.,
from the published writings of the physiologists themselves, Messrs. Schiff,
Béclard, Gavarret, Bert, &c., recording their own experiments?   If a man's
own account of his own act be " testimony open to much doubt," which must
be " received with caution and *charity* " (save the mark !), we ask, what kind
of testimony ought to be taken as conclusive ?   The above quotation is a typical

the same purpose which has appeared in the *Times*, the *Standard*, and the medical papers, a simple person might imagine that the writers either never saw the Parliamentary Blue Book and took all they wrote from some garbled extracts, or else that they possessed a calm assurance that their readers would never compare their statements with that recondite volume—as inaccessible apparently to the "general reader" as if it were the *Codex Vaticanus.* The Report of the Royal Commission, with the Minutes of Evidence, is nevertheless to be obtained by any humble member of the community, at the reasonable price of four shillings and fourpence, through the Parliamentary publisher, Mr. King, of King Street, or any other bookseller; or may be consulted *gratis* by anyone all day long at 1 Victoria Street, at the office of the Society for Protection of Animals liable to Vivisection.

An attentive perusal of this, not mysterious, volume will establish a few important facts.

1st. The Royal Commission was so constituted as to afford every advantage of fair play to the physiologists.* Of the seven gentlemen who received Her Majesty's Commission "to inquire into the practice of subjecting live animals to experiments," the first four were eminent statesmen, the fifth a surgeon, the sixth a professed physiologist, and the seventh the editor of a political

instance of the soft words with no definite sense wherewith the advocates of Vivisection are in the habit of smoothing down the feelings of tearful old ladies, who come to them and say : "Oh, dear doctor ! tell me if those dreadful things can be true which it is said are done to poor animals by physiologists ?"—"My dear madam, I assure you that we need pay no attention to these 'vague reports'; the testimony on which they are based is 'open to much doubt,' and should be 'received with the utmost caution and charity'." (Old lady dries her tears, asks the doctor to luncheon, and resolves not to send that cheque of £5 to the Society for Protection of Animals.)

* It was, for example, not a little astonishing when one witness (Mr. Jesse) read out the record of an experiment which he deemed sufficiently cruel to deserve the attention of the Commission, to find that one of the Commissioners unexpectedly observed (6459) : "Those experiments were *made by me*," &c., &c. It is a singular position for a gentleman to be called to report on the morality of his own actions.

and literary newspaper.   There were thus two *experts* on the side of science ; and the progress of the inquiry shows that these two gentlemen acted throughout as counsel—the one for the physiologists, and the other for the medical profession.   The present writer does not presume to question whether a public inquiry of this kind ought to be carried on in this forensic manner ; but, assuming that such a course was befitting, it certainly seems to follow, as a matter of plain justice, that there should have been, on the humanitarian side, some gentleman no less well versed in so abstruse a subject, and able to draw forth from the witnesses such facts as might bear in an opposite direction.   The great ability and acuteness displayed by Mr. Hutton, who acted as counsel on behalf of the victims of experiment, could not possibly supply the lack of technical knowledge possessed by Messrs. Huxley and Erichsen.

2nd.   This constitution of the Commission being borne in mind, the results at which its members unanimously arrived will appear noteworthy, *not* for any sweeping exoneration of vivisectors—which is not to be found therein, albeit Mr. Lowe's observations would make us suppose it to be the principal conclusion, —but for the very weighty observations made in the opposite sense, and for the final decision that legislation was unquestionably necessary.   The Commissioners say indeed that "they have great satisfaction in assuring Her Majesty that at the present time a general sentiment of humanity appears to pervade all classes in this country," and that Mr. Darwin's principle, that the infliction of unnecessary pain " deserves detestation and abhorrence," is "accepted generally by the very highly educated men whose lives are devoted either to scientific investigation or to the mitigation of the sufferings of their fellow-creatures, though *differences of degree in regard to its practical application* will be easily discernible by those who study the evidence laid before us ".   The Commissioners proceed to say that Dr. Sharpey gave no small testimony of humane sentiment by quitting Majendie's lectures in disgust ; that several instructors bore testimony to the good feeling of students ; and that Mr. Colam said he " did not know a single case of wanton cruelty " among English physiologists.   This is absolutely all that is to be found in the Report resembling that perfect acquittal of the physiologists by the Commissioners which Mr. Lowe would have us think rendered the subsequent promulgation of a restrictive law an act of absurd inconsequence on the part of the Government. If "whitewashing" was to be done, we may be pardoned for saying could scarcely have been effected with a less expenditure of lime. However this may be, the Commissioners having paid their compliments, as they saw fit, to the physiologists, proceed immediately to the business of legislative interference, and remark that they have found in some minds, as in the case of Mr. Lister, a decided "prepossession" against it, but that from such prepossession "many of those whose position and character entitle them to the greatest weight are wholly free"; and they go on to give their reasons for legislation, which, to any unbiased reader, appear very much more weighty utterances than their vague compliments to the humane sentiments of all classes—physiologists included. They say (p. xvii.) that "*it is not to be doubted that inhumanity may be found in persons of very high position as physiologists*"; that "it cannot be doubted *that very severe experiments are constantly performed*, and *that witnesses have spoken from personal knowledge of the sufferings which they say have been often unnecessarily inflicted in the name of science*". They add, that "they have had evidence that cases have arisen in which the unpractised *student has taken upon himself, without guidance, in his private lodgings, to expose animals to torture without anæsthetics*". And, besides the cases in which inhumanity exists, "they are satisfied that there are others *in which carelessness and indifference prevail to an extent sufficient to form a ground for legislative interference*".* In accordance with these facts, demonstrated to their conviction, and from the consideration that the "practice is, from its very nature, liable to great abuse," the Commissioners proceed to sketch the outline of the legislation they recommend, of which the Government Bill was (Mr. Lowe confesses) the substantial embodiment.

Will anybody readily believe that the gifted member for London

* Report, p. xvii.

University had this report actually under his vision when he wrote in this *Review* (p. 716): The Commissioners "proceeded to consider to what restrictions they should subject the humane and excellent persons in whose favour they had *so decidedly reported.* Their proceeding was very singular. They *acquitted* the accused, and sentenced them to be under the surveillance of the police for life "—?

Having ventured to offer these corrections of Mr. Lowe's cardinal positions, namely, that the indignation of the physiologists at the Government Bill was "just," and that the Royal Commission reported "decidedly in their favour," I shall leave the right honourable gentleman's criticism of the new Act,—which I am in no way concerned to defend *in the shape to which his friends have reduced it,*—and add only a few incidental remarks.

That exasperating form of procrastination which consists in always suggesting the duty of doing B when it is proposed to do A, and urging the solemn obligation to attend to D when we have just spoken on behalf of C, has probably never had more lively exemplification than during the course of this weary controversy. No sooner was a novel and peculiarly hateful kind of cruelty brought to light and denounced, than every other cruelty under the sun was adduced as affording good reason why we should not meddle with it. Of course it is nearly as rational to refer to fox-hunting, rabbit-gins, and Strasburg geese as arguments against endeavouring to check the cutting up of living dogs and cats in a laboratory, as it would have been, when cholera or diphtheria first invaded us, to discountenance all efforts to stop their ravages till we had cured all the gouty and consumptive patients in the kingdom. The anti-vivisectionists simply endeavoured to put down *the worst form of cruelty they knew,* and, especially, that worst form directed against the *most sensitive animals,* whose sufferings under any injury indefinitely exceed those of less highly organised or nervous creatures. For this confession of weakness (seeing that *if* they were omnipotent they might have stopped all cruelty at once) they have been severely criticised by Mr. Lowe, whose "real anxiety" to prevent "all

wanton and unnecessary cruelty to any animal " (p.723) embraces
so vast a circuit of benevolence that we have reason to apprehend
he will suffer no Bill henceforth to pass which does not protect
from torture " all other animals " beside those now under partial
shelter—a principle which of course involves the advent ere long
of a state of things wherein the coats of right honourable gentlemen will resemble the hospitable cassock of the "sainted Aloys,"
whose small fellow-lodgers never received notice to quit :

> " Kind, tender, forgiving, to everything living ;
> From injury still he'd endeavour to screen 'em ;
> Fish, flesh, and fowl, no difference between 'em,
> *Nihil putavit a se alienum* ".

In our inability to extend our hopes to such a millennium of
parasites, common sense and common morality tell us to protect
first, and to extend the more complete protection to, the highest
animals ; and, though Mr. Lowe sneers at us for craving for immunity from torture for our " pets " (as if any shame were involved in gratitude for their love and service !), and tells us that
it is " low, paltry, and worthless " to make any such distinctions,
we must continue to urge their paramount claims so long as a
line must be drawn short of the flea and the zoophyte.

A noteworthy point connected with the agitation concerning
the fifth clause of the Act (the complete prohibition, as it originally stood, of experiments on dogs and cats) is the diversity
of the reasons given for opposing such immunity. Mr. Lowe
repeats the assertion that these animals, " from certain simi-
larities in their structure and functions to those of man, were
peculiarly adapted for experimental purposes " ; and we presume
he is cognisant of the fact that the most important experiments
are commonly made at their expense. Why, then, we may reasonably ask, whenever the advocates of Vivisection need, for the purposes of their rhetoric, to contrast the vast benefits to man which
they hope to obtain, against the sufferings of animals—*why* do they
invariably ignore the all-important part played by the tortured dogs
and cats, and raise a laugh among their sympathetic audience by
talking of " scratching a newt's tail " ? Let us understand what

they really mean, and be told whether it be the sacrifice of 14,000 dogs by one professor in variety of torture, which the advocates of Vivisection intend to defend, and which they demand liberty to copy? If so, let them, like honest men, cease to repeat contemptuous jests about this frightful slaughter-house work, and to make misleading allusions to "newts' tails". On the other hand, if trifling experiments on humble reptiles be actually (as their words would lead us to suppose) their sole pursuit, let them permit us to assure ourselves by law that the noble creatures we love, and who return our affection, will never be left to endure the agonies of their torture-troughs.

Though Mr. Lowe thinks it " low, paltry, and worthless " to make distinctions between domestic and wild animals, he thinks it a " disaster" (p. 722) that the word " invertebrate " was substituted at the last moment in the Bill for " cold-blooded," and that thus " uncontrolled power over the frog is lost to physiologists, and their absolute dominion is restricted to creatures of structure and functions very far removed from the human race". Thus in one breath he condemns Mr. Cross for not extending an equal measure of protection to all animals, and for not leaving frogs to the uncovenanted mercies of the physiologists!

Marshall Hall (in our humble opinion rather blasphemously) called the frog " God's gift to the physiologist ". How shocking of the Home Secretary to dream of placing any restrictions (even, alas ! the very feeble and ineffective ones of the new Act) on his " uncontrolled power " over that miserable creature !

Again, among the disingenuities of the vivisectors and their friends must be reckoned the habit of representing their experiments as few in number, pursued only by a mere handful of highly-gifted scientific inquirers throughout Europe, and quite insignificant in amount compared to the magnitude of the beneficent results which may be anticipated from them. This idea they have managed to convey deeply into the minds of those innumerable persons who know scarcely anything about the subject, and are only too happy to have the painful suggestions of anti-vivisectors laid to rest. I shall not attempt to refute the notion at any great length, but shall first invite the reader to glance over the plates forming vol. ii. of the celebrated *Handbook of the Physiological Laboratory*, and then over the still larger and more splendid volume of illustrations in the atlas to Cyon's *Methodik der Physiologischen experimente-und-vivisectionem.** Among these engravings they will find representations of costly and elaborate instruments, made by various noted manufacturers in Paris and elsewhere, commencing by a score or two of peculiar lancets, scalpels, saws, &c., and ascending to dozens of exquisitely delicate and complicated machines, under which the poor victim to be sacrificed sometimes appears as an insignificant detail.

Can any rational being for an instant suppose that all these infernal instruments of torture are invented, manufactured, engraved, and recommended as best made here or there over Europe, to perform experiments either few or trifling? Direct evidence of what actually goes on in a great physiological laboratory is unattainable, because no one is permitted to witness it who is not pledged by honour or interest to hold his peace. But the indirect evidence afforded by these plates of the enormous scale on which vivisections take place is more convincing than the testimony of a hundred sworn witnesses. In the face of them the jokes of eminent physicians and surgeons concerning "newts' tails" may perhaps to some readers seem to deserve stronger epithets than the present writer thinks fit to use.

We must now sorrowfully admit that the effort of the friends of animals to obtain a compromise which should fulfil the aspirations of the Commissioners and "make the progress of medical knowledge compatible with the just requirements of humanity" has for the time been defeated. There is little doubt that, had the physiologists so pleased, it was possible to secure liberty for the performance of most of the experiments from which any hope of real benefit to humanity can be derived, while at the same time guarding the animals against torture. The behaviour of the physiologists has unhappily left us to conclude that they would prefer

---

* Both may be inspected by anybody, gratis, from 11 till 5 o'clock every day, at the office of the Society for the Protection of Animals, 20 Victoria Street.

that a thousand unhappy brutes should suffer useless agony under random experiment rather than that the "profession" should submit to the necessary machinery of State inspection, or a physiologist be put to the trouble of procuring a certificate.   It is *they* who have virtually forced on the friends of animals the dilemma of either resting satisfied while torture may be going on all around them unchecked, or else adopting an attitude of uncompromising hostility to a practice which they find they cannot succeed in guarding by any sufficient legal machinery from horrible abuse.   To such as think with me there can be little doubt as to which of these alternatives ought to be adopted. The vast and mighty advantages to be derived from Vivisection— so freely prophesied, so poorly hitherto performed !—cannot in our view, even were they tenfold greater than they are, be set against the crime of inflicting excruciating pain upon unoffending creatures, and transforming into a curse the lives which God meant to be a blessing.   There is no use in taunting us with our inability to form a judgment of the scientific value of experiments, or of the " necessity " for making them of extreme severity.   We leave the physiologists to decide these matters for themselves, but simply hold that, *whatever* be the value of that scientific discovery which must be obtained by *torture*, it is morally forbidden to us, just as if it were to be gained by robbery, rapine, perfidy, or any other crime between man and man.   We are not sentimentalists, though it is a favourite sneer at us to say so ; and few or none of the anti-vivisection party would, I believe, have taken any action in the matter had the experiments of physiologists been kept within such limits of suffering, as, for example, the existing Prevention of Cruelty Act is ordinarily ruled to reach.   *De minimis non curat lex.*   It would have been absurd and Quixotic to interfere with the vivisector if he never did anything worse to animals than the sportsman or the farmer does every day.   It is because Vivisection as now practised not seldom involves protracted and hideous *tortures*,—tortures which make the whole existence of the victim to appear a frightful wrong and evil under Heaven,—that we denounce and condemn it.

And when we are told, as by Mr. Hutchinson, to "trust a specially qualified class," and "believe that the humanity of this class is on a fair average with that of mankind generally,"* we reply that we find it utterly impossible to do so for two reasons. The first of these is, that it is idle to quote the merits of persons as reassuring us respecting their actions when we have in our hands their own avowals that they *have already done* what we deprecate. Where the question at issue in any case is, "whether certain men have done certain things," testimony to their good character is highly valuable as showing, for example, that a generally honest man is not *likely* to have done a dishonest thing, nor a generally humane one exhibited cruelty. But where there is no doubt at all about the fact of the deed being done, or of the individuals who did it, nothing can be gained (unless it be another mournful lesson of the inconsistency of human nature) by reference to those virtues which *did not hinder the offence.* And the second reason why we cannot trust "a specially qualified class" is that the "qualification" which fits physiologists to judge of the *scientific* value of experiments appears to us to have distinctly detracted from their ability to see the *moral* issues of the question as they appear to an onlooker who is not carried away by the passion of discovery, and whose feelings have not been blunted by familiarity with the spectacle of agonised creatures. The expressions of several of the witnesses before the Royal Commission seem to us to display a callousness regarding animal suffering little short of absolute moral blindness, and proving most distinctly to our judgment the fatal influences of their pursuit upon the human heart.†

---

* *Fortnightly Review*, September, 1876, p. 309.

† Mr. Hutton says: "The inquiry of the Royal Commission has convinced me that, while foreign physiologists have come, in very many cases, to think little or nothing of the sufferings inflicted . . . even English physiologists, though not so reckless, recognise a very different standard of morality in these matters from that by which they abide in ordinary life. . . . The truth is, that nothing seems easier than for a scientific man to believe, without much or any evidence, that the signs of pain which a creature exhibits, if it does exhibit any, are all due to 'reflex action'. . . . An eager mind, with a great appetite for knowledge, has an immense power of overleaping the considerations which

All this line of argument, in short, in the mouths of the pro-vivisectors, may be turned, with the utmost nicety of parallel reasoning, into a defence of the Spanish Inquisition, and an exoneration of the Civil Power in Spain for leaving the members of the highest of all professions (that of Divinity) to decide whether the application of the stake and the rack were, or were not, "necessary," in the case of interests of a still more important kind than the cure of physical disease. Arguing from the exalted and disinterested character of Torquemada and many of his associates, who,—it may be asked,—should presume to question whether *such* men were not fitly trusted, as a "specially qualified class," to judge concerning the "necessity" of an *auto da fè?*

These things being so, it is obviously impossible for those who have engaged in this most painful contest to repose the required confidence in the vivisectors, or in any way to allow the matter to stop at its present most unsatisfactory point.

It is true that during the six months which have elapsed since the Act came into force there has been (as Mr. Cross's Returns promise to prove) a considerable abatement of painful experiments in the kingdom, and for this much we are heartily thankful. None of us will grudge the depressing labour of the last two years if even a few poor brutes have been protected from torture, and if (for example) a certain hideous series of experiments at Edinburgh have been stopped, and a dozen of "Greyfriars Bobby's" comrades have been mercifully spared to die in peace, instead of perishing in the long-drawn agonies destined for them by the local professor of this true "Dismal Science".

But such restrictions as the Act has placed on scientific cruelty just now are only too probably to be classed among the proverbial efficiencies of "new brooms," to be relaxed the moment that public interest is diverted from the subject. And,

obstruct its search. . . . It is in this way, I believe, that humane men will justify, when applied to the lower animals, which cannot tell us what they feel, elaborate tortures, which they would shrink, as the greatest wickedness, from inflicting on the lowest criminal in the condemned cells of our gaols." (*The University of London and Vivisection*, p. 11).

still more certainly, the entire force of the law, such as it is, rests exclusively on the discretion and sentiment of a single man—the Home Secretary for the time being. As a change of Ministry, or even a different distribution of offices in the Cabinet, may give us to-morrow a Home Secretary who entertains the opinions of Mr. Lowe on the desirability of leaving Vivisection wholly un-restrained, it is absurd to suppose that we can acquiesce in such a state of things as a final settlement of the question.*

We have been defeated in the endeavour to obtain a very moderate concession of mercy to the brutes, and we must now persistently go on asking for more, even for the entire prohibition of all painful experiments upon them, and the placing as stern and efficient legal restrictions upon the scientific and refined cruelty of the laboratory as upon the merely brutal and stupid cruelty of the streets, the bull-ring, and the cock-pit. Mr. Holt's Bill, in which this principle is maintained, will not pass this year, perhaps it will not pass for twenty years, but the agitation will never be allowed to drop till it or some equivalent measure be granted by the Legislature. During the interval the public sentiment of disgust

---

* The following is an excellent summary of the benefits and defects of the new Act (39 and 40 Vict., c. 77), published by the London Anti-Vivisection Society :

The only absolute prohibitions are, that experiments shall not be per-formed for the attainment of manual skill ; nor as a public exhibition.

The only restriction, without exception, is that the operator must be a licensed person.

The only absolute prohibition of pain is found in the case of demonstra-tion to students, in which the use of an anæsthetic is absolutely required, and in which, further, it is possible that the law may be enforced under the provisions for the registration and inspection of places for experimental instruction.

Except as above, the Act really provides no safeguard whatever against the infliction of pain. Its safeguards are only against the performance of experiments by unauthorised persons ; and as the cruelties which have outraged public feeling have been performed by physiologists, and these are the very men who under the Act will obtain licences and certificates to do what they please, in secret places, uncontrolled, the alleged safeguards are in reality useless.

and indignation against the vivisectors must necessarily be exasperated. As we have just seen, these gentlemen are already at this early stage so well aware of the existence of such feeling among a section of the nation large enough to be formidable, that their advocates have abjectly pressed the Home Secretary to conceal their names when giving to Parliament the demanded Return of their Licences—thus introducing into British affairs the novel and anomalous system of Secret Licensing—for the express purpose of shielding men who *possess superlative humanity* from the indignation of their countrymen !*   These things are "done in the green tree ".   It will be only worse, I apprehend, for the vivisectors if it prove necessary to maintain the agitation year after year, till Vivisection becomes utterly infamous, ere we succeed in making it illegal.   Of course this will not be speedily accomplished.   It is a long and heavy task which lies before those who desire to place a breakwater against the wave of scientific cruelty which threatens to spread over the civilised world.   But it will surely be accomplished at last, though not, perhaps, till the whole moral sense of England, nay, of Europe and America, has been aroused, and the duty of mankind towards the inferior animals has been reviewed afresh, and placed on loftier, truer ground ; perhaps, yet further, not till men have learned that the law of Love and Mercy is alone Divine, while the thirst for Knowledge may be the passion of a devil.   When this is done, the practice of *torturing animals in the cause of science* will be looked on with the same abhorrence and condemnation as the civilised world now regards the once equally well established practice of *torturing men in the cause of justice.*

In conclusion, a few words must be said respecting the recent reference to this subject by Dr. Tyndall at Glasgow.

It appears from this very solemn announcement of the learned Professor that, after all, one point has been discovered concerning the UNKNOWN AND UNKNOWABLE.   It is—that He approves of vivisection !   We had grown accustomed to hear from a variety of

* Since the above was written the names of Licencees are published in the *Returns.*

quarters that the practice in question was " harmless,"—was " justifiable,"—was even a Moral Duty. It was reserved for Professor
Tyndall to discover that it is Religious, and that the new God is
henceforth, it would seem, to be chiefly " propitiated" (the word
is Dr. Tyndall's, not ours) by Vivisection. After speaking of the
" hideous cruelty" of those who would enact "short-sighted
restrictions upon physiological investigations" as being a "zeal
for God, but not according to knowledge," and describing all
that he hopes physiologists will discover by-and-by about epidemic diseases (though as yet their achievements seem limited,
like those of Pharaoh's magicians, to *causing* the plagues without
curing them), the eloquent Professor is reported * to have burst
forth as follows :

"Men of Glasgow! Facts like these excite in me thoughts
that the rule and governance of this universe are different from
what we in our youth supposed it to be—that the inscrutable
Power, at once terrible and beneficent, in whom we live and move
and have our being and our end, is to be propitiated by means
different from those usually resorted to. The first requisite towards such propitiation is knowledge," &c.

With all my soul I agree with Professor Tyndall, that *if* the
great Power above is to be "propitiated" by any such methods
as he has indicated—nay, more, if that Power will in any wise
bless to the true welfare of mankind any knowledge obtained by
such means—then, indeed, is His rule of the universe *very* different
from that which we have believed it to be, either in our youth or
in our later age. And if that terrible Power will in truth "scourge"
us with a hundred diseases unless we thus propitiate Him, then
would I, for one, deliberately pray, " Let these dread diseases
overtake me, and let me die, sooner than share any benefit from
such foul rites, or ever say to this Moloch of Science,—Thou art
my God ".

* *Scotsman*, October 20.

XII.

THE BRITISH MEDICAL MANIFESTO.

On the 9th November, 1881, a circular was issued by the General Secretary of the British Medical Association to the 8000 members of that body, enclosing a copy (or in some cases, we have heard, as many as six copies, with proffers of more) of Prof. Humphry's address on Vivisection, delivered at Ryde on the previous 11th of August.*

This Address, which must now be assumed to constitute the best justification of Vivisection which the British Medical Association can put forward, had previously appeared in two or three provincial newspapers, but was scarcely noticed by zoophilists. They were deafened a little, perhaps, by the grand chorus of "Great is Vivisection," which was taken up successively during the autumn at all the Congresses of London, Ryde, York, and even in Dublin, where the cutting up of living animals was, for the first time, recognised as a branch of Social Science. Since Prof. Humphry has now been brought forward as the Goliath of the scientific host, it will be proper to take heed of his remarks and offer some response to them, albeit the initial task of construing his English is not altogether an easy one. Probably Prof. Humphry's studies of the brains and entrails of tortured brutes have left him too little leisure to cultivate the humbler sciences of grammar and syntax. Here, for example, is the first sentence

* The President of the Ryde Congress, who introduced Prof. Humphry with strong expressions of sympathy, B. Barrow, Esq., is President of the Ryde Branch of the Royal (Jermyn Street) Society for the Prevention of Cruelty to Animals.

with which we have to deal, and which seems (if we may venture
to borrow a simile from Prof. Humphry's profession) to be suffering from the disease called elephantiasis :

> "I mentioned it (this subject) to a considerable number of the other members
> of the Association ; and they all, everyone to whom I spoke, agreed with me,
> that, whereas there is so much of misrepresentation and exaggeration, to say
> the least of it, placed before the public on this subject, which is tending to
> bring the minds of many persons, and, I am sorry to say, of our legislators, to
> wrong opinions on this matter, it was the duty of us, as members of the pro-
> fession and of the Association, who know what is actually done, who know
> what is the real position of the matter, who know the real importance of Vivi-
> section to the advancement of our profession and the welfare of the community
> —it was our duty, less, indeed, in the interest of our profession than for the
> general welfare of the public, that we should speak out and state distinctly what
> we think."

The "real importance of Vivisection to the *advancement of our
profession,*" which the professor here puts, first before, and then
after, the "welfare of the community," may be great or small.
Medical men are themselves the judges whether to heal the
diseases of mankind will not suffice to constitute a "noble profession" unless there be added an exceptional permission to
torture brutes.   But of the "general welfare of the public"
laymen may speak as well as doctors ; and our speech shall
be brief.   We simply do not believe that the "welfare of the
public" is to be attained by any such means as Vivisection.
Professor Humphry, like all his colleagues, talks bombast about
the grand discoveries made by his favourite practice ; but one
thing is clear to the meanest capacity, and that is, that, if physiologists have partially satisfied their own curiosity, that achievement has served exceedingly little to alleviate the woes of humbler
mortals.   The dread scourges of disease in its most direful forms
hang over our heads in 1881, as they did over the heads of our
grandfathers in 1781, and of their forefathers in 1681.   Tens of
thousands of harmless animals have perished in hideous torments
during those two centuries, adding no mean item to the sum of
agony in a groaning world ; but consumption, cholera, cancer,
insanity, confront us as of old, unconquered and unconquerable.

The very cattle-plague baffles the physiologist, who with infinite pomp turns from his long and costly experiments at the Brown Institute and solemnly counsels us, "Stamp it out!" All the boasts of the doctors come practically down to this. Here and there in surgery and medicine they profess to have found out some improved mode of treatment which sometimes keeps patients, like poor President Garfield, in lingering death for a few months, or others in miserable life for a few years.* Here is what one of the wisest of physicians, Dr. Mortimer Granville, frankly confesses as the upshot of the whole improved medicine of the present generation : " In result of a somewhat large acquaintance with the facts held to indicate the state and progress of human health, I

---

* This case of President Garfield is a typical one, illustrative of the boasted achievements of modern medical science due to Vivisection. The most eminent surgeons in America (a country supposed to be foremost in this particular branch of the Healing Art) attended the unfortunate man incessantly, and charged the State for their attendance (as the *British Medical Journal* informs us) at the respective rates of 100 dollars a day for the local practitioners, and 1000 dollars a day for Messrs. Hamilton and Askew. Yet at the end what was the result? In the language of Dr. W. A. Hammond (ex-Surgeon-General to the United States), reported in the *Boston Journal:* "There can only be one opinion among medical men concerning the surgical treatment of President Garfield's case from beginning to end. It was based *on entire misconception of the facts.*" A private correspondent, with special means of information, writes under date, Boston, Nov. 3, as follows : " Since our good President's death we have been agitated by a terrible discussion concerning his treatment by the attendant surgeons and physicians. The autopsy revealed the fact that not one of them knew the condition of their patient, the location of the ball, or the real cause of death. They had issued bulletins concerning his condition three, four, and half-a-dozen times daily, which were sent all over the country. But in the light received from the autopsy these bulletins were *wilful, deliberate lies,* or *gigantic blunders.* The papers of to-day announce a terrible arraignment of the attending physicians made by one of the leading physicians of the country in one of the medical journals, who says, as does Dr. Hammond, that President Garfield need not have died had he been properly treated. All the disputing doctors are high up in the profession. How baseless were their arrogant claims to little less than infallible knowledge !" Since the publication of the above, the story of the sad illness and death of "Frederick the Noble" has more than capped that of President Garfield as an example of modern medico-scientific achievement.

fear my testimony must be given to show that the *improvement* effected by science consists in a prolongation of the passive endurance of life, rather than an extension of the period of true *vitality*, or any increase of the opportunity for good work and real intellectual enjoyment. We may ' live ' longer, but our lives are not either happier or more useful for the excessive energy recently devoted to the conservation of health, or the inordinate and laborious means taken to avoid disease and death. . . . I think men were happier and better, and lived nobler lives, before the pursuit of health and the yearning for longevity became a craze, almost amounting to madness. *

Nay, more.   If physiologists had attained tenfold greater success in the therapeutics than they have done, had they really restored us to healthful life, we should still say with Schiller—

> " Das Leben ist der Güter höchstes nicht,
> Der Uebel grösstes aber ist die Schuld ".†

The contagion of cruelty communicated by vivisectors to their students, and from them to their companions and to the community at large, is in our judgment a deadlier malady than any which can affect the bodies of men, and we would "stamp out" *that* disease even if it cost us any amount of physical pain.

Again, while the law of libel stands as it does, Professor Humphry may safely challenge us to point out any special vivisectors who have been demoralised by their practice. We may, however, say this: that there are few men outside the profession who will read through the six thousand replies of the physiologists to the questions of the Royal Commission, and arise from the perusal with any other feeling than that of contempt for the whole prevaricating and pitiless crew.

The main defence of Vivisection against the charge of inhumanity is of course, as usual, based by Professor Humphry on the delusion of anæsthetics.   Here is what he assures us is the

---

* Letter in *Spectator*, July 30, 1881.

† Life is not the highest good,
  But the greatest evil is guilt.

truth on this vexed question : "Gentlemen, I know something of Vivisection. I know that it is practised, whenever it can be so practised, under anæsthesia. Now this is not admitted ; but it is a fact. I have never seen an animal tortured when that torture could be prevented. Anæsthetics are almost invariably used, unless there is some special reason against them. I wish this to go forth to the world ; and I think the manner in which this is overlooked or not stated is too bad. Anæsthetics, I repeat, are always used when it is posssible to use them ; and experiments are not performed unless there is a real object for the performance." Here, then, let us pause and join issue since we have something tangible to deal with. "Anæsthetics are almost invariably used, unless there is some special reason against them." The same assertion was repeated by nearly every vivisector examined before the Royal Commission. To what does it amount ?

There was, in the last century, a dull and profane joke called "Being sworn at Highgate". People went to that cheerful suburb for a day's pleasure, and the turnpike-man tendered to them an oath binding them not to do a hundred things, *unless* they liked them,—as, for example, not to eat brown bread, *unless* they preferred it to white. It was, in short, a practical form of the jest of M. La Palisse and of Madame Blaise.

There is a great virtue in "unless," in these matters. Anæsthetics are invariably used *unless* there is some special reason against them. What sort of "special reasons" are there likely to be in the case ? Let us first enumerate offhand the vast classes of experiments in which the use of anæsthetics is obviously and avowedly impracticable without vitiating the results.

1. Experiments on the nervous system (the most fashionable of all at the present moment).

2. Experiments on the temperature of the arteries (also in fashion).

3. Experiments on the phenomena of pain.

4. Boiling alive.

5. Baking alive.

6. Stewing alive.

7. Drowning.
8. Starving to death.
9. Experiments in Alcoholisation.
10. Feeding on substances incapable of sustaining life.

It goes without saying that for all these classes of experiments the use of anæsthetics is *altogether* prohibited by the necessities of the case.

We may next consider the immense number of experiments in which, as in the case of Professor Rutherford's dogs, Professor Brunton's cats, and Professor Ferrier's monkeys, the initial operation may be performed while the animal is in a state of anæsthesia, but of which the effects endure for hours, days, and weeks of misery before the victim dies and after the anæsthetic has ceased to operate.

Having now eliminated all these classes of Vivisection experiments, we find a residue to which anæsthetics may properly and thoroughly be applied. We do not deny (having no means of ascertaining the fact) that they are so applied, but we beg respectfully to ask *what* anæsthetic is used on these occasions by Professor Humphry and his colleagues? Is it chloroform? And does he use it on dogs? There is a good deal of difficulty and risk, it seems, in this process. Here is what Professor Pritchard (Professor of Anatomy, Royal Veterinary College) told the Royal Commission on this head (Minutes, 797) : "With regard to dogs I should never think of applying chloroform at all. . . . They appear for some time not to be under the influence of it at all, and then suddenly they come under the influence of it and we find it impossible to bring them round."

Or is it, perhaps, some preparation of opium which Prof. Humphry considers an anæsthetic, like Dr. Lauder-Brunton, who, with a grave face, told the Commission (5772) it is "*decidedly* an anæsthetic". Here is *per contra* what a greater physiologist than either Humphry or Brunton says in his last great work (*La Physiologie Opératoire*, Paris, 1879, p. 155), of the finest preparation of the drug. After a large dose of morphia he says the dog still feels pain : " Placé dans la gouttiere à vivisection il y demeure immobile et stupéfié, jamais il ne cherche à mordre, quelque opération qu'on lui fasse subir. *Il sent la douleur,* mais il a, pour ainsi dire, perdu l'idée de la défense."

There is but too much reason to fear that the anæsthetic which is "invariably" used, according to Prof. Humphry, must be neither more nor less than the sham anæsthetic, curare; the "hellish wourali," which paralyses motion but leaves the nerves of sensation alive to what Claude Bernard describes (*Revue des Deux Mondes,* Sept., 1864) as the "most atrocious sufferings which the imagination of man can conceive". Even Professor Schiff, who will not be credited with morbid sensibility on the subject, observes respecting curare: "It is nothing but hypocrisy to wish to impose on one's self or on others the belief that the curarised animal does not feel pain" (*Sopra il Metodo,* &c., p. 34). The use of this substance is not forbidden by the Vivisection Act of 1876, as many suppose: it is only ruled not to be an anæsthetic for the purposes of the Act. A licensed vivisector who has a certificate to dispense with anæsthetics may use it as often as he pleases in his laboratory; and this is the testimony which the same oft-quoted Prince of Vivisectors has given to its almost universal employment in those torture-chambers so lately as 1879: "Curare is now employed in a vast number of experiments as a means of restraint for animals. There are but few observations of which the narrative does not commence by notifying that they were performed on a curarised dog" (*La Physiologie Opératoire,* par Claude Bernard, p. 168).

So much for Professor Humphry's Highgate-Oath about anæsthetics! Finally, Dr. Humphry makes a very strange statement at page 6 of his address, and not, we believe, for the first time. He says: "What we may call dead structure is pretty much worked out: it is living processes that need to be investigated". Coming from the proprietor and editor of the *Journal of Anatomy,* the assertion that "dead structure is pretty much worked out" is startling. If the case be so, we must anticipate the immediate dissolution of that respectable periodical which is at present three-fourths filled with the results of very interesting microscopic investigations of the aforesaid "dead structure".

There remains only one other point to be noticed in this address. Vivisection must indeed be an elevating pursuit, since it renders its professors unable even to imagine that anybody can labour for a humane object without a pecuniary interest in the same. Here is what our opponent says of the workers in the Anti-Vivisection cause : " Therefore, I do hope that our countrymen will become more reasonable upon this point, and exercise their own reason and their own thought, and not be led away by the various publications which are issued respecting it, for which, and for the statements that are made in them, I have some difficulty in accounting. I sometimes think there must be money to be made by them. I have been told there is " (Address, p. 6).

There is " money to be made," and there are also Fellowships in the Royal Society, and, in one notorious case, a remarkable plurality of lucrative posts to be obtained, *by Vivisection*, or by the advocacy of the practice ; but as for the money to be made by *opposing* Vivisection, we regret to say we have never yet heard of it. Some of the officials connected with the different societies, it is true, receive salaries, but only such as their abilities could command in other fields, perhaps to a greater extent. In other cases the burden has been borne by private individuals, who, so far from reaping any pay, have given up remunerative employment to carry on for years this heavy and heart-sickening work altogether gratuitously. The charge of Professor Humphry, then, is as groundless as it is base, and thus forms a fitting conclusion to his argument on behalf of Vivisection.

On the last page of the Ridiculous Address is printed a Letter written by Professor Humphry to the *Hampstead Express* in reply to some comments made in that journal on the subject. Not unnaturally the British Medical Association has not further appended the crushing rejoinder which that letter received from a lady antagonist, well known for her mastery of the controversy. I am sure she will permit me, as her friend, to quote it in full.

"*From the* 'HAMPSTEAD AND HIGHGATE EXPRESS,' *Oct.* 29, 1881.

"*To the Editor of the* ' EXPRESS '.

"VIVISECTION.

"SIR,—Professor Humphry appears to think that I am ignorant of the fact that Harvey was a vivisector, and in order to prove to me that this distinguished physiologist was a ruthless experimenter he refers to three chapters of Harvey's work containing his observations on dissected living animals. But although the fact of Harvey's vivisection must be sorrowfully admitted, it by no means follows that these researches were of any avail in helping him onwards to his great discovery. On the contrary, the careful reading of his writings would incline one to the belief that it was his persistence in making observations on the living animal rather than on the dead subject which brought him into that condition of confusion and 'unsettlement' so vividly described in his own words :

"'When I first gave my mind to vivisections as a means of discovering the motions and uses of the heart, and sought to discover these from actual inspection and not from the writings of others, I found the task so truly arduous— so full of difficulties— that I was almost tempted to think with Frascatorius that the motion of the heart was only to be comprehended by God. . . . My *mind was therefore greatly unsettled*, nor did I know what I should myself conclude, nor what believe from others.' This confusion is not to be wondered at if he were engaged in attempting to do that which, according to high medical testimony, is impossible.

"I will take the evidence of George Macilwain, F.R.C.S., as given before the Royal Commission. Blue Book, page 96 : ' *You could not discover the circulation in a living body ?*—I do not see how it is possible to do it. If you had a dead body then it is so easy to discover the circulation that it is difficult to understand how it was not done before, because if you inject by the arteries you find that it is returned by the veins. Harvey was a pupil of Fabricius, of Aquapendente, and Fabricius discovered the valves in the superficial veins—(of course the blood can only move in one direction)—but Fabricius did not see that, Harvey *did*—and that is the real seed of his discovery.'

"In the passage specially selected by Professor Humphry from Dr. Barclay's Harveian oration—as conclusive on *his* side of the controversy—we find no definite statement, only, 'I *thought* that I had attained to the truth—that I *should* extricate myself from this labyrinth'. And it is noteworthy that in the conversation held with Harvey shortly before his death, as reported by Robert Boyle, when, to use Boyle's own words, 'I asked our famous Harvey what were the things that induced him to think of a circulation of the blood,' there is no reference to Vivisection as having been the means of his discovery.

"Now the facts from which, by a brilliant process of inductive reasoning, Harvey worked up his theory of the circulation *nearly* to the point of demonstration, were, as Dr. Robert Willis asserts in his biography, 'familiarly known, most of them, to his predecessors for nearly a century, *all* of them to his teachers and immediate contemporaries'.

"In their great desire to claim this distinction for an Englishman, our countrymen seem to have to some extent overlooked the fact that others had come very close to being the authors of the discovery. We know Italians consider that Cesalpino shares the honour with Harvey, and it would seem as though Servetus might have anticipated the English physiologist but for his premature and violent death. Again, is not Dr. Barclay going too far when he speaks of Harvey as having 'obtained the sure answer to his questions, the *proof* of his hypothesis'? As we read the history of the discovery, it would certainly appear that Harvey had left *one* link wanting, which was not supplied until four years after his death, when Malpighi, the Pope's physician, demonstrated by the aid of the microscope the passage of blood through the smallest blood-vessels, and so established the reality of the communication between the arteries and the veins.

"Dr. Willis writes : 'Harvey left the doctrine of the circulation as an *inference* or induction only, not as a sensible demonstration

He adduced certain circumstances and quoted various anatomical facts which made a continuous transit of the blood from the arteries into the veins, and from the veins into the arteries a *necessary* consequence, but he never *saw* the transit.   His idea of the way in which it was accomplished was even defective ; he had no notion of the one order of sanguiferous vessels ending by uninterrupted continuity, or by an intermediate vascular network in the other order.   *This was the demonstration of a later day*, and of one who first saw the light (Malpighi) in the course of the very year when Harvey's work on the heart was published.'

"If the question, ' Whether or not Vivisection had helped or hindered Harvey in his discovery of the circulation?' were to be settled, as Professor Humphry wishes to persuade your readers, by a ' cursory glance at his great work,' how comes it that when Dr. Acland, Regius Professor of Medicine in the University of Oxford, was examined before the Royal Commission, his reply should be : ' It is not quite certain what argumentation led Harvey to *that*, whether it was the observation of the living structure or the contemplation of the dead structure '.

"And how is it that Dr. Lauder-Brunton, himself a vivisector, and therefore not likely to strain a point on *our* side, should state in one of his lectures : ' Harvey himself was led to form his ideas regarding the course taken by the blood from the position of the valves in the veins, and might possibly have been able to discover it exactly without making a single experiment' (Goulstonian Lectures, *British Medical Journal*, 17th March, 1877).

"And again, how could Dr. J. H. Bridges, in his article in the *Fortnightly Review*, commit himself to such an emphatic statement as the following : ' The more Harvey's immortal work—a master-piece of inductive and co-ordinate reasoning—is studied, the more palpable is the fallacy that his discovery resulted from any such process of direct inspection as Vivisection is supposed to give. . . . No such verification by the process of direct inspection ever has been made, or by the nature of things can be ' (' Harvey and Vivisection,' *Fortnightly Review*, 1st July, 1876, pp. 10-14).

"I fail to appreciate the force of Dr. Humphry's implied rebuke when he writes : 'Your correspondent, for the purpose of refuting an assertion which I did not make, writes,' &c., for if your readers will refer to the Ryde speech, they will notice this passage : 'Our knowledge of the movement of the blood . . . of the functions of the nervous system . . . of every nerve which passes from the brain and spinal cord, of the influence of those nerves over every organ and structure of the body . . . is almost entirely due to Vivisection '.

"I thought when I wrote—I think so still—that on this head a quotation from Sir Charles Bell's work on the nervous system was strictly to the point. Professor Humphry must excuse my presumption in venturing to suggest that the personal application of his own excellent prescription—'that the writings of an author should be read before undertaking to refute another from them '—might have led him—not to stop at page 31 of Sir Charles Bell's book, but—to have read as far as page 217, where occurs this passage : ' In concluding these papers I hope I may be permitted to offer a few words in favour of anatomy as better adapted for discovery than experiment. Anatomy is already looked upon with prejudice by the thoughtless and ignorant—let not its professors unnecessarily incur the censures of the humane. *Experiments have never been the means of discovery*, and a survey of what has been attempted of late years in physiology will prove that the opening of living animals has done more to perpetuate error than to confirm the just views taken from the study of anatomy and natural motions. In a foreign review of my former papers the results have been considered as a further proof in favour of experiments. They are, *on the contrary*, deductions from anatomy, and I have had recourse to experiments, *not to form my own opinions*, but to impress them upon others. It must be my apology that my utmost efforts of persuasion were lost while I urged my statements on the grounds of anatomy alone. For my own part, I cannot believe that Providence should intend that the secrets of nature are to be discovered by the means of cruelty ; and I am sure that those who are guilty of protracted cruelties do not possess minds capable of appreciating the laws of nature' (*Nervous System*, page 217—'Nerves of the Orbit').

"One more quotation from Bell, and I close this already too lengthy letter. Let me remark that the following words occur in Sir Charles Bell's essay on 'The Forces which Circulate the Blood,' where, if anywhere, the author would have been likely to refer to Harvey's discovery as having been the result of knowledge acquired by Vivisection : 'In what follows, as in what had preceded, I have endeavoured to discover the truth by the examination of the structure and the observation of the phenomena of life without torturing living animals.

"'It is too common a belief that, in physiology, experiments on living animals is the best and surest way of pursuing an inquiry, although it is certain that the supposed issue of experiments is as much affected by the preconception as the process of reasoning can be. The experimenter on brutes is not to be called a Philosopher merely because he goes counter to the natural feelings of mankind, nor is he more entitled to favour that he gives a character of cruelty to the medical profession, thereby contracting its sphere of usefulness.

"'It is but a poor manner of acquiring fame to multiply experiments on brutes and take the chances of discovery. We ought at least to try to get at the truth without cruelty, and to form a judgment without having recourse to torture.'

"In a note Sir Charles Bell adds : 'I can affirm, for my own part, that conviction has never reached *me* by means of experiments on brutes, neither when I have attempted them myself nor in reading what experimenters have done. It would be arraigning Providence to suppose that we were permitted to penetrate the mysteries of nature by perpetrating cruelties which are ever against our instinctive feelings. I am therefore happy in believing that the examination of the natural structure and the watchful observance of the phenomena of life will go further to give us just notions in physiology than the dissections of living animals.'

"Yours faithfully,

"ELLEN ELCUM REES.

"HAMPSTEAD, *October* 25, 1881."

XIII.

LIGHT IN DARK PLACES.

THE following pages are intended to convey, in the briefest and simplest form, ocular illustration of the meaning of the much disputed word *Vivisection*. Some of the tools and some of the furniture of the physiological laboratory, various modes of fastening the victims, and a selection of instances of divers experiments, have been arranged with the view of affording the reader by a few moments' inspection a truer idea of the work of the "torture-chambers of science" than can be obtained by the perusal of a vast quantity of letterpress description. Every one of the illustrations is a reproduction, in most cases of reduced size, by photo-zincography, of the engravings and woodcuts in the standard works of the most eminent physiologists. In every case the reference to the original work is given, and the perfect accuracy of the reproduction guaranteed. Nothing has been added and nothing has been taken away, except somewhat of the strength and vividness of the larger originals, which have been lost in the reproduction. Thus every illustration in this pamphlet may be taken with certainty to be *a vivisector's own picture of his own work*, such as he himself has chosen to publish it.

Further, it must be borne in mind that the experiments here exhibited, with the exception of two or three peculiar ones at the end, are not, as might be supposed, single instances of severe operations performed once or twice in a way by one particular physiologist. The greater number are, so to speak, *stock* experiments. They are gone over by each new recruit in the army of science who takes up the study of the organs concerned, and may be likened more properly to the scales and exercises of the musical practitioner than to the purposeful operations of the surgeon.　In the editor's (Dr. Burdon-Sanderson's) Preface to the English *Handbook of the Physiological Laboratory*, he says : "This book is intended for beginners in physiological work.　It is a book of methods . . . designed for workers . . ."　The whole large volume is in the form of a Receipt-book for cookery.　"Proceed as above . . ." "Divide the lingual nerve . . ." "A cannula having been placed in the carotid, a second manometer is placed," &c.　"For this purpose (asphyxia) a cannula must be fixed air-tight in the trachea," &c.　"In these spasms, which accompany the final gasps of an asphyxiated animal, the head is thrown back, and they must be carefully distinguished by the student from the expiratory convulsions previously described,"—and so on through 558 pages.　The great foreign treatises of Cyon, Claude Bernard, Paul Bert, and Livon are to the same purpose.

Finally, as regards anæsthetics, it is needful that the reader should dispel from his mind all illusion on the subject.　No defence of Vivisection is so frequently offered and so generally accepted as the assertion that, in the vast majority of experiments, the animals are rendered wholly insensible to pain by means of anæsthetics.　Persons who shrink from the miserable subject naturally seize on this assurance with relief, and thenceforth turn a deaf ear to the advocates of the suppression of the practice. What is the truth of the case?

There are to be considered : 1st.　Real anæsthetics (chloroform, ether, nitrous oxide, &c.).　2nd. Narcotics (opium, chloral, &c.). 3rd.　Mock anæsthetics (curare).

1.　Speaking of REAL ANÆSTHETICS, Dr. Hoggan observed in a letter to the *Spectator*, May 29, 1875 :

"The incalculable advantages which mankind has derived from chloroform as a means of destroying the sense of pain have remained a dead-letter as regards the lower animals, in consequence of the very unsatisfactory state of our knowledge of the line which separates insensibility from death, especially in some of those classes of animals which are most generally employed as the subjects of physiological experimentation. Many of these die, apparently before they can become insensible through chloroform, some of them, indeed, as soon as it has been administered. The practical consequence of this uncertainty is, that complete and conscientious anæsthesia is seldom even attempted, the animal getting at most a slight whiff of chloroform, by way of satisfying the conscience of the operator, or of enabling him to make statements of a humane character. Not only, however, are those numerous cases to be regarded with due suspicion in which a slight whiff of chloroform is recommended to be given, but we have also to bear in mind that, even where complete insensibility has been produced at the beginning of an operation, this effect only endures at most for a minute or two, and during the rest of the operation, extending perhaps to hours, the animal must bear its torture as best it may. Continued insensibility could only be maintained by continued careful administration by a special assistant, whose undivided attention would require to be concentrated upon this object. This, I believe, is seldom, if ever, done; and even if it were so we should be leaving entirely out of sight that numerous class of operations in which anæsthetics cannot be used, as they would interfere with the correctness of the results; and where, if used, they would render the experiment worse than useless. . . .

"In cases of operations on the human subject, a special assistant gives his whole attention to the administration of the anæsthetic, so as to prevent either a wakening to sensibility on the one hand, or a sleeping-away into death on the other. Yet, in spite of the exercise of the greatest care, fatal results often occur, so often, indeed, that some medical men make a speciality of the administration of anæsthetics, and undertake no other practice. . . .

"Personally, I may add that the first experiments which I attempted to make as a student in my own private room failed, because in my anxiety to produce anæsthesia I found that the animal had died before the experiment could be commenced; this, too, at a time when I had much experience in administering chloroform in the operating theatre of the hospital. I, therefore, gave up the idea of trying such experiments until I had had an opportunity of seeing how experienced vivisectors managed it. I have since then had ample opportunity of seeing, and the result of my experience was embodied in a remark I made in a letter published three months ago, that 'I am inclined to look upon anæsthetics as the greatest curse to vivisectible animals'."

2. As to NARCOTICS, this is what Claude Bernard says of the most important of them (*Revue des Cours Scientifiques*, vol. vi., p. 263):

"Morphia is not an anæsthetic, but a narcotic *(stupéfiant)*. When it has taken effect on a dog, he does not seek to escape; he has not the knowledge of where he is; he no longer notices his master. Nevertheless, sensibility persists, for, if we pinch the animal, he moves and cries. At the same time, morphia plunges dogs into a state of immobility which permits us to place them on an experimenting-trough without tying or muzzling them."

Thus neither real anæsthetics nor narcotics avail much to assuage the agonies endured by the victims of Vivisection.

3. There remains the third alternative, the MOCK ANÆSTHETIC, curare. Here again Dr. Hoggan bear testimony:

"If there be anything reliable in the results obtained by experimental physiology, it is the ingeniously ascertained effects of curare. Could these now be disproved, it would establish the truth of the sneer so often heard, 'that Vivisection only requires to prove a thing, in order that fresh hecatombs of animals be tortured to disprove it'.

"Claude Bernard, the greatest authority upon, as he is the greatest discoverer of, the effects of curare, says of it in *Revue Scientifique* for 1871-2, p. 892: 'Curare acting on the nervous system only suppresses the action of the motor nerves, leaving sensation intact. Curare is not an anæsthetic.' Vol. vi., p. 591: 'Curare renders all movement impossible, but it does not hinder the animal from suffering and from being conscious of pain'. These opinions of his are to be found repeated twenty times in the same work, in which he also mentions that they were proved on a human patient, operated upon under the influence of curare, who was quite sensible throughout, and suffered frightful pain. Even in his latest remarks on the same subject (vol. 1874-75, p. 1117) he refers to experiments where the patients on their recovery had been able to relate 'that during paralysis they had been fully aware of their existence, and of all that happened around them'. Vulpian also, the next best authority, says in the latest work (*Leçons sur l'appareil locomoteur*, Paris, 1875, p. 660) : 'Curare does not act on the sensory nerves, or, at least, does not abolish their function'."

Again, Claude Bernard, in his classic paper "On Curare," in the *Revue des Deux Mondes* for September, 1864, after quoting the opinion of travellers, and more especially of Waterton, says (p. 173) :

"Thus all their descriptions offer us a pleasant and tranquil picture of death by curare. A gentle sleep seems to occupy the transition from life to death. But it is nothing of the sort; the external appearances are deceitful. In this paper it will be our duty to point out how much we may be in error relative to the interpretation of natural phenomena where science has not taught us the cause and unveiled the mechanism. If, in fact, we pursue the essential part of our subject by means of experiments into the organic analysis of vital extinction, we discover that this death, which appears to steal on in so gentle a manner and so exempt from pain, is, on the contrary, accompanied by the most atrocious sufferings that the imagination of man can conceive." (And *ante*, p. 162) : "In this motionless body, behind that glazing eye, and with all the appearance of death, sensitiveness and intelligence persist in their entirety. The corpse before us hears and distinguishes all that is done around it. It suffers when pinched or irritated; in a word, it has still consciousness and volition, but it has lost the instruments which serve to manifest them."

Can we require any more decisive evidence of the entire indifference of physiologists to the agonies they cause than to read in a subsequent volume by the same writer the complacent statements, made without a syllable of reproval or regret, to his fellow labourers in the torture-field :

"Curare is now employed in a vast number of experiments as a means of restraining the animals. There are but few observations of which the narrative does not commence by notifying that they were made on a curarised dog" (*Leçons de Physiologie Opératoire*, Paris, 1879, p. 168).

He believes that it creates "the most atrocious sufferings which the imagination of man can conceive" ("des souffrances les plus atroces que l'imagination de l'homme puisse concevoir "), and yet he is perfectly satisfied that it should be "employed in a vast number of experiments as a means of restraining the animals !"

I now proceed to show what are the simplest tools of vivisectors.

The following are taken (much reduced) from Bernard's last

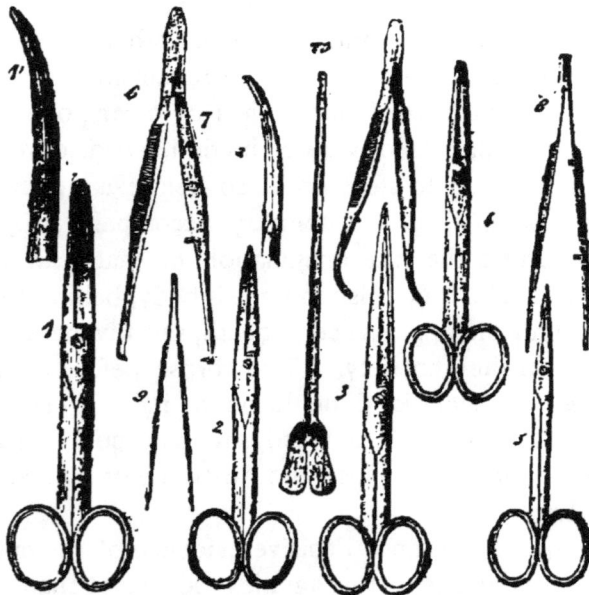

From Bernard's *Physiologic Opératoire*, p. 184.

great work, the *Physiologie Opératoire* (Paris, Bailliere et Cie, 1879). They consist of various forms of scissors, pincers with claws, crooked pincers, scalpels, forceps, saws, and knives.

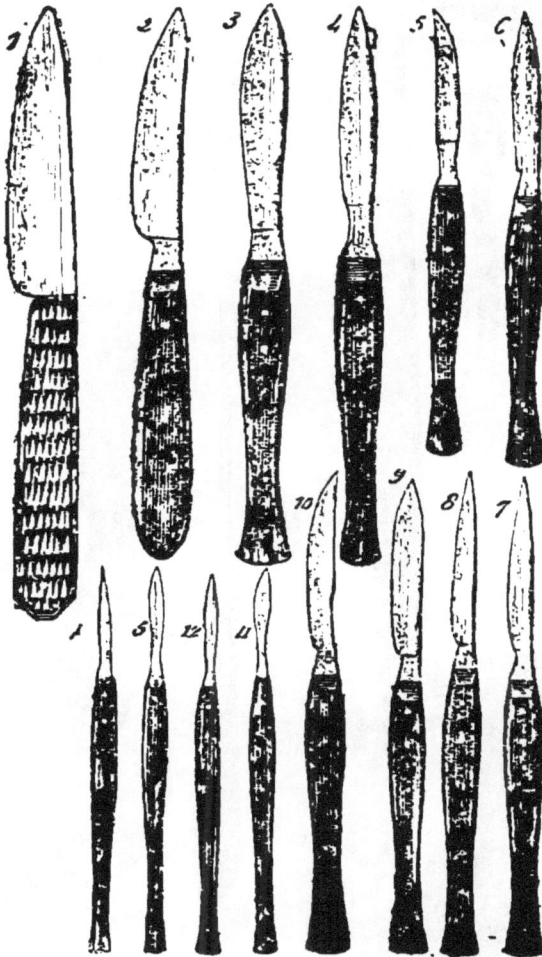

From Bernard's *Physiologie Opératoire*, p. 186.

The next illustration (page 189) is taken from Livon's *Manuel de Vivisection* (Bailliere, Paris), p. 8, a book issued in 1882 from the new school of Vivisection in Marseilles. The three instruments are described respectively as—

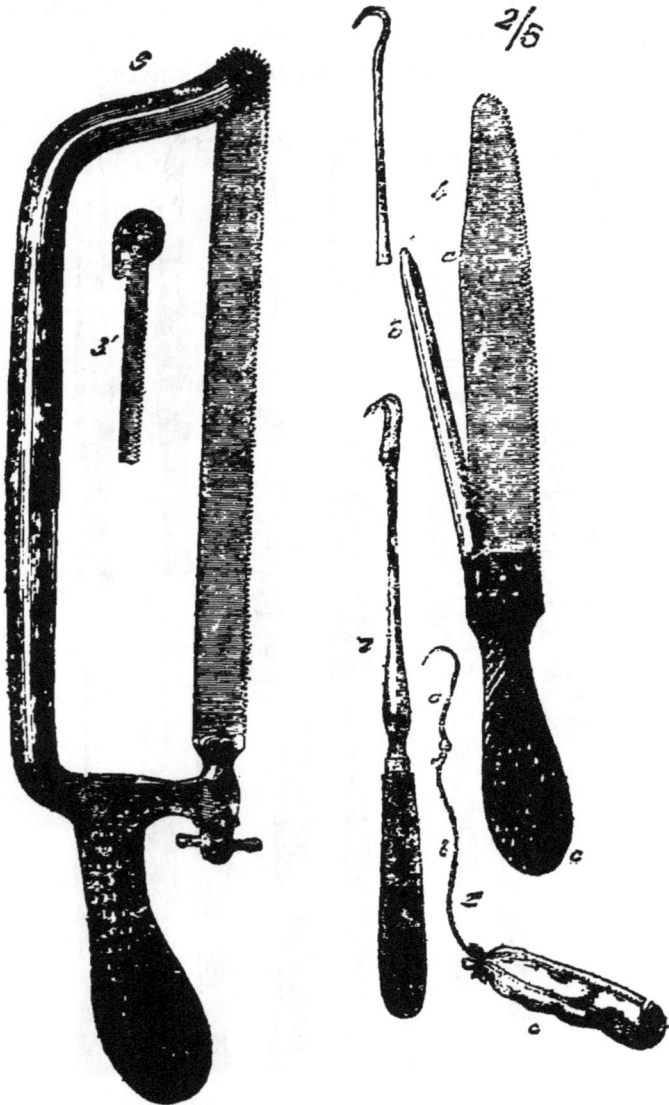

From Bernard's *Physiologie Opératoire*, p. 188.

" A little saw for sawing the vertebræ ";

" Bone forceps to open the vertebral canal ";

" Forceps of which the teeth cross like scissors, intended to cut the bones of old animals ".

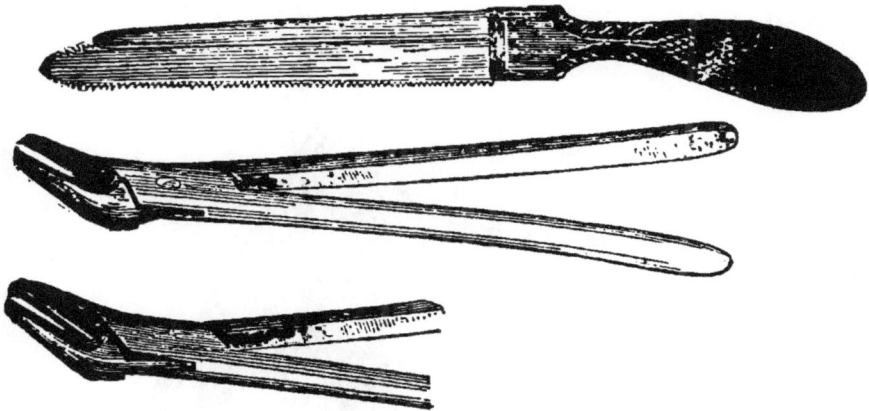

Livon's *Manuel de Vivisection*, p. 8.

We next reach (page 190) one of the many instruments in use (this is Schwann's) for sustaining Artificial Respiration. It is to be understood that when an animal is curarised the muscles are so completely paralysed that it ceases to breathe, and would immediately die were not artificial breathing kept up by pumping air into the lungs. This is sometimes done by hand, but in large laboratories it is customary to keep a water-engine or steam-engine at work for the purpose. In Ludwig's laboratory it has been stated that the engine in question never ceases playing day or night, sustaining life in the dogs and other animals extended on the vivisecting tables around.

There are an immense number of other instruments, some infinitely more elaborate and costly than this, in use in laboratories, and figured in the various treatises; and their various makers in London (Messrs. Hawksley, Messrs. Cettie & Co., Messrs. Elliot & Co.), and in Paris, Heidelberg, Berlin, Wurzburg, &c., are variously specified and recommended (*vide* in particular the list of such instruments, and places where they can best be procured, in Dr Burdon-Sanderson's *Handbook*, p. 573). Plates exhibiting these costly instruments fill 43 large pages of Cyon's *Atlas* and 21 of the English *Handbook*, and afford convincing proof of the enormous extent of a practice which can require and defray the expense of manufacturing such tools.

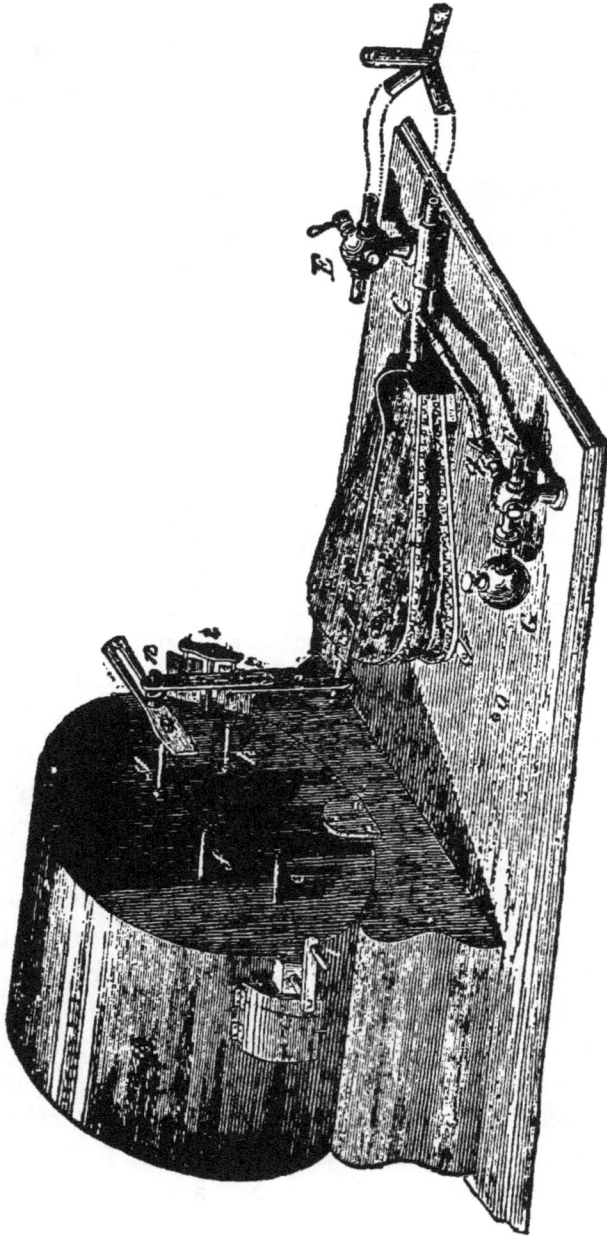

Instrument for producing Artificial Respiration.
From Bernard's *Physiologie Opératoire*, p. 227.

From Bernard's *Physiologic Opératoire*, p. 126.

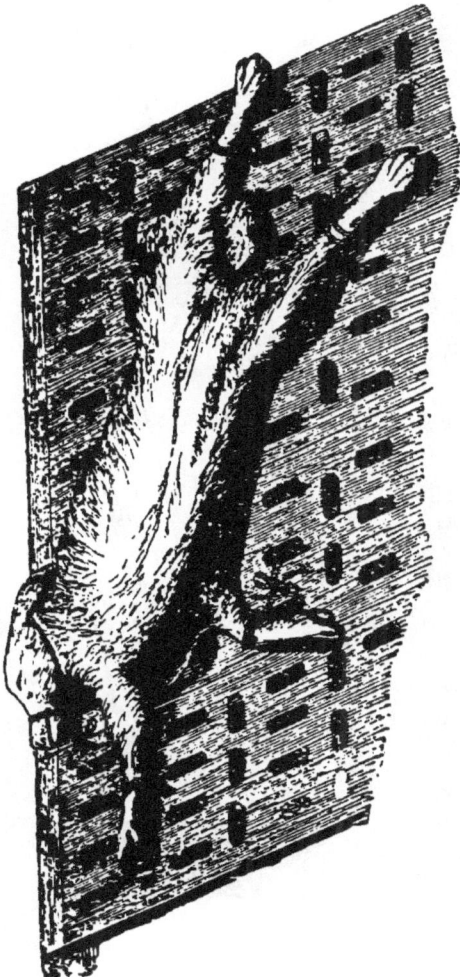

From Bernard's *Physiologie*
Opératoire, p. 125.

From Bernard's *Physiologie*
Opératoire, p. 135.

I next pass to the various forms of the vivisecting tables—or torture-troughs as they have been called—in use in every laboratory. From the simple tables with holes, through which cords are conveniently passed to bind the limbs of the animal (page 191)

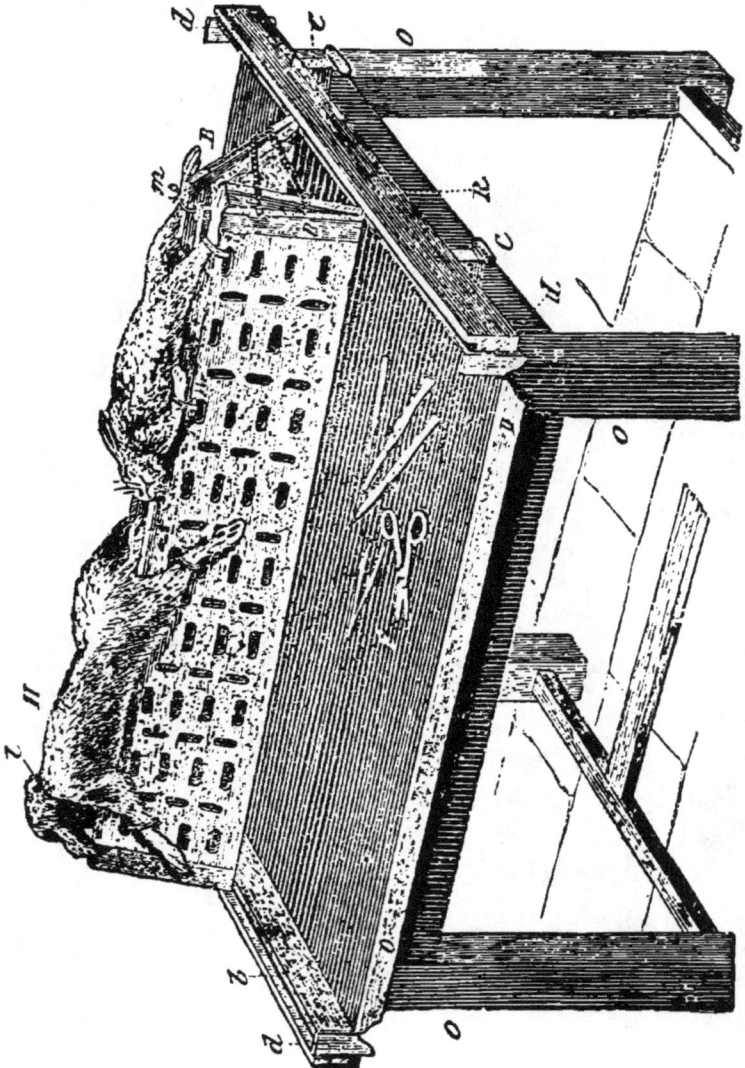

A Dog and Rabbit on a Torture Trough.
From Bernard's *Physiologic Opératoire*, p. 131.

to the more elaborate trough and double trough (page 192) the illustrations explain themselves.

With respect to the last illustration, of the rabbit and dog on the trough with an elevated ridge, it will be seen how well the instrument would serve for the experiment lately shown to students in Florence, described in the *Zoophilist* for May 1, as follows :

"The following story has been sent us on the best authority from Florence :

"A young man, son of a well-known and respected veterinary surgeon, gives this account of the spectacle he witnessed at a lecture :

"'A dog, with its four feet fastened to a table, and supported by a sort of *chevalet*' (no doubt the usual vivisecting trough reversed), 'had its skin cut and turned back all along the back

Cyon, Plate xxvi. Fig. 7.

13

from the neck to the tail.   This was done in such a way that the
spinal canal was laid bare, and the nerve roots exposed so that
they could be touched like the strings of an instrument with a
pair of forceps.   To each touch responded a cry of agony like the
notes of a violin.   The scene was so revolting that after a time
the young man left the place.' "

Again, we have illustrations of elaborate methods of suspending
a dog's body in an upright position (page 193), to be maintained
for several days, as in the treating of gastric or hepatic fistulas, and
of a dog's head when the jaw is to be kept open, as below.

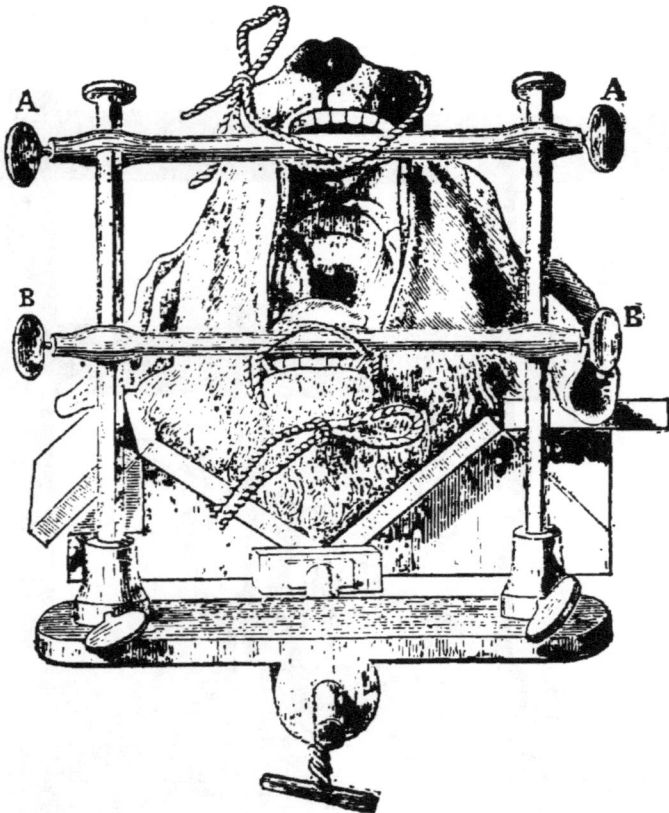

From Bernard's *Physiologie Opératoire*, p. 137.

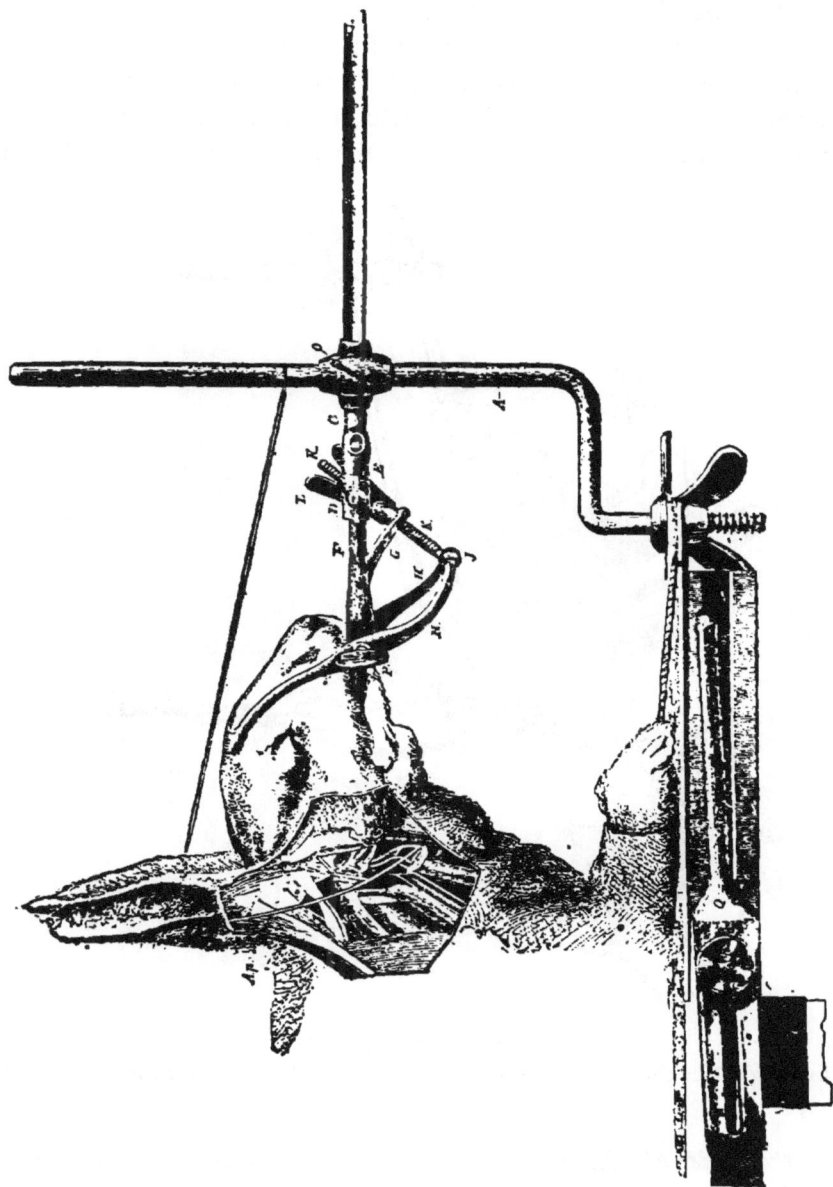

Cyon, Plate vii.
Czermak's Rabbit-holder, with nerves of rabbit dissected out, and anatomy of the parts.

The next illustration (page 195) represents an instrument very frequently mentioned in these works (Czermak's rabbit-holder), with the rabbit's head fixed in it, and the nerves of the neck dissected out. This illustration (including some anatomy of the parts as well as the actual vivisection) is from M. de Cyon's

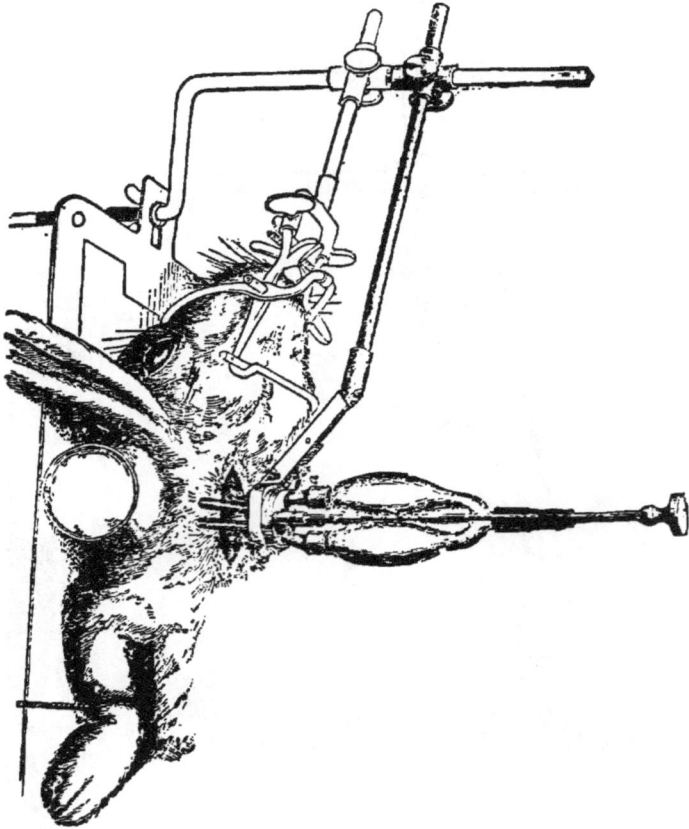

Cyon, Plate xxii.
Ludwig's Machine for measuring the rate of the blood-current in arteries of rabbits.

Methodik der physiologischen Experimente und Vivisectionen (Giessen, St. Petersburg, 1876).

It is in the preface to these volumes that M. de Cyon gives his well-known description of a true vivisector:

"The true vivisector must approach a difficult vivisection with the same joyful excitement and the same delight wherewith a surgeon undertakes a difficult operation from which he expects extraordinary consequences. He who shrinks from cutting into a living animal, he who approaches a vivisection as a disagreeable

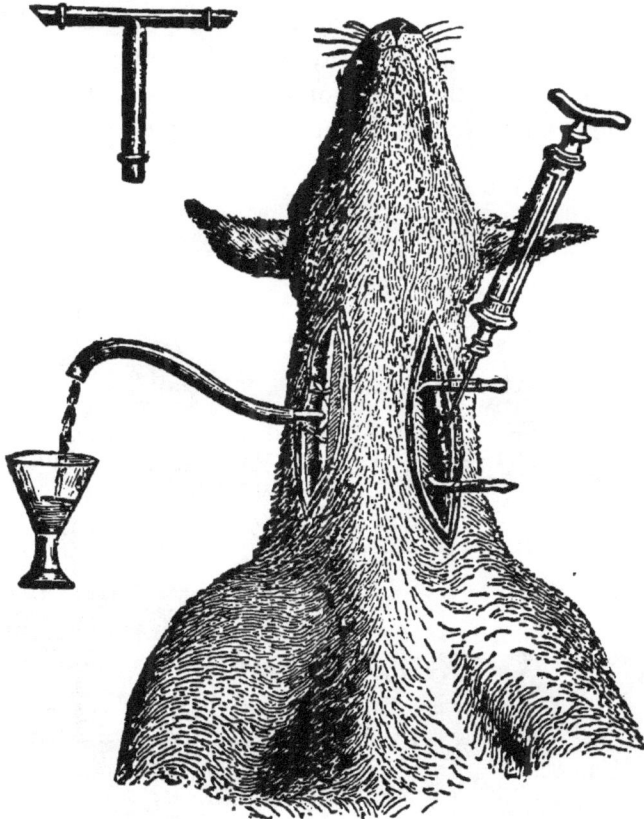

Experiment for testing the time required for injected poisons to traverse the circulation.
From Bernard's *Physiologic Opératoire*, p. 372.

necessity, may very likely be able to repeat one or two vivisections, but will never become an artist in Vivisection. He who cannot follow some fine nerve-thread, scarcely visible to the naked eye, into the depths, if possible sometimes tracing it to a new branching, with joyful alertness for hours at a time; he who feels no enjoyment when at last, parted from its surroundings and isolated, he can subject that nerve to electrical stimulation ; or when, in some deep cavity, guided only by the sense of touch of his finger-ends, he ligatures and divides an invisible vessel,—to such a one there is wanting that which is most necessary for a successful vivisector. The pleasure of triumphing over difficulties held hitherto insuperable is always one of the highest delights of the vivisector. And the sensation of the physiologist, when from a gruesome wound, full of blood and mangled tissue, he draws

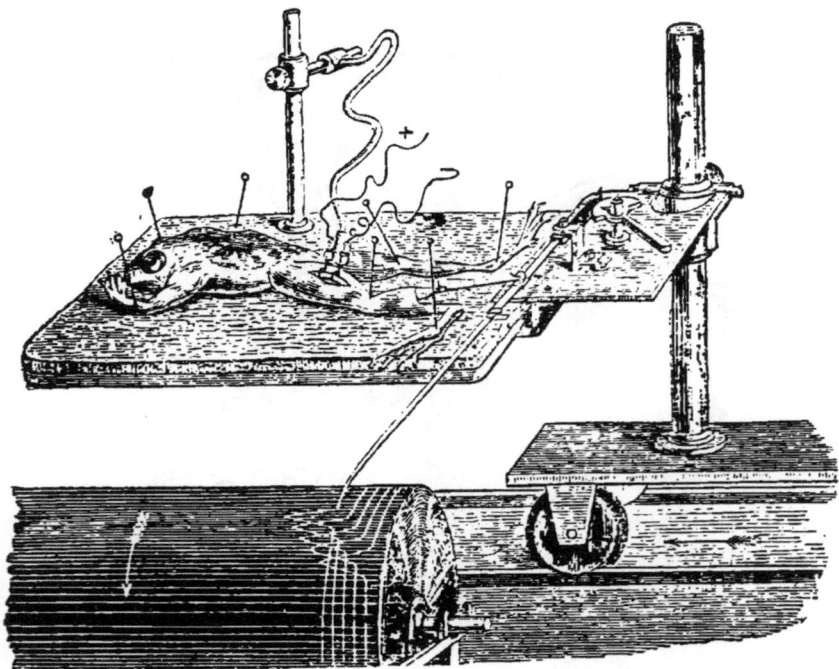

Handbook of the Physiological Laboratory, Plate ciii.

forth some delicate nerve-branch, and calls back to life a function which was already extinguished,—this sensation has much in common with that which inspires a sculptor, when he shapes forth fair living forms from a shapeless mass of marble" (*Methodik*, p. 15).

Here is another machine, invented by Ludwig, one of the

leading members of the Leipzig Society for Protection of Animals, and, at the same time, the head of the largest physiological laboratory in the world (p. 196).

The next illustration (page 197) exhibits one of the minor processes of Vivisection, an experiment intended to test the time required for poisons to circulate through the system.

Bernard's *Leçons sur la Chaleur Animale*, p. 347.

Here (page 198) is an experiment (not a painful one, for the frog is already pithed and practically dead), exhibiting the manner in which frogs—the poor creatures which Marshall Hall blasphemously called "God's gift to the Physiologist"—are pinioned on a piece of cork for experiments with what is termed a mycograph.

The illustration is taken from the second volume of the *Hand-book of the Physiological Laboratory*, Plate ciii.

We now come (page 199) to an illustration which will be recognised by many readers—the first of the two stoves invented and

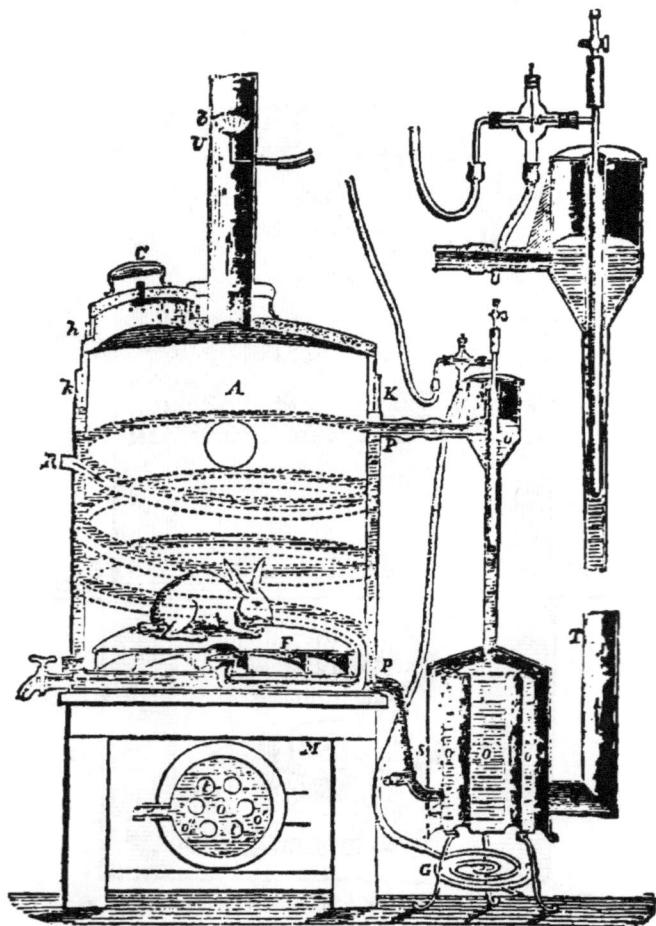

Bernard's *Leçons sur la Chaleur Animale*, p. 363.

used by Claude Bernard. It is taken from his *Leçons sur la Chaleur Animale*, (Paris, 1876, p. 347), and represents, as M. Bernard states, his "first apparatus for the study of the Mechanism of Death by Heat". Of the results of experiments made with it he prints several tables. These tables show how dogs, pigeons, and rabbits baked in the stove expired at the temperatures of 90° or 100° Cent. in six minutes, ten minutes, twenty-four minutes, &c.,

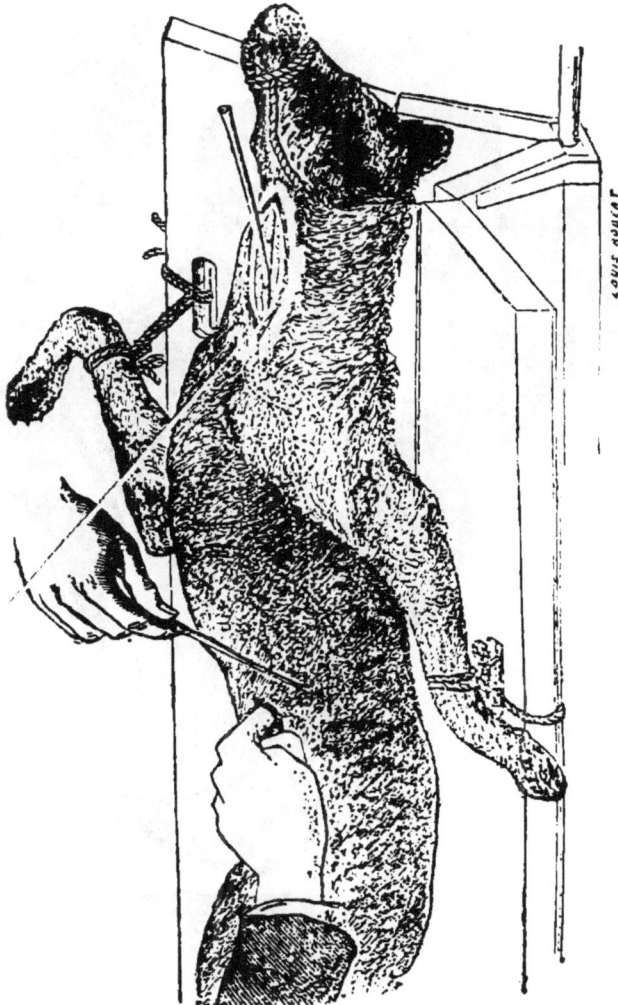

From Bernard's *Physiologic Opératoire*, p. 282.

and at higher temperatures at different intervals; and again how, when the apparatus formed a hot bath (*i.e.*, the animal was boiled instead of baked alive), a different scale of heat and subsequent

death was observed. A small dog placed in a temperature of 55°
expired after eight minutes, and so on. Again, another series of
results were obtained when the head of the victim was kept out-

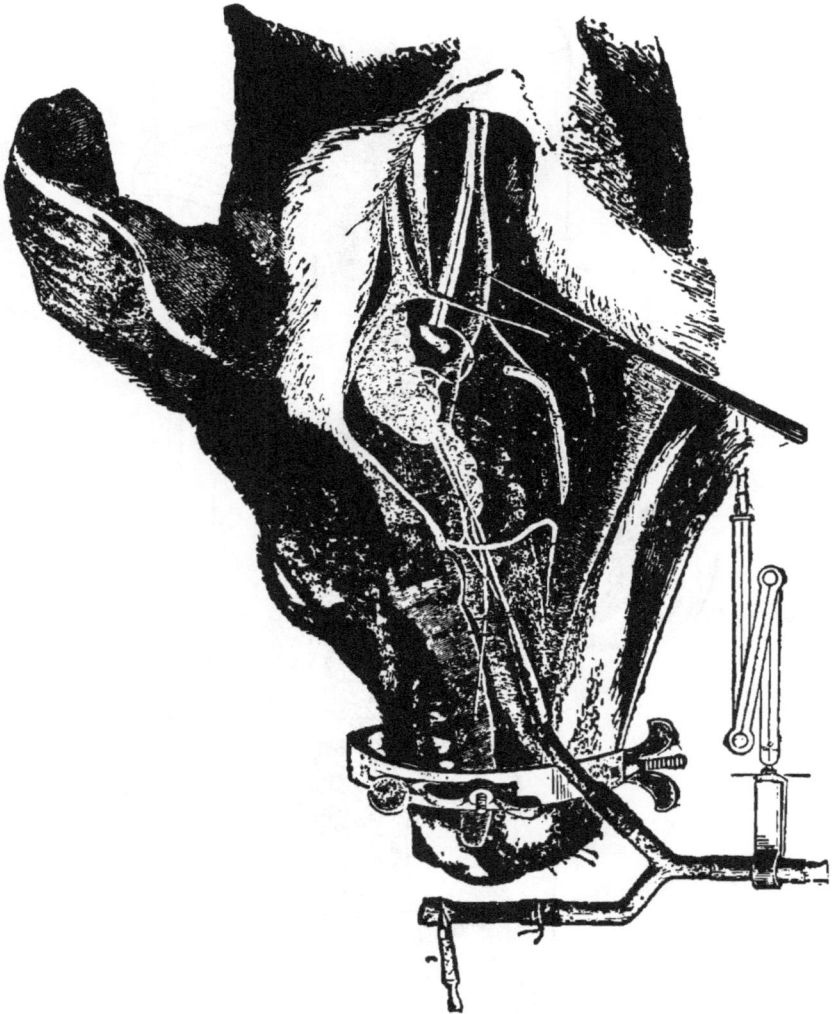

From Cyon's *Atlas*, Plate xv.

side the stove, while its body was baked or boiled. "The animals"
(M. Bernard notes, page 356) "exhibit a series of symptoms
always the same and characteristic. At first the creature is a little

agitated. Soon the respiration and circulation are quickened. The animal opens its mouth and breathes hard. Soon it becomes impossible to count its pantings ; at last it falls into convulsions, and dies generally in uttering a cry."

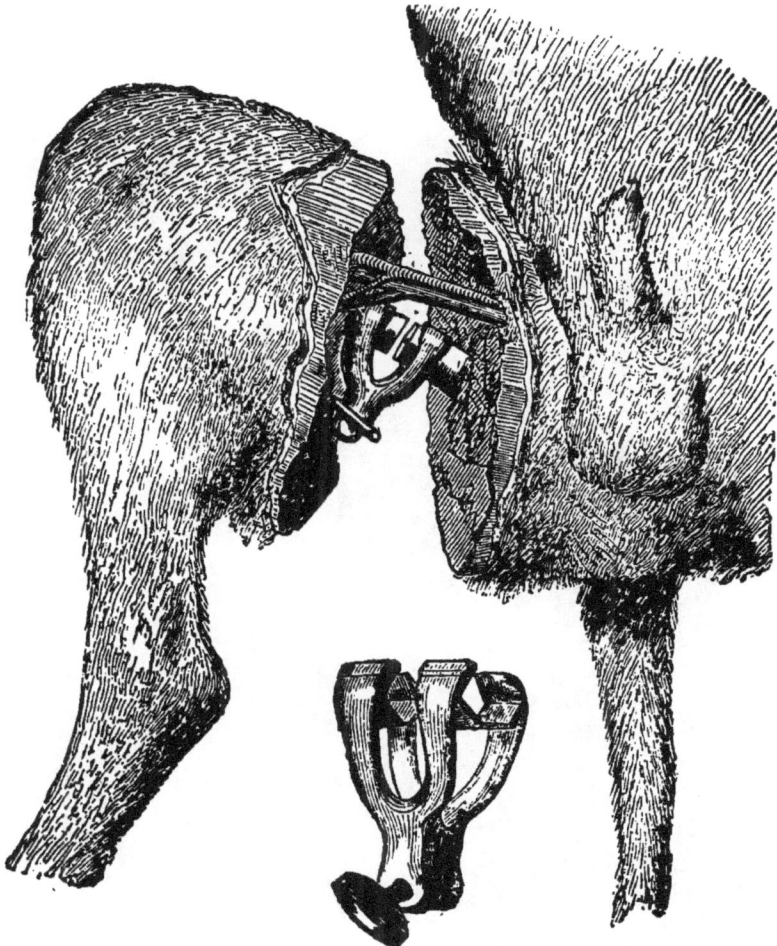

From Bernard's *Physiologie Opératoire*, p. 337.

In a subsequent table M. Bernard gives the particulars of the deaths in this apparatus of seventeen dogs and of numerous rabbits and pigeons ; and then proceeds in the next lecture to show his audience the diagram of another and more elaborate stove, in which many other series of animals were sacrificed.

Here (page 206) is the second and more elaborate stove invented

Paul Bert's *Pression Barométrique*, p. 800.

and used by M. Bernard, of which the aspect is less familiar.　He says of it (p. 361): "The machine which served our first experiments presented an imperfection which rather complicated the

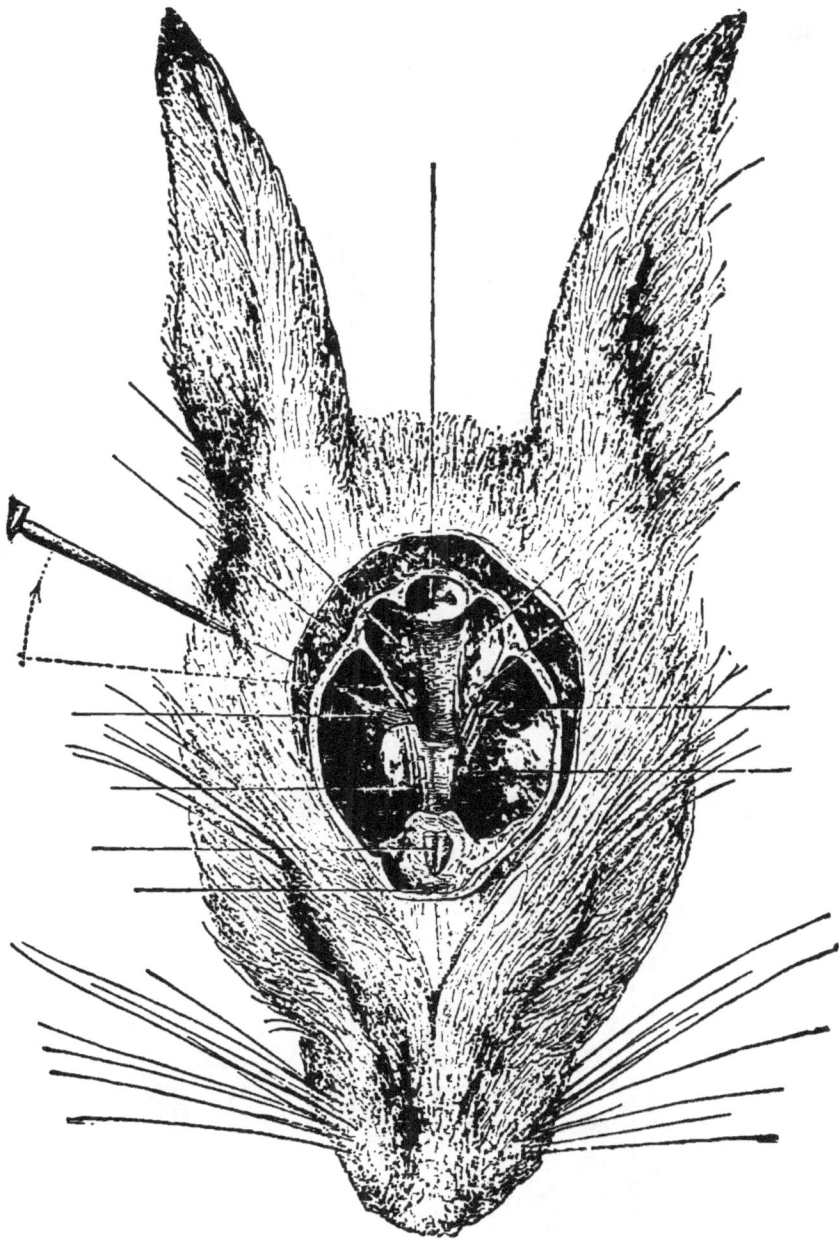

Cyon's *Atlas*, Table xxxv.

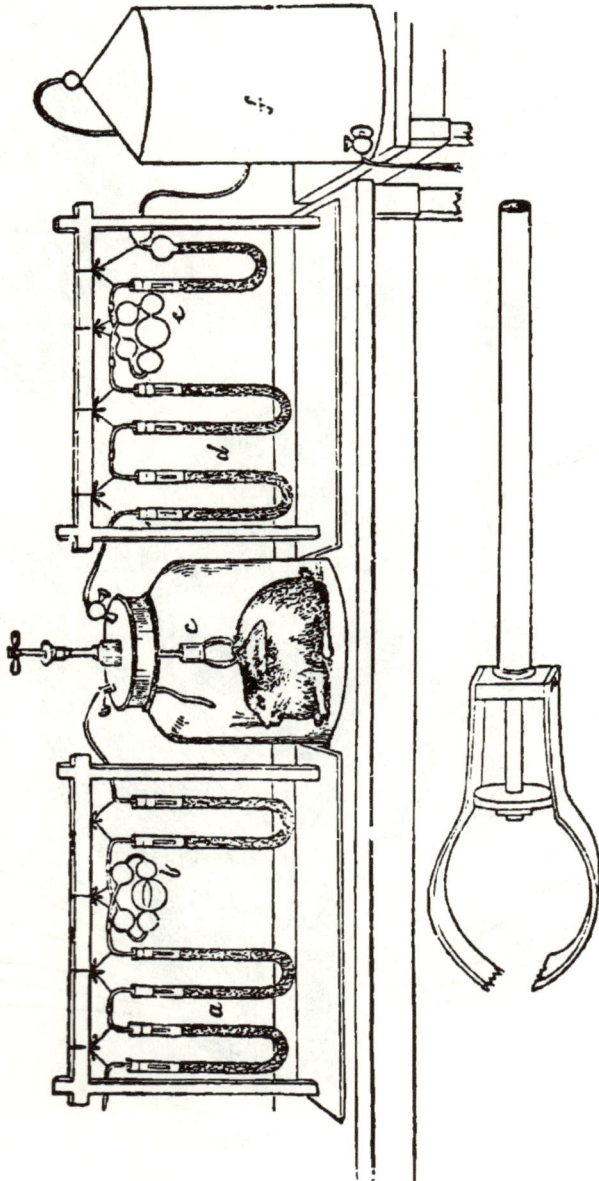

Mantegazza, *Del Dolore*, p. 98.

phenomena, and might in a certain degree vitiate the appreciation of the action of temperatures on living beings. . . . The machine of which we have recently availed ourselves has not this inconvenience." (Then follows a long description.)

"In the stove we place a sparrow. The temperature is about 65° (Centigrade). At the end of a minute we see the animal open its beak, manifest an anxiety which becomes more and more lively, breathe tumultuously, then fall and die. . . .

"We try the same experiment on a rabbit. The same series of phenomena are exhibited, but more slowly, for it only dies at the end of twenty minutes. . . ."

I now come to experiments in what is called Catheterism. They are described at great length in Claude Bernard's *Physiologie Opératoire.* The illustration (page 201) represents catheterism of the blood-vessels, showing how long flexible tubes are inserted at some convenient part of a blood-vessel, and then pushed along into the different parts of the heart and blood-vessels. Blood may thus be obtained from a given part for analysis ; or the temperature may be ascertained by pushing thermometers into such otherwise inaccessible regions. In these experiments there is no pretence of giving anæsthetics ; and as a matter of fact as well as logic none are given, for they would greatly interfere with the results when a careful analysis is to be made of the blood so obtained from special regions, or when it is a question of the temperature which normally exists there.

To the above description we may add that the jugular vein in the neck of the bound-down and muzzled animal has first been carefully dissected out and opened into, and, through the opening thus made, the bent tube or catheter has been inserted and pushed down through the heart into the great vein which brings the blood from the liver and hinder part of the body.

The next figure (page 202) represents a dog with the salivary glands, and the nerves supplying those glands, exposed. A cannula (small pipe) is fixed into the duct of the gland. A muzzle of an elaborate kind is placed upon the jaws.

M. de Cyon, in his article in the *Contemporary Review*, April, 1883, mentions this drawing (which was one of those exhibited life-size on the hoardings of London in 1877), and asserts that it was drawn from the dead body of the animal. It may be possible that the actual dog from which M. de Cyon made his sketch was at that moment no longer living, but that the hideous mutilations exhibited in the drawing had been inflicted while it was still living is proved by two circumstances : one, by the presence of the elaborate muzzle, which assuredly no one would have placed on the corpse of a dog ; and, secondly, by the presence of the cannula fixed into the duct of the salivary gland, a gland which, of course, like any other, ceases to secrete at death, and into which therefore it is absurd to suppose a cannula would have been inserted after death. M. de Cyon's assertion that the dog represented is a dead one is also thoroughly disposed of by an extract from his own book quoted in an excellent letter by Mr. Ernest Bell, published in the *Spectator*, April 7, 1883. Speaking of the plates in M. Cyon's work—

"When he tells us that these plates are, 'of course, drawn from the dead body of the animals,' he probably is speaking the literal truth as regards the plates, but in as far as he wishes us to infer that the operations they represent were done on the dead body, he is saying what his books show to be untrue. For, concerning one of the plates (No. xv.), I find on p. 264 of the work the following paragraph :

" ' If the experiment is made only for demonstration, one can drug the animal beforehand with chloral, chloroform, or curare ; and if the last-named poison is applied, artificial respiration must be used. If, on the other hand, one wishes to use the experiment for purposes of observation, particularly if the investigation concerns the influence of the circulation on the activity of the glands, it is better to avoid these drugs, on account of their influence on the circulation. One should choose for the experiment strong, lively animals, which have been well fed for a few days previously.' "

The next figure (p. 203) shows the limb of a dog entirely severed, including the bone, with the exception of the main artery and the vein through which strychnine when injected passes into the trunk. This experiment is now done under anæsthetics, but

Majendie devised and continually repeated it many years before chloroform was discovered.

The following illustration (page 204) is the triumph of M. Paul Bert's genius, and certainly exhibits, in a remarkable degree the fitness of that gentleman to exercise (as he did a few years ago) the function, in the French Government, of Minister of Worship and Public Instruction. So proud was M. Bert of this achievement in thus transforming a living dog into the resemblance of a piece of wood (*un morceau de bois*) that his portrait has been exhibited in Paris holding up the tortured animal in the attitude depicted.

"Let us come," says M. Bert, in his large book on *La Pression Barométrique*, p. 800, "to the description of the convulsive attack (produced by placing the victim for hours under compressed oxygen). It is really curious and frightful" (*effrayante*).

"Let us take a case of medium intensity. When the animal is taken out of the machine it is generally in full tonic convulsions. The four paws are stiffened, the trunk is recurved backwards, the eyes are starting from the head, the jaws clenched. Soon there is a sort of loosening, to which succeeds a new crisis of stiffenings with clonic convulsions, resembling at once a crisis of strychnine poisoning, and an attack of tetanus. . . . Sensibility is preserved. . . .

"In lighter cases, instead of attacks so violent as this, one may lift the animal by one paw like a piece of wood, as Figure 61 shows. We observe disordered movements and local convulsions," &c.

The next figure (page 205) shows the head of a dead rabbit, of which the brain and top of the skull is removed to show the position of the nerves, and the instrument is exhibited piercing the head and reaching the nerve (the trigeminus) on which it is desired to operate. The description given by Cyon of the method of operation (*Methodik*, p. 512) is as follows : "The rabbit is firmly fastened to the ordinary vivisecting table by means of Czermak's holder.   Then the rabbit's head is held by the left hand, so that the thumb of that hand rests on the condyle of the lower jaw. This is used as a *point d'appui* for the insertion of the knife. . . . To reach the hollow of the temple the instrument must be guided forward and upward, thus avoiding the hard portion of the temporal bone and leading the knife directly into the cranial cavity. . . . The trigeminus then comes under the knife. Now holding the head of the animal very firmly, the blade of the knife is directed backwards and downwards, and pressed hard in this direction against the base of the skull.   The nerve is then generally cut behind the Gasserian ganglion, which is announced by a violent cry of agony (*einen heftigen Schmerzensschrei*) of the animal."

The experiments of Ferrier on monkeys and of Goltz on the brains of dogs involve different mutilations, with scooping out of the brains, till, in some cases, they resemble, as Goltz has said, a "lately-hoed potato-field".

Lastly, we arrive at an illustration (page 206) which cannot be quite classed with the preceding, having been (so far as I know) merely the private delight or toy (he avows he has used it *con molto amore*) of a single physiologist.

Signor Paolo Mantegazza, a brilliant Italian Senator, and *Bel'uomo*, author of books of travels, of tender reminiscences of *La Mia Mammà;* of treatises on "Good and Evil," and on the "Hygiene of Love"; set himself to study the physiology and philosophy of Pain, on which he afterwards composed a work, *La Fisiologia del Dolore* (Florence, Felice Paggi, editore, 1880), from whence we derive our information and our illustration.   To study pain properly it was necessary, so Professor Mantegazza thought, to create the most intense pain he could possibly contrive ; and with this object in view he devised various combinations.   One, which he found excellent, consisted in "planting nails, sharp and numerous, through the feet of the animal, in such a manner as to render the creature almost motionless, because in every movement it would have felt its torment more acutely" (*piantando chiodi acuti e numerosi attraverso le piante dei piedi in modo da rendere immobile o quasi l'animale, perchè ad ogni movimento avrebbe sentito molto più acuto il suo tormento).* Further on he mentions that, to produce still more intense pain (*dolore intenso*), he was obliged to employ wounds followed by inflammation.

Going a little further, he devised, and, with the help of an ingenious machinist in Milan, brought into working order, the instrument depicted in our illustration, which is exactly reproduced from his book (p. 98). This machine enabled him to grip any part of an animal with pincers with iron teeth, and to crush or tear, or lift up the victim, "so as to produce pain in every possible way". The first series of his experiments, Signor Mantegazza informs us, were tried on twelve animals, chiefly rabbits and guinea-pigs, of which several were pregnant. One poor little creature, "far advanced in pregnancy," was made to endure *dolori atrocissimi*, so that it was impossible to make any observations in consequence of its convulsions. In the second series of experiments twenty-eight animals were sacrificed, some of them taken from nursing their young, exposed to torture for an hour or two, then allowed to rest an hour, and usually replaced in the machine, to be crushed or torn by the Professor for periods of from two to six hours more. In the table wherein these experiments are summed up, the terms *molto dolore* and *crudeli dolori* are delicately distinguished, the latter being apparently reserved for the cases when the victims were, as the Professor expresses it, *lardellati di chiodi* (larded with nails).

In conclusion, the author informs us (p. 27) that these experiments were all conducted *con molto amore e pazienza*.

Such are a few out of scores of illustrations which might be added of the practice of Vivisection which its advocates strive to make the British Parliament and public believe is almost wholly painless to the victims, and involves nothing more serious than "scratching a newt's tail" or "exhibiting a frog's foot under a microscope".

XIV.

THE FALLACY OF RESTRICTION APPLIED TO VIVISECTION.

To those who have taken part in the Vivisection agitation since it began in England in 1874, there is no need to address any argument concerning the right policy to be adopted by the opponents of the practice. They know, and no doubt the vivisectors know equally well, that it is a case of "all or nothing". The cruel and misleading Method of Research must either continue to be legalised, and used *as a Method,*—with or without a few formalities, possibly harassing to the physiologists, but of little or no practical use to the victims,—or it must be forbidden *as a method,* and Mr. Lawson Tait's aspiration be fulfilled and the practice "stopped in the interests of Science, so that the energy and skill of investigators may be turned into better and safer channels".

A new generation of anti-vivisectionists has, however, risen up since those distant days of our first warfare against scientific cruelty, and some have very naturally questioned the necessity for assuming our extreme position. They perceive the sad remoteness of the fulfilment of our hopes in the final suppression of Vivisection, at once by law and public opinion, and, in their humane impatience on behalf of the poor brutes, they cast about for some compromise which may be obtained, as they fancy, much more quickly. They cannot persuade themselves that the "reconciliation of Humanity and Science," which the Royal Commission pointed out as the proper goal of legislation, is really unattainable, or, if it should prove so, that it is impracticable for them so cunningly to frame an Act of Parliament as that, while seeming to those who pass it to leave scope for Science, it shall actually secure the claims of Humanity, and make any really cruel experiment impossible under its provisions. Thinking in this way, it is inevitable that these friends should regard us, who hold tenaciously to the programme of Abolition, as injudicious and fanatical; and they repeat to us once more the proverb which has become one of the stock-phrases of our weary controversy, that "half a loaf is better than no bread"; to which we would fain reply, "Not so, if the half loaf be mere flummery, and by accepting it we relinquish the whole loaf for ever".

In the hope (always a precarious one!) of conveying to our friends the fruit of our own hard-earned experience, we propose here to state as succinctly as possible the reasons why we hold it to be a grievous mistake to demand anything short of the total prohibition of Vivisection.

Let the history of the Victoria Street Society be briefly reviewed at starting, that the moderation of its policy, and the caution wherewith its leaders have advanced, may be borne in mind.

In November, 1874, a Memorial to the Royal Society for the Prevention of Cruelty to Animals was prepared by the present writer, and, on the 25th January, 1875, presented to the Committee of that Society, with the signatures of 600 persons, praying that action might be taken to obtain the legal restriction of Vivisection. On the 4th of May, 1875, a Bill for Regulating the Practice of Vivisection, drawn up at the same writer's instance (after consultation with Lord Coleridge and many other men of experience), was introduced into the House of Lords by Lord Henniker. Then followed the Royal Commission, and it became evident that a Society was needed to carry on the work. The Association, afterwards named the Victoria Street Society, was founded in November, 1875, and was awkwardly, but most carefully, named the "Society for the Protection of Animals *liable to* Vivisection". Its prospectus announced that its aim was "*to obtain the utmost possible protection for*" such animals. The Society so constituted, in the following March, urged on the Home Office the introduction of a Bill to carry out the recommendations of the Royal Commission, and the Committee subsequently sketched the measure which Lord Carnarvon introduced on behalf of the Government, and which, while affording entire immunity from Vivisection to dogs, cats, horses, and asses, placed the Vivisection of other vertebrate animals under a restrictive system of licence s. In July a great Medical Deputation invaded the Home Office, and induced Sir Richard Cross (into whose hands the Bill had passed for presentation in the House of Commons) to mutilate it so deplorably that, on becoming law as the Act 39 and 40 Vict., c. 77, it has proved the almost futile measure we know it to be.

Up to this epoch the hope that a really effective restrictive measure was possible, and might be obtained from Parliament, never deserted the founders of the Victoria Street Society ; and the obvious moral difference between painful and painless experimentation was insisted on by no one more anxiously than by the present writer, with a view to attaining the apparently feasible object of a valid "reconciliation of science and humanity," and of preventing the strength of the agitation being wasted by the larger and (as she was often assured) hopeless demands of the *International* and the *London* total Abolition Societies, already at work. But the utter transformation of Lord Carnarvon's Bill by the aid of the "amendments" of Sir Richard Cross, and the subsequent exasperating experience of the Inspector's delusive Returns, were lessons which the most bigoted adherent of half-measures could not fail to learn, and which the whole body of the Victoria Street Society, with very few exceptions, and after endless discussions, actually learned. In the case of the honorary secretary the change of policy was likewise enforced by the growing conviction (derived from study of the principal Manuals of Vivisection, and only to be conveyed by such cumulative evidence as they afford) that the aims, sentiments, and methods of vivisectors are not, and never can be, amenable to humane restrictions. On the 27th April, 1877, a great meeting of the Society supported Mr. Holt's Bill for total prohibition ; and on the 7th August, 1878, the Committee, by the advice of Lord Shaftesbury and of nearly all the leaders of the Society, passed the following resolution : " That the Committee will henceforth appeal to public opinion in favour of the Total Abolition of Vivisection ". Thus it was not till nearly four years' experience of Parliamentary action on the subject, and of very arduous and painful study, that the programme of Restriction was finally abandoned by the originators of the movement.   To find themselves just now told by those who have come at the eleventh hour into the vineyard that they have been hasty, and understand much less than these novices of the practical working of such a cause in Parliament, and of the real nature of Vivisection, is, it must be owned, a little difficult to understand.   But we hasten now to give as clearly as may be some of the reasons which induced the late Lord Shaftesbury, and we may presume also Lord Coleridge, Cardinal Manning, the Bishop of Winchester, Mr. Stansfeld, Lord Tennyson, Lord Mount-Temple, Mr. Browning, and all the other honoured Vice-Presidents of the Society as at present constituted, to accept the principle of Total Prohibition instead of Restriction.

1. No Restrictive Act of Parliament which human ingenuity may devise can afford efficient protection to animals delivered over to a vivisector.   The advocates of Restriction fondly imagine that they *can* devise such provisions ; but, with all respect for them, we unhesitatingly assert that no one who understands the *purposes and methods of vivisectional research* can believe that such provisions are possible.   It is of course easy to devise a Bill, which, *e.g.*, might provide that every vivisection should be described exactly beforehand and announced for a month in the *Times ;* and that it should take place on a table, in the middle of Exeter Hall, in the presence of the Committee of the Jermyn Street Society.   But no one who has read the books of Claude Bernard, Cyon, and Burdon-Sanderson could for an instant suppose that any such plan would meet the ever-varying, ever-shifting suggestions of scientific curiosity ; or that infinitely delicate and difficult experiments (often extending over days and weeks and requiring perpetual variation) could be performed under any similar circumstances.   A Bill embodying provisions in any way resembling these would be simply held by all physiologists to be practically a Bill for the total prohibition of Vivisection ; and though its pro-

moters might say "*tant mieux* if it prove so," the general opinion would be that such a Bill was an insult to Parliament; and, in any case, it would as certainly be thrown out as a Bill frankly prohibiting the practice altogether,—with the additional scoff that its promoters stultified themselves by admitting that Vivisection *ought* to be sanctioned, and then practically sought to make it impossible.

Again, the advocates of Restriction fall back on the old fallacy of anæsthetics, and vaguely conceive they could pass a measure forbidding all experiments except on animals under complete anæsthesia. But even a superficial acquaintance with the works of vivisectors shows us that they would be stopped at every turn could such a condition of experiments be really secured. That it could *not* be secured by any conceivable precautions, is almost equally clear. Once more the words of Dr. Hoggan in his famous letter are verified. "Anæsthetics" (by the delusions which humane people indulge about them) "have proved the greatest curse to vivisectible animals."

If Vivisection can neither be performed under full public inspection, nor under any certainty of complete anæsthesia of the victims, it becomes obvious that real safeguards against abuses of the practice cannot be obtained. A poor dumb brute shut up in a laboratory with one or two, or half-a-dozen physiologists and students, all imbued with the "joyful excitement" wherewith Cyon says they should "approach a difficult vivisection," can, from the very nature of the case, have *no* protection against the uttermost extremity of torture. In other words, there can be no line drawn by the Legislature between the Use of Vivisection, and the cruellest Abuses into which it has perpetually and notoriously fallen. But whenever the abuses of a practice are very great, and they cannot be separated from the use, then, according to a well recognised principle of legislation, the use itself must be forbidden. This principle has been already actually carried out by Parliament in the case of Animals. By the Act 12 and 13 Vict., c. 60, the employment of Dogs for draught of any kind is totally prohibited.

2. The incentive to Vivisection is unquestionably, in the

vast majority of cases, the honour and distinction obtained among the confraternity by successful researches respecting large or small points in physiology,—such distinctions culminating in the statue recently erected in Paris to Claude Bernard, which represents him as standing beside a torture-trough. To obtain such *kudos* it is indispensable that the vivisector's experiments be *published in the scientific journals.* So long then, as, under any restrictive law, Vivisection is permitted in a country, so long such publications (with due caution in alleging the use of anæsthetics or submission to other legal conditions) may safely go on ; and if anti-vivisectionists attempt through such publications to bring the experimenters before a court of law, friendly witnesses (such as appeared in the Ferrier case in Bow Street in 1881) may, no doubt, always be relied on to get the vivisector triumphantly out of his scrape. But if, on the other hand, Vivisection be *uncon-ditionally forbidden*, then, and then only, the great incentive to the practice will be removed. No vivisector will dare publish any experiment at all ; and it may be safely prophesied that the zeal of the investigators will thenceforward be very quickly turned into other channels, and, like other heroes, they will "go where glory waits them ". It is also to be noted in this connection that the trade of dog and cat stealing and selling for Vivisection might be stopped under a prohibitive, but not under a restrictive, law.

3. The results of Vivisection being, according to our unani-mous contention, worse than *nil*—misleading and injurious to science—we shall best befriend science itself by closing up that false path altogether, and not making a stile to enable travellers to walk therein. In pretending merely to restrict it we are practi-cally admitting our opponents' assertion of its utility ; and if we do this, we involve ourselves in inextricable difficulties to deter-mine, next, the point where a little pain, or a greater pain, to one animal or to a thousand animals, ought to be sanctioned to obtain benefit for mankind ; and how great or direct that benefit ought to be, and how far it must be likely of attainment. We fight the battle, in short, thenceforth on our enemy's ground ; and must infallibly be pushed back and back, till all the excesses of scien-

tific cruelty be justified, just as they were by the different witnesses before the Royal Commission.

4. Every imaginable law sanctioning in any measure Vivisection is not only fallacious as regards the protection of animals, but *demoralising to the men* who pursue the practice, and injurious to the community, which, at one and the same moment, institutes Bands of Mercy, and treats domestic creatures as pets, servants, and playmates, and then is called on to authorise men to dissect them alive as mere parcels of bone and tissue. Either Vivisection ought to be wholly scouted and forbidden, or the whole movement on behalf of kindness to animals which has been the glory of England since the days of Erskine and Martin ought to be abandoned, and the hypocrisy renounced of caressing a dog to-day and consenting to his vivisection—restricted or unrestricted— to-morrow. So long as we regard a sentient and intelligent creature as a mere mechanical clock which we may open at will to see how it works; so long as we think of a brain which holds all the wondrous instincts and reasonings of the dog and the ape as a lump of grey matter to be scooped out and broken up, as Goltz says, "like a potato field," to note what happens after its mutilation; so long as we think of the little heart which beats with joy for the return of a beloved master, or breaks for sorrow on his grave, as a "muscle" into which it is "interesting" to push a catheter to ascertain its exact temperature—so long the spirit of a Cyon will spread like a hideous disease amongst us. Nothing but absolutely forbidding a practice, linked and associated for ever with the most reckless cruelty (even when for the nonce carried out without actual offence), can stop the contagion of this New Vice of scientific cruelty.

To sum up our conclusions. No Restrictive Bill could be devised which would protect vivisected animals from torture ; and if such a measure could be drawn, it would meet in Parliament precisely the same opposition as our Bill for the Prohibition of Vivisection, for the simple reason that it would be tantamount to Prohibition. Exactly in proportion as a Bill afforded real checks and not sham ones, it would be virulently opposed, and only suffered in the last resort to pass when the efficiency of the checks had been nullified by Amendments. To introduce such a measure would therefore be only to lower our flag; to admit that Vivisection is useful; to consent to educate the rising generation in Cyon's sentiments; and, finally, to open the way to a fresh series of hoodwinkings and deceptions of the public worse than those miserable ones which accompanied and have followed the Act of 1876.

Neither a Total Prohibition Bill nor any Restriction Bill has, alas! any chance of passing into law for a long time to come; and the latter not a day sooner than the former, unless it be a mere sham and wholly inoperative for its purpose. But there is this essential difference between the two programmes: *Public opinion cannot be educated on the subject by men who treat Vivisection as a thing to be sanctioned under restrictions;* and, should they ever succeed in passing some measure in accordance with their views, the result would be the cessation of all agitation, the disbandment of the Anti-vivisection Societies, and the enjoyment thenceforward by the physiologists, *first,* of such easy terms as the new law may allow, and soon of such unopposed liberty to torture, and teach the art of torturing, as they may please to take. On the other hand, when, at last, the public opinion of the nation has been educated by our patient efforts up to the point of recognising Vivisection to be, as Lord Shaftesbury called it, "an abominable sin," *then* the practice will be absolutely stopped simultaneously by that public opinion, and by an Act of Parliament following thereon—stopped utterly, completely, and *for ever.* Were the Restrictionists to carry their point, the vivisecting table would remain to all future generations a well-used instrument of research. When we, Abolitionists, carry ours, that hideous implement will be consigned to the museums of old chains and thumbscrews, and will be described by the historian of the future as the barbarous invention of Science in his cruel boyhood—to be bracketed with the rack of the mediæval judge, and the stake of the inquisitor, as things over which men may blush and angels weep.

XV.

FOUR REASONS FOR TOTAL PROHIBITION
OF VIVISECTION.

1. Because the Vivisection Act of 1876 (39 and 40 Vict., c. 77) fails to stop the scientific torture of animals.

a. It does not prohibit the extremest torture, but provides for certificates to be obtained by licensed vivisectors for " Performance of experiments without anæsthetics " (no limit being assigned to the severity of such experiments); and for " Dispensing with the obligation to kill the animal before recovering from anæsthetics " (Clause 3).

b. It leaves all vertebrate animals,—with the sole exception of horses, asses, and mules—to be freely vivisected by every Licensee without special certificate ; the only condition annexed being one whereof it is impossible to obtain any guarantee of fulfilment— namely, the exhibition of anæsthetics. Thus the most sensitive and intelligent of animals, dogs, cats, and monkeys, are placed by the Act on the same level, as regards liability to torture, with toads and snakes (Clause 5).*

c. It does not prohibit the employment of curare, but merely provides that it " shall not, for the purposes of the Act, be deemed an anæsthetic," thus leaving to the option of the vivisector to

---

* And this while the " Arrangement of Clauses " at the head of the Act, and also the margin, describe this clause as "*Special restrictions on painful experiments on dogs, cats,*" &c., and the Parliamentary Returns each year contain a column for certificates "*permitting experiments on cats, dogs, horses, asses, or mules*"—the truth being that no such special restrictions exist, and no such certificates are required as regards either dogs or cats.

double all the sufferings entailed by his experiments and to render
the exhibition of genuine anæsthetics abortive (Clause 4).*

As there is nothing in the contents of the Act prohibiting
torture, so neither is there anything in the machinery which it
provides to secure the carrying out of the very limited protection it proposes to afford to animals liable to Vivisection.

d. Applications for licences and certificates must be signed
exclusively by scientific authorities.   These are, however, in
several cases themselves vivisectors ; and, as their signature of the
applications is a matter of course, the formality is merely illusory.

e. The appointment of Inspectors under the Act is left to the
discretion of the Home Secretary, without stipulation that the
appointed persons shall have previously given any—the smallest—
guarantee of humane feeling towards animals, or shall not be
themselves advocates of unlimited Vivisection, or officers of
Societies whereof the leading members are vivisectors. †

f. The duty of the Inspectors personally to visit "all registered
places from time to time for the purpose of securing compliance
with the provisions of the Act," though defined by the Act (Clause
10), has not been enforced by any clause requiring the registration
of such personal visits.   No assurance exists that the Inspectors
actually "inspect" any such registered places ; much less "all" of
them all over the Kingdom, either "from time to time"—when
their visits may, or may not, be expected, or at any time ; or that
they often do more than register and tabulate for the use of the
Home Office and of Parliament such reports of their experiments
as it may please the vivisectors themselves to furnish.

g. Prosecutions against licensees for breach of the Act can only
be instituted with the consent in writing of the Secretary of State
for the Home Department (Clause 21).

* Again this fourth clause is described, in the heading and in the margin,
" *Use of curare as an anæsthetic prohibited !* "

† In a correspondence with the Secretary of the Victoria Street Society,
the late Inspector for England spoke of the movement which originated the
Act which it is his duty to carry out, as a " senseless and mischievous
agitation ".

All these deficiencies make the Act of 1876, even theoretically and at the best, a feeble and limited restriction of scientific torture. But it not only fails on paper, both as regards its provisions and the machinery for carrying them out, it has practically proved insufficient to stop some of the most cruel experiments ever performed in any age or country—as, for example, the well-known series of experiments which have been performed at Edinburgh and at Cambridge. (See *Twelve Years Trial of the Vivisection Act*, Sonnenschein & Co., London, 1889, price 3d.)

2. Because, not only is the existing Restrictive Act theoretically and practically insufficient to afford protection to animals liable to Vivisection, but every possible amendment of that Act must, from the nature of the case, prove insufficient likewise. No ingenuity of bill-drafting can frame a measure which shall extend *bonâ fide* protection to an animal which has been delivered to a vivisector and bound down upon the torture-trough in his laboratory, hidden from every eye ; nor can any legal regulation control the scalpel of the ardent physiologist who works unwatched upon his dumb victim. It would be voluntarily to delude ourselves, and to betray our trust as protectors of animals, to attempt to tinker the Act of 1876 with any such hope. Vivisection (it cannot be too often impressed on the public mind) is not the occasional resource of baffled inquiry, but a *Method of Research*, pursued with unflagging zeal and pertinacity by at least 250 professional physiologists in Europe, many of whom repeat again and again, with endlessly varying results, every experiment which each one devises. A mere glance at the volumes of engravings of the arsenal of costly instruments manufactured for the express purpose of Vivisection is sufficient to demonstrate the exorbitant extent to which this method is pursued. *As a Method* then, it must be either freely sanctioned, or else abolished and suppressed.

3. Because every actual or possible legal restriction of Vivisection is not only fallacious as regards the protection of Animals, but demoralising to mankind. Every system of law is a system

of education, and, in extending legal sanction to the scientific torture of animals, the State educates the nation in a false view of the relations of man to the lower creatures, encourages selfishness and cruelty and the disregard of the rights of the weak by the strong, and nullifies the elevating influence of the noble legislation which has been the glory of England since the days of Erskine and Martin. Even if it were expedient (which it is not) in the interests of Science and the Healing Art to sanction Vivisection, a still higher expediency would demand that such benefits as might be thence obtained should be foregone, rather than that the rising current of humane sentiment in the nation should be driven back, and the portentous type of character formed by the practice of Vivisection be developed at the summit of our educational system.*

4. Because, by prohibiting Vivisection, we shall not retard the progress of Science or of the Healing Art, but, on the contrary, by barring a misleading path, we shall drive investigation into the true and legitimate roads to discovery, namely, clinical observation and microscopical research. On this point opinions may differ, and no true anti-vivisector will consent to rest a question essentially moral on the issue of a scientific controversy. But it is a source of satisfaction to those who oppose Vivisection primarily on ethical grounds, and who support abolition because nothing short of it

* Cyon and Bernard, two of the greatest vivisectors of the age, thus draw the portraits of the ideal of their profession. Bernard says that the vivisector " does not hear the animal's cries of pain, and is blind to the blood that flows. He sees nothing but his idea and the organisms which conceal from him the secrets he is resolved to discover " (*Introd. à l'Etude de la Médicine Exp.*, p. 180). Cyon describes him still more forcibly. " The true vivisector must approach a difficult vivisection with *joyful excitement*. . . . He who shrinks from cutting into a living animal, he who approaches a vivisection as a disagreeable necessity, may be able to repeat one or two vivisections, but he will never be an artist in Vivisection. . . . The sensation of the physiologist when, from a gruesome wound, full of blood and mangled tissue, he draws forth some delicate nerve thread . . . has much in common with that of a sculptor " (*Methodik*, p. 15).

will clear the air of the moral infection of the practice, to be assured by one of the greatest medical authorities in the kingdom, that "Vivisection has proved useless and misleading; and that, in the interests of true science, its employment ought to be stopped, so that the energy and skill of investigators should be turned into better and safer channels ".*

* See *Uselessness of Vivisection.* By Lawson Tait, Esq., F.R.C.S. Published at the office of the Victoria Street Society.

XVI.

MAD DOG!!

RABIES, until recently, has been a very rare disease. Edward Mayhew—one of the greatest authorities on veterinary subjects—observes in his book on *Dogs and their Management* (p. 164) that "it is rarely that more than one mad dog appears at a time in England. Even at present when the number has, for some occult reason, vastly increased, it remains a fact that not one man in a hundred thousand, perhaps not one in a million, has ever so much as seen a rabid dog in his life. Naturally, then, much ignorance prevails on the subject, and the use of the misleading word "madness" applied to the disease may be suspected of having introduced much popular misapprehension concerning it. The majority of people imagine that a rabid dog is "mad" in the sense in which a man *non compos mentis* is mad; and as human insanity is not necessarily a condition of physical suffering, the common notion of canine madness is connected merely with erratic and alarming behaviour, terrifying from its possible consequences to the spectators but not appealing to their compassion, as it would do were it understood to be the dumb expression of unbearable agony. To find the true human parallel to the dog's so-called "madness," it is probable that we ought to see a strong man driven to shriek and yell and tear himself by burning torture—a Servetus at the stake. From these two causes of popular ignorance and misapprehension it has come to pass that numbers of humane persons have judged of Pasteur's researches without taking into consideration the very important element in the case which is furnished by the atrocious suffering which he has caused numberless animals to undergo, and which must continue to be inflicted on other wretched creatures almost *ad infinitum*, if his supposed discovery is to be utilised. With a view to dispelling the errors which have obscured the subject and enabling the reader to count the cost of "mitigated virus," we propose to make a few extracts from reliable authorities respecting the true nature of Rabies.

The first are taken from an MS. note-book of the late Sir Thomas Watson, President of the Royal College of Physicians, who appears to have written after attendance at a course of lectures on the subject delivered by Youatt at London University; adding thereto his own and other observations.

"The symptoms (of rabies) then are : Melancholy, anxiety of the countenance (for to one familiar with them dogs have expressive countenances), a horror and dread of some unknown evil oppressing the animal's mind. He steadfastly gazes on and caresses his master, apparently reasoning thus : 'No ! you cannot be the cause of this which so distresses me !' Mr. Y. has seen this 1000 times. It is one of the earliest symptoms. (Next)—The dog hides himself, comes out of his retreat hesitatingly, becomes irritable or rather fidgety, cannot remain quiet or in the same place,—shifts his posture ; his eyes wander, and he is constantly making his bed, not as dogs usually do, but he scrapes the straw into a long pillow and then lies down with his chest opposite the diaphragm, upon the pillow. This he does again and again. . . . Contemporaneously with this, and occurring at a very early symptom, is licking some part, biting it, nay, savagely biting it—his own foot, for example—growling over it and even drawing blood. . . . Depraved appetite is an early symptom. Parlour dogs will pick up scraps of thread, &c., &c. The dog also begins to drop his natural food out of his mouth either from some paralysis of the muscles of the jaws or from disgust. . . . (Next)—The countenance changes: from anxious it becomes louring, but is occasionally lighted up by flashes as it were ; strabismus occurs, not as it merely appears to do (from some alteration in the *membrane nictitans*) in distemper, but actual squinting ; a still more fixed gaze, and then wandering of the eyes as if pursuing the course of some imaginary object. This . . . is peculiar to Rabies and occurs in no other disease. . . . It is the same in man. (See Dr. Bardsley's account of the horror at some imaginary object shown by patients, their hiding themselves under the bed clothes, &c.)

"Again the countenance (of the dog) undergoes another change. The eyes are lighted up with a brilliancy scarcely conceivable by those who have not witnessed it—the dog's eyes become two terrible globes of fire.

"A reeling motion is another symptom, an affection of the loins. . . . He catches uncertainly at the food offered him. . . . There next comes a change of temper. He is irritable if meddled with, like the human patient: is impatient of control, even of the control of his owner. This irritability increases, he (then) *seeks* objects on which to display it. He mumbles the hand or the foot, at first without biting them. . . . The dog will bite the dress also, and then in *his* way, by crouching, &c., ask pardon for his fault.

"Discharge of saliva from the mouth (is) no characteristic; it occurs indeed, but only for a short time, from 12 till 20 hours. It is common to many diseases. Insatiable thirst follows this. The dread of water is *not* a symptom. In one case only (a setter of Count Münster's) did he (Youatt) see anything like it. In that dog a spasm, horrible to see, followed ineffectual attempts to lap. From paralysis of muscles of the jaw the lapping is often ineffectual, but where they can drink they drink enormously. (There is) tenacious mucous which human patients (in hydrophobia) are busy pulling, while dogs scratch it from the corners of the mouth.

"There is no distinction between dumb and furious rabies. They are merely different stages of the same disease.

"The paralysis never degenerates into fits. The rabid dog has no fits. Where you see epilepsy there is not rabies. Mad dogs have a howl quite characteristic of the disease—not the howl of a dog in confinement or anger. It begins in a bark, somewhat hoarser than natural, and terminates in a howl. This is not to be mistaken. Towards the last there is partial spasmodic closure or twitching of one eye, more than of the other. The animal

becomes at length deaf and blind. The eye is of a bottle-green
and completely disorganised."

(Another authority describes the eye of the dying dog as a
" mass of ulceration ".)

Our second extracts are from the well-known pages of Edward
Mayhew, one of the most experienced as well as humane of
veterinarians (*The Dog and its Management*, pp. 155-163).

" The dog is naturally the most nervous of all the dumb tribe.
His intense affection, his ever-watchful jealousy, his method of
attack, the blindness of his rage, and his insensibility to consequences, all bespeak a creature whose nervous system is
developed in the highest degree. . . . *Dreadful as hydrophobia
may be to the human being, rabies is worse to the dog.* It makes its
approaches more gradually. It lasts longer, and it is more intense
while it endures. The dog that is going mad feels unwell for a
long time prior to the full development of the disease. He is
very ill . . . dissatisfied with everything, and, greatly against
his better nature, very snappish. Feeling thus, he longs to avoid
annoyance by being alone. . . . There is another reason which
decides his choice of a resting place. The light inflicts upon him
intense agony. The sun is to him an instrument of torture,
which he therefore studies to avoid, for his brain aches. This
induces the poor brute to find out the holes and corners in which
he is least likely to be noticed and into which the light is unable
to enter. In solitude and darkness he passes his day. If his
retreat be discovered and the master's voice calls him to come
forth, the affectionate creature's countenance brightens, his tail
beats the ground, and he leaves his hiding place, anxious to obey
the loved authority. But before he has gone half the distance a
sensation comes over him which produces an instantaneous change
in his whole appearance. He seems to say, 'Why cannot you let
me alone? Go away. Do go away! You trouble, you pain me!'
And thereon he suddenly turns tail and darts back into his dark
corner. If let alone there he will remain, perhaps frothing a
little at the mouth, and drinking a great deal of water, but not
issuing from his hiding place to seek food. His appetites are

changed ; hair, straw, rags, tin shavings, stones, the most noisome
and unnatural substances are then the delicacies for which the
poor dog, changed by disease, longs and swallows in hopes to ease
a burning stomach. He is now (in the more advanced stage)
altogether changed. Still he does not desire to bite, he rather
endeavours to avoid society. He takes long journeys of thirty or
forty miles in extent, lengthened by all kinds of accidents, to
vent his restless desire for motion. When on these journeys he
does not walk. This would be too formal and measured a pace
for an animal whose frame quivers with excitement He does not
run. That would be too great an exertion for an animal whose
whole body is the abode of a deadly sickness. He proceeds in a
slouching manner—in a kind of trot—a movement neither a run
nor a walk, and his aspect is dejected. His eyes do not glare and
stare" [as they did at first], "but they are dull and retracted.
His appearance is very characteristic, and, if once seen, can never
afterwards be mistaken. In this state he will travel the most
dusty roads, his tongue hanging dry from his open mouth, from
which there drops no foam. His course is not straight. How
could it be since it is doubtful whether at this period he sees at
all? His desire is to journey unnoticed. If no one notices him,
he gladly passes by. He is very ill. He cannot stay to bite. If,
nevertheless, anything oppose his progress, he will, as if by impulse,
snap, as a man in a similar state might strike, and tell the person
to 'get out of the way'. He may take his road across a field
in which there are sheep. Could these creatures only make room
for him and stand motionless, the dog would pass on and leave
them uninjured. But they begin to run, and at the sound the
dog pricks up. Rage takes possession of him. He flies at one,
and then at another. He does not mangle, nor is his bite,
simply considered, terrible. He snaps and rushes forward, till,
fairly exhausted, he sinks down.

"If he escape and return home from these excursions he seeks
the darkness and quiet of his former abode. His thirst increases,
but with it comes the swelling of the throat. He will plunge his
head into water, so ravenous is his desire, but not a drop of the

liquid can he swallow, though its surface is covered with bubbles in consequence of the efforts he makes to gulp the smallest quantity. The throat is enlarged to that extent which will permit nothing to pass. He is the victim of the most horrible inflammation of the stomach and intense inflammation of the bowels. His state of suffering is most pitiable. He flies at and pulls to pieces anything that is within his reach. One animal in this condition being confined near a fire, flew at the burning mass, pulled out the live coals, and in his fury scrunched them."

[Had Mayhew lived in 1886, he might have cited the following illustrative incident recorded by one of the admiring visitors at Pasteur's laboratory :—"On kicking the cage the dog rushed and gnashed furiously at the bars. When the end of a heavy iron rod was pushed in he seized it in his jaws, and bit it so fiercely that it was difficult to make him loose his hold. It was the same when the end of the bar *had been previously heated.*" From the succeeding paragraph it appears that M. Pasteur was standing by while his visitor thus diverted himself by kicking the dog's cage and stirring it with a *previously heated* iron bar. We return to Mayhew.]

" He " (the rabid dog in the last stage) " emits the most hideous cries. The noise he makes is incessant and peculiar. It begins as a bark, which sound, being too torturing to be continued, is quickly changed to a howl, which is suddenly cut short in the middle. And so the poor wretch at last falls, fairly worn out by a terrible disease."

[After mentioning that Youatt imagines the mad dog to be moved by malice, Mayhew says] "There can be no malice in a raging fever which vents itself on any object within its reach, animate and inanimate. The poor beast is urged by some power too mighty for its control which lashes it beyond all restraint. . . . There is something likewise in the disposition which causes it to quit the society of all it loves and to leave the house in which those for whom its life would cheerfully be sacrificed dwell, to inhabit a dark and noisome corner. It is not mischief which makes the animal respond to its master's voice so long as memory has power. There is no malice in the end of the disease ; it is blind and indiscriminate fury which would much rather vent itself on things than on beings, even finding pleasure in injuring itself, gnawing, biting, and tearing its own flesh ; and so truly is the fury *blind* that most frequently the eyes ulcerate, the humours escape, and the rabid dog becomes absolutely sightless."

[After death it appears that] "The entire glandular system seems to be in the highest degree inflamed, and, besides this, the brain, the organs of deglutition, digestion, and, occasionally, of respiration are acutely involved. *The entire animal is inflamed.*"

Such is the malady which that "Benefactor of Humanity," that "God-sent Healer," as his admirers have styled M. Louis Pasteur, has deliberately produced by injecting the virus from one to another of "innumerable" dogs ! A disease which twenty years ago was so rare that only one case at a time was believed to exist in England, now torments scores of unhappy creatures with all its agonies—nay, with somewhat enhanced agonies, since instead of being left to perish in their retreats, or quickly put out of misery by a merciful gun-shot, they are now kept in iron cages in the glare of light, and disturbed and prodded with heated bars as fancy may dictate to M. Pasteur's visitors.*

The reader of the foregoing pages will, I hope, be inclined to sympathise with the final remarks of Mayhew in the chapter I have cited, when (after describing the ineffectual efforts of French vivisectors of his day to induce rabies artificially in forty dogs on which they experimented by causing them to perish of thirst, &c.) he concluded as follows (p. 164) :—

---

* On this point the *Referee*, 2nd August, had some excellent observations :— " . . . . My objections (to M. Pasteur) is that in the interests of vivisection his establishment has been advertised by illegitimate means. The panic would have died out long ago, but it has been fomented by the press in the interests of Pasteurism, and when the mad dog has not been available for sensational treatment a mad dog has been invented. One thing is certain. The present epidemic of rabies did not commence till M. Pasteur was ready for it. If he were to-morrow to abandon his experiments in this direction, and turn his attention, say, to small-pox or cholera, we should hear of very few cases of mad dogs. The best way to stamp out hydrophobia would be to unmuzzle all the dogs and send Pasteur to the North Pole !"

"They,—these French philosophers,—have only demonstrated that the utmost malice of the human being can be vented on his poor dumb slave without producing rabies." (Alas ! they *now* know how to produce it !) "They have held themselves up to the world, and in their books have duly reported themselves, as capable of preverting science to the most hideous abuses, and under its name contemplating evils and beholding sufferings at which the feelings of humanity recoil with disgust."

XVII.

PHILANTHROPY AND ZOOPHILY.

WE are pained to remark that many philanthropic associations (notably the new and admirable one for the Protection of Children) rarely issue appeals for support without making invidious reference to the large funds subscribed for the protection of Animals. The comparison is, of course, absurd on the face of it. At the end of some three-score years since the earliest was founded, the various Zoophilite Societies in the Kingdom—Societies for Prevention of Cruelty, Anti-Vivisection Societies, and Homes for Horses and for Lost Dogs—may possibly possess, including legacies and subscriptions, some forty thousand a-year between them all. On the other hand, the voluntary subscriptions and endowments allotted to human sufferers in the vast heterogeneous charities of Hospitals, Asylums for deaf, blind, idiots, and aged ; Orphanages ; Homes ; Widows' funds, &c., are estimated (in the *Charity Organization Review*, August, 1888, p. 356),—omitting Educational and Missionary Charities,—at £2,457,695, for London only. Adding to this £2,258,029, the amount of the Metropolitan Poor Rates, we have a total of £4,715,724. Thus for every £1 given throughout the United Kingdom to relieve the sufferings of animals, more than £100 is given in *London alone* to relieve those of human beings. The Metropolitan Hospital Sunday Fund by itself exceeds all that is subscribed and bequeathed throughout England, Scotland, and Ireland in the whole year, for the benefit of the entire animal creation. Even as regards individual donors, for a single guinea or poor half-crown which a humane person, touched for once with pity or affected by some solitary sermon, thinks fit to bestow on a society for protection of animals, the same benevolent person will usually be found to have subscribed ten guineas apiece to two or three Hospitals, and perhaps fifty to some pet Orphanage or Convalescent Home, or to a fund for charity dinners, or to give town children a holiday in the country. We do not complain of this ; we think it perfectly right, fit, and natural that human sufferers should have preference of relief. But when the small driblets of subscriptions which come to help our sore and necessarily costly struggle on behalf of the tortured brutes are grudged and pointed at (as not unfrequently happens), as if every penny of it were actually *robbed* from men and women, we feel disposed to turn on our accusers in some such words as these :

"Do you really think, O short-sighted Philanthropists ! that you can benefit suffering men and ill-used women and children by suppressing, or paralysing by impoverishment, the few feeble agencies yet at work to protect animals from brutal violence, and to expose and check the lawlessness of scientific curiosity? Are you so utterly ignorant of human nature as not to know that cruelty grows by what it feeds upon, and becomes stronger and bolder every day that it is permitted to prey upon the weak and defenceless? Do you not understand that the boy who has been allowed to torture a cat, to beat a starving donkey, to stone a dog, will in a few years be the man who will kick his wife with hobnailed shoes, and dash his infant against the wall? Do you not consider, you who mostly make appeal in the name of religion and of Christianity, that, by leaving cruelty to animals to pass unpunished and unchecked, you would be leaving the *souls of men* to grow harder year by year, more brutal and selfish, and with more ungovernable passions, till they were further than ever from the spirit of Christ?

" And, further, and as regards our own especial work, is it not for the benefit of Man, as well as beast, that we labour to stop Vivisection? Have we not again and again demonstrated that it is quite as much for the moral interests of humanity that we seek to put an end to the abominable practice as for the physical interests of the brutes? The descriptions of the 'true vivisector' as given of themselves and their brethren by Cyon and Claude Bernard are descriptions of beings out of whom the most divine attributes of humanity have ebbed and vanished; in whom the 'ardour of research' has dried up the fount of mercy till they find, as they tell us, in 'gruesome wounds' and 'mangled tissue' a 'joyful excitement' which might well be shared by the very devils of the pit. Is it to do nothing for the good of *humanity* that we should stop this demon-creating practice? Is it nothing that we should endeavour to deter young men from entering on the course which leads to such perdition?

"Even if we did not (as we hope and trust may be the case) save some young souls from the deadly vice of scientific cruelty, we might still claim to be friends of the *physical* welfare of men and women just as truly as those who compass sea and land to gather subscriptions for the hospitals. Those very Hospitals of London, the typical monuments of English philanthropy, are diverted, as we now know, from their benevolent purpose, and turned into what may better be called Museums of Disease. In them doctors may experiment, and students may learn, but the patients are continually sacrificed to the demands of insatiable science. The exposure of this heinous iniquity, this gross misuse of public charity, has come, not from the philanthropist's, but from the anti-vivisectionist's camp; and it is the same spirit of pitiless curiosity which we have denounced in its treatment of Animals, which we hold up to public execration when applied to hospital patients. It would have been long, we think, before the professed philanthropists would have plucked up courage to roll away the stones from the whited sepulchres which many of these great Hospitals have become and exhibit the rottenness within, as has been done by the author of *St. Bernard's* and *Dying Scientifically.* If the great evils signalised in those books be ever stopped, and men and women patients relieved from useless operations and endless experimentation, it will be thanks to those who have denounced scientific cruelty exercised alike on beast and man."

No! There is nothing to be gained by setting one kind of charity against another; still less by invidiously disparaging the charity which aims to relieve the agonies of the humblest of God's creatures—of creatures who can only *suffer*, who can neither write touching appeals in the newspapers, nor organise turbulent meetings to ventilate their wrongs; nor even, when all is done, thank or recognise those who have saved them from worse than death. There is a solidarity in all real charity; and to help one order of sufferers is to help all, for it is to keep alive in human hearts those feelings of justice and compassion on which not only charity, but civilisation itself is founded. And there is no less certainly a solidarity in all kinds of cruelty and wrong-doing; and those who would leave it unrepressed—either in the low places where rough men misuse beasts of burden, or in the high places where Science offers her bloody sacrifices—may count upon seeing it burst out sooner or later in acts of savage barbarity to men, women, and children.

XVIII.

SCIENCE IN EXCELSIS.

A NEW VISION OF JUDGMENT.

———————

SCENE 1.

An outlying region of Paradise. A group of Cherubim reclining on clouds. In the midst, the Archangel St. Raphael on a crimson bank of sunset. Eloa, the sister of the Angels (the Angel of Pity), leaning on the frustrum of a rainbow in the background.

ST. RAPHAEL. My friends and fellow Cherubim, it seems to me that we and some of our former associates, now in "another place," have dissertated long enough on Fixed Fate, Free Will, Foreknowledge Absolute. If I mistake not, it is nearly nine hundred thousand years since the subject was first mooted by my illustrious brother Saint Uriel, and since that epoch we have spent many ages in talking the matter over, without arriving at any satisfactory conclusion. In fact (as one of these poor little intelligent creatures who move on the planet Tellus ventured to surmise), we have—

" Found no end, in wandering mazes lost ".

It is high time, surely, for us to turn to some more practical study, lest our special glory of being the "Spirits who *know* most" be eclipsed, and no question will remain but that the Seraphim, who *love* most, have the better of us.

THE ANGEL ISRAFEL. I rise to second the motion of the most wise and noble Archangel. His observation is just. We have spent time enough on scholastic and metaphysical riddles which no Angel can be expected to understand. Science, as everyone now admits, is superior both to Learning and Philosophy. Let us turn our attention to it forthwith.

MANY CHERUBIM AT ONCE. By all means! By all means! Let us immediately establish a "Celestial Association for the Promotion of Science".

RAPHAEL (*graciously*). I am pleased, my friends, to see that my suggestion meets your approval. We will take up Science with angelic vigour forthwith. Let us consider a moment how we shall pursue the various branches. As to Astronomy (for which we possess, of course, very special advantages), I think our Celestial Association might very properly "endow research" by sending out an Exploring Expedition round the Universe, to bring us in the latest intelligence from all the worlds of space. A Report drawn up on such a scale would be both instructive and entertaining.

THE ANGEL SAMIASA. A splendid proposal, Saint Raphael! I am ready to volunteer for the Expedition on the spot.

MANY OTHER ANGELS. And I! And I! And I!

RAPHAEL. This is highly gratifying. Our distinguished colleagues will doubtless return, within a million years or so, laden with interesting intelligence. I would only warn the less far-sighted not to lose themselves by mischance in a Nebula, a misfortune to which scientists in general seem liable. The next science to be considered (since we need not trouble ourselves with petty details, such as Geography or Geology) is Physiology; and here, I venture to foretell, our most interesting studies will be found. What do any of us, Angels, know, for example, of that singular little Automaton, Man—a tiny creature of bone and muscle, blood and nerves, who yet sends his thoughts up to our very dwelling-place, looks through our ethereal forms with his telescope even to the remotest suns, penetrates the history of past ages, and writes poems which, like the *Divina Commedia* and *Paradise Lost*, even Angels are wont to peruse with satisfaction? How, I ask, does that little lump of pulpy matter which the creature calls his Brain help him to do these things? How does he move his little legs and arms by those bands he calls his muscles; and what is the meaning of that curious internal bag, into which he is always cramming bread and fruit and (horrible to think!) the flesh of other animals? Truly, I believe, my dear fellow-cherubim, we could scarcely find, in any of the hundred million spheres around us, a more interesting point whereat to commence our studies than this very Physiology of Man; and I for my part, as the Archangelic Healer, confidently hope to hit on some beneficent discoveries which, as in the case of Tobit, may enable me to cure these poor creatures' maladies.

[*All the Angels tumultuously applaud, and St. Raphael continues :*]

To effect our purpose, it will be desirable to adopt their own method of scientific research and make investigations into the structure of these little beings, especially into their nervous systems; and to collect and verify as many facts as possible about their various organs—how they are kept alive, and how long it takes to kill them when they are dipped in boiling water, or starved, or put in an oven, and so on.

ELOA (*starting up*). Oh, Saint Raphael! you don't mean to say you would suffocate, or starve, or bake those miserable creatures? Consider, they are evidently sensitive to pain.

RAPHAEL (*reprovingly*). Dear Eloa! do not be so excitable! Nothing will be attempted, I can assure you, beyond the legitimate demands of Science. Grave doubts may be entertained as to whether Men are anything more than Automata; but, even granting they have some dim feelings of pain and pleasure, it would surely be absurd for a moment to put their sensations in competition with the noble thirst for knowledge now stirring in the Angelic mind? Only think of placing a *man's* existence or suffering in the balance against the acquirement of some great truth by Archangels like Gabriel, Michael, or myself!

ELOA (*weeping and clasping her hands*). Oh, Saint Raphael! when you speak thus, and draw up your majestic form a thousand fathoms high, and shake your iridescent wings, I feel how poor

16

and low, and all too base, to claim your consideration, are the feeble creatures of earth! But yet, O mighty and wise and generous Archangel, have pity on these miserable beings! To the greater part of them Science is but a name, a word of no meaning. To live their little day in the sun ; to play and eat and sleep ; to love their mates and their offspring ; this is what existence is to them—harmless, even if ignoble. Say, great and glorious St. Raphael, that you will not turn that humble existence into a curse by putting them to tortures of which they can understand neither reason nor end ?

[*Two or three Cherubim touch her on the shoulder.*]

Sister Eloa! It is a pity when charming Angels talk of things which they don't understand.

St. Raphael. Well, well, Eloa shall have her way thus far. We will not try any experiments on those simple mortals for whom she pleads, who know nothing about the glories of Science, and cannot be supposed to take any sympathetic interest in our investigations into their brains and stomachs. We will confine our researches entirely to those eminent Physiologists who have devoted themselves to the same pursuit, and have tried every experiment upon creatures nearly as much lower than they as they are lower than we ; I mean on cats, dogs, and monkeys. They have been so ingenious in inventing and so candid in recording all their practices, that we shall have nothing to do but to order up a few of their *Handbooks* and *Reports*, and then set to work to go over the contents *seriatim* on their own persons. At the end—though it seems doubtful whether these human Physiologists have obtained anything of value by tormenting the brutes—of course we, with our keener vision and deeper knowledge, shall advance Science much more by experimenting on the higher animal.

The Angel Ithuriel. Nothing can be more to the purpose than our great President's observation. I only wish to know how his Wisdom means to proceed.

Raphael. Well, I think we must first command a new Physiological Laboratory to be built in connection with our College of Science, and let it be placed in such a position that it cannot be overlooked, and also where good south and north light may be obtained. So far as my recollection goes, there has not hitherto been any edifice of the kind in Heaven, though there are several closely resembling it in an opposite locality. Then we shall furnish it suitably with tables, Bernard's gags, experiment troughs, forceps, saws, clamps, chisels, cannulæ, knives and actual cauteries ; a furnace or two, and an engine for maintaining artificial respiration when the subjects are curarised. When all is ready, Azrael will, I am sure, be so obliging as to run down and tell all the Physiologists they are "wanted" up here; and we may then immediately set to work without further delay.

ALL THE CHERUBIM. An excellent plan ! So be it. Glory to Science in the highest ! Amen.

[*Scene closes.*]

SCENE II.

A celestial Laboratory, or lofty hall, filled with a variety of singular troughs and tables of sundry shapes. A formidable collection of instruments is ranged along the wall. An engine works in the corner. Galvanic batteries, kymographions, hæmodromometers, and other philosophical machines, lie about the tables. Over the door is the inscription LICENSED AS THE ACT DIRECTS, FOR THE TORTURE OF VERTEBRATE ANIMALS, *beneath which a boy-cherub has written in chalk* "MANGLING DONE HERE". *Enter Raphael and the Cheribum. Eloa timidly following.*

RAPHAEL. Our architect has done his work with his usual rapidity. Our Laboratory has "risen like an exhalation". I hope, my friends, we shall soon be enabled to quench our noble thirst for knowledge at the fountains of life. Ha! here comes the ever-punctual Azrael and our "subjects".

[*Enter Azrael (the Angel of Death), leading in a score of eminent Physiologists, who stand, pale and shivering, near the door.*]

GERMAN PHYSIOLOGIST. Mein Gott! What is that for a place! It mooch remind me of a well-known spot.

FRENCH PHYSIOLOGIST. Mais qu'est-ce que c'est donc? Un Laboratoire de physiologie? But where are the dogs, and the cats, and the rabbits? Mon Dieu! serait-il possible que. . . .

ENGLISH PHYSIOLOGIST. Well! what do those tremendous swells of Angels over there want with us? Can they intend to take some lessons out of our Handbook of the Physiological Laboratory, and do they mean to invite us to give them a course of lectures, like the students at the dear old Hospital?

RAPHAEL *(approaching, with a smile).* Not so far wrong, most learned doctor. We mean to learn Physiology from you, only not perhaps quite in the way you expect. You have always loudly proclaimed that theory without experiment is of little worth, so we intend to try some of your own choice examples on yourself and your friends.

ALL THE PHYSIOLOGISTS IN CHORUS. Oh! oh! oh! No! no! no! Oh, how shocking! Oh, how cruel! Oh, how insulting to Science!

RAPHAEL *(turning to the Cherubim).* Did you ever hear anything so inconsistent? Why, these are the very men who have been repeating again and again that only by actual Vivisection could Physiological Science be advanced, and that Science is an end so noble and glorious that it was not worth while considering the pain any creature might endure to advance it! I have really no patience with them; but still I will condescend just to say a few words in explanation. [*He beckons to the Physiologists, and whistles, as if calling dogs.*] Come hither, you poor little two-legged trembling creatures! Don't growl and whine, but think yourselves very much honoured by what we Cherubim are going to do to you.

PHYSIOLOGISTS. Oh, my Lord! Oh, your Saintship! Oh, your Holiness! Don't try your experiments on us! We were not made to be experimented on—indeed we were not; and we are *quite certain* the UNKNOWN AND UNKNOWABLE would not approve of it at all!

RAPHAEL. I should like to know why you are not to be experimented on, when you have tried your own devices on nearly every creature which breathes.

PHYSIOLOGISTS. Why? Because we are men and they were brutes. We had of course a right to do as we pleased with them.

RAPHAEL. Well! we are angels and you are men; and by the same logic *we* have a right to do as we please with you, being quite as much above you as you are above the dogs and monkeys. Moreover, these same monkeys, by your own showing, are your near relations; whereas we angels disclaim any kind of connection with you miserable mortals.

PHYSIOLOGISTS. Oh, but, you see, we are intelligent beings.

RAPHAEL. If I am not greatly mistaken, dogs are intelligent too; much nearer to the level of your intelligence than you are to ours.

PHYSIOLOGISTS. We have reason.

RAPHAEL. So have they!

PHYSIOLOGISTS. We have affections.

RAPHAEL. So have they! More than you, I suspect.

ENGLISH PHYSIOLOGIST. We have immortal souls.

RAPHAEL. *A la bonne heure!* I was waiting for somebody to say that; and I suppose the French and German and Italian Physiologists felt a little diffidence in bringing out the argument. You have certainly immortal souls, as your presence here, after Azrael has delivered his death-warrant, sufficiently testifies. But will you please to explain to me why the fact that an animal has (as you imagine) only one life should justify you in making that solitary life such a curse as that it were better it had never been given?

GERMAN PHYSIOLOGIST (*loftily*). We don't want to be justified. We are Philosophers, and can allow no superstitious moral considerations derived merely from the inherited prejudices of our ancestors to interfere with our pursuit of knowledge.

RAPHAEL. Herr Professor! though you don't believe in the story of Adam and the Forbidden Tree of Knowledge, you talk uncommonly like one of his descendants. May I ask if you think it equally becoming for a Philosopher to steal and lie and cheat, as well as to be cruel, for sake of knowledge ?

FRENCH PHYSIOLOGIST.   Quel tracasserie àpropos de quelques malheureux chiens !   Enfin—we are the strongest, and that is the long and the short of the matter.

RAPHAEL.   Perfectly true, Monsieur !   You have hit the nail on the head.   Your argument is unanswerable, and of course you will acquiesce cheerfully in our application of it to the present case.   We Cherubim are stronger than you men, and we mean to treat you precisely as you treated the dogs.

[*Physiologists are silent and stand, with chattering teeth, looking at the apparatus and at the Cherubim, who are tucking up their sleeves.*]

ELOA (*sinking on her knees*).   Oh, my beloved Archangel, have mercy upon them !

RAPHAEL.   Tut-tut !   Eloa, you are really too weak, I cannot let these creatures escape.   The slight resemblances which exist between their nature and ours make them (as they have said of dogs) " creatures which it would be a pity to withdraw from research "; and in the sacred interests of Science——

ALL THE CHERUBIM.   Oh, yes !   The sacred interests of Science !   The sacred interests of Science !

PHYSIOLOGISTS (*unanimously*).   D—n Science !

RAPHAEL.   Come, come ; we have no time to lose.   Just hand me that curly-haired one, Sandalphon, and I'll begin by paralys-ing him with curare !

PHYSIOLOGISTS (*screaming*).   O mercy, mercy ! not curare !

RAPHAEL.   What a miserable cur it is, whining and crying be-fore he is hurt !   We can have no more of this.   Let the assist-ants secure the whole pack as fast as possible on the operating troughs.   Where are their books ?

ATTENDANT CHERUB.   Here, your Grace.   Here is the *Hand-book of the Physiological Laboratory*, and the *Lezioni di Fisiologia Sperimentale*, and the *Leçons sur le Système Nerveux*, and the *Physiologie Opératoire*, and the *Pression Barométrique*, and the

Méthodik, and the *Archives de Physiologie*, and the *Centralblatt*, and many more lectures and papers.

RAPHAEL. Enough for the present. Let us begin at once and take the Englishmen, for their experiments are not quite so ingeniously cruel as the others. When we have sawn through their backbones, and irritated the stumps of the nerves, and rubbed caustic on their eyes, and made a few other interesting demonstrations, we shall be in better mood to bake, and skin, and try many curious experiments with the rest. See, here is quite a facetious idea. [*Aside.*]

"It seems, indeed, wonderful to see animals (of course Men are included) sometimes, after a slight puncture of some part of the encephalon with a needle, turn round just like a horse in a circus, or roll over and over, for hours, and sometimes for days. . . . The animal is bent like a corkscrew as much as the bones allow, in cases of rolling." *

Think how instructive it will be to see a philosopher rolling over and over, twisted over like a corkscrew, for hours and days together ! Then there are many other experiments to be verified. I say deliberately *verified*, because it seems that after being tried on dogs and cats and horses, even if all the Physiologists come to the same conclusion, which is very seldom, it always remains doubtful whether the same result will follow in the case of man. [*Turns over the books.*] Here is a good case for one of our English —or ought I to say Scotch?—subjects. It is recorded, I find, in the *British Medical Journal* for Oct. 23, 1875—a periodical, I think, edited by the very gentleman who so loudly proclaimed, in a newspaper called *The Times*, that no cruelties are ever practised by vivisectors. [*Aside.*] I hope you have not forgotten to bring him up, Azrael? Of the whole crew he will be the most entertaining subject, as we shall be able to see what sort of brain secretes these kind of statements. [*Aloud.*] Well, our Professor, like his dogs, will need to be starved for eighteen hours. Then we shall curarise him and establish artificial respiration, and when

* Lecture by Dr. Brown-Séquard, *Lancet*, vol. ii., p. 600.

this is done we shall cut open his abdomen, squeeze out his gall-bladder, clamp his cystic-duct, dissect out his bile-duct, tie a tube in it, inject various things into his intestine, and carefully note the results. It will not take more than seven or eight hours, it appears, to do all that is needful.

Here is another very amusing experiment to be tried upon one of the authors of the *Handbook of the Laboratory*. He directs it to be tried by the student on the eye of a " frog or small mammal," but I have little doubt a large mammal will answer quite as well. We must first take off the Professor's spectacles, and then " scrape the cornea of the eye, so as to remove the epithelium completely. Hereupon, the caustic is to be rubbed two or three times lightly over the whole surface, after which the eye is washed with saline solution, and the animal (or professor) is left to itself for twenty or thirty minutes," during which interval spectators have recorded that it is apt to perform antics of a very diverting description.

But we will not be severe on these Englishmen, who, as I said, are not so cruel *yet* as their continental colleagues. Here, good Israfel, will you be so obliging as to catch that slippery little German who gives the *Lezioni di Fisiologia* to his pupils? We will just try two of his tricks mentioned in his book, pages 38 and 40. First, we will take hold of the sciatic nerve (the great nerve of the thigh, my dear fellow-cherubim, which in all these earthly creatures is exquisitely sensitive), and *tear out its roots at the pelvis*, as he did to the nerve of a dog. After a little while we shall then treat him to a curious experiment he is fond of trying on frogs. We will force open his mouth, seize the epiglottis with a hook, pull up the lungs, and snip them off with scissors.

As to the French gentlemen, we have plenty of interesting experiments to make on them. Here is one or two we will try on the author of the *Traité de Physiologie Humaine :*

" We must first strip the skin completely off the legs and lay bare the nerves, and then apply to the nervous branches some exciting substance ".

Still more instructive will be this :

"In order to suppress the functions of the skin, it is advisable to lay bare, by shaving, the whole skin of a dog, sheep, or horse (it will not be necessary to shave the man), and to cover the exposed surface with a thick drying varnish. Animals thus treated rarely survive twelve hours. After death the organs are found gorged with black blood."

The state of the creature while it is thus simmered alive in its own blood must be very curious indeed to witness ; indeed, it would seem there can be little use in the experiment, except to afford pastime to the spectators. Quite a new interest will be afforded by baking some of these gentlemen in ovens variously prepared at different degrees of heat. Several of them have ascertained in this way, as M. Gavarret mentions, that dogs bear being kept in an oven at 120° *centigrade* for eighteen minutes, or survive for thirty minutes if the oven be only heated to 80°.* It will be new to see how long Men can endure having the blood parched in their living veins like these animals.

Lastly, we shall take one peculiarly ingenious gentleman, and treat him as he tells us he treated a "middle-sized, vigorous dog".† We shall place some curare under his skin, which, we are told, ‡ "will cause him to become perfectly paralysed ; while his intelligence, his sensitiveness, and his will, will remain intact" —"a condition," we are assured by the same great authority, "accompanied by the most atrocious sufferings which the imagination of man can conceive". When our friend is in this state of redoubled sensitiveness, but utter helplessness, we shall make him breathe, by means of a machine blowing through a hole in his wind-pipe, and then we shall dissect out the nerves of his face, neck, fore-arm, interior of abdomen, and hip. We shall continue to excite them with electricity for ten hours, and then we shall leave him with the engine working on him, while we go and

* See M. Gavarret's Treatise, p. 156.
† *Archives de Physiologie*, vol. ii., p. 650.
‡ *Revue des Deux Mondes*, Sept. 1, 1864, pp. 173, 182.

refresh ourselves for a second bout of the same interesting experiments.

ELOA (*whose eyes have grown large with horror during this reading, flings herself into the arms of St. Raphael.* Oh, my brother! my glorious Archangel! spare these poor wretches! It is impossible your noble nature can descend to inflict such torment even on the meanest of God's creatures.

RAPHAEL. Dear Eloa! Must I remind you that your unfortunate habit of compassionating unworthy objects has ere now led you into terrible mistakes? Do you forget how you followed Lucifer himself into Gehenna when he told you his pitiful tale, and how, when he had got you there, he clutched you fast, and said you should remain and be lost with him for ever; and how it was JUSTICE, and not PITY, which delivered you, so that you might warn your sex never to follow your foolish example?

BAHMAN, LORD OF THE ANIMALS* (*here stands forward among the group of student-Cherubim*). Most noble Archangel and brother Cherubim! I think it becomes me to speak in this matter. Do you understand, beloved and gentle Eloa, that these men have already done all these hideous things to my poor, harmless, unoffending birds and brutes? Do you know that they have tortured them for hours and days, by scores and by hundreds, and taught thoughtless youths to stifle every emotion of compassion and do the like, multiplying and repeating every form and kind of agony again and yet again? Do you know that the clanking engines, which maintain breath in the curarised and doubly-suffering creatures, never cease working in their accursed laboratories by day or night; and that they lie down to sleep leaving their mangled victims on their torture-troughs, waiting for the morrow's fresh anguish? Do you know that one of these men alone has been known to have tried his infernal devices on no less than fourteen thousand dogs, beside uncounted numbers of other sensitive creatures?

[*Eloa sobs convulsively, and at last covers her face and slowly leaves the hall.*]

* One of the seven Amshaspands. *Vide* Zend-Avesto.!

RAPHAEL. My brother Angels! there now remains nothing to stay our hands. PITY has fled before SCIENCE, who alone will henceforth direct our proceedings.

[*A veil falls and conceals the scene.*]
A voice from behind the veil :

With what measure ye mete, it shall be measured to you again.

An Anthem of Seraphs heard from a great distance :

Blessed are the merciful, for they shall obtain mercy !

XIX.

"THOSE WHO ARE APPOINTED TO DIE." *

AMONG the anomalies of human sentiment there is one which seems to have hitherto escaped notice. It is a peculiar *hardness* which takes possession of people, otherwise of average humanity, when they deal with animals doomed to death. Prior to experience we should have imagined that the knowledge that a creature is about to be killed—struck out of existence for ever, as is generally supposed—would move some impulse of compassion even towards vermin; but the reverse is certainly the case. Possibly this hardness arises from an instinctive steeling of the heart to spare our own pain in performing or witnessing the slaughter. Probably rather from the uprising in us of the old savage *Heteropathy* still lurking in our half-reclaimed natures; that antithesis of Sympathy which makes birds, brutes, and barbarous tribes of men destroy their sick or aged companions, and which only yields by slow degrees to Aversion, such as the Greeks felt for Philoctetes; and that Aversion again, at last, to Compassion and Tenderness. From whatever cause derived, it is a mournful fact that, as a rule, the slaughtering of animals is done with a haste and a roughness partaking of barbarity. Of course humanity itself demands that there should be no needless dawdling to prolong the terror and pain of the dying creature. But it is not this swiftness of care and precaution which is commonly exhibited, but, on the contrary, a selfish, brutal hurry to make an end of the expiring life, which has in it a character quite *sui generis*.

* From the *Zoophilist*.

Hasty, redoubled blows are repeated again and again with growing fierceness, rather than a single well-aimed one delivered with all the strength of the slaughterer. If a superannuated or diseased dog or cat, or a superfluous puppy or kitten is to be drowned (a cruel mode of dispatch at best), it is not carefully put into a sack or hamper with stones, or tied securely to a heavy weight and then dropped into deep water; but it is flung into the pond or stream and beaten back again and again as it struggles to swim to shore; dying at last more of blows and exhaustion than of the comparatively merciful suffocation under water. Even when the creature is, more humanely, sent to the chemist to be poisoned, the mistress who "feels too much" (as she will tell her friends) to supervise the administration of the death drops, will give the animal in charge to anybody,—generally to a *boy*,—who undertakes the job rather as a treat than otherwise. Her caresses, long lavished to excess while the creature was in health and beauty, come to an end altogether when age and suffering and terror would make them of real comfort; and strange rough hands clutching its neck replace the delicate fingers which so long stroked its glossy coat and the lips which kissed its silky head. It Italy, sheep and kids which have been house-pets from their birth are no sooner devoted to the butcher than they are slung up in an atrociously cruel fashion by all four legs together; while calves may, in every country, be seen carried on carts to the slaughter with their heads pendulous in agonising positions. Fowls and pigs in the same way, long familiarised with the farmer's wife and children, seem to become objects almost of ridicule in their death struggles to the family who stand talking and laughing amid their piteous cries and yells of terror and pain. We have elsewhere quoted a recent instance of this barbarity, where young boys were allowed to find so much amusement in the killing of a pig that they, next day, cut the throat of their baby brother to repeat the scene for their own enjoyment.

It is enough to awaken the attention of thoughtful men and women to the existence of this peculiar sentiment of *heteropathy* towards dying animals, to suggest the necessity for very special care in every arrangement connected with the death either of household creatures or of cattle, or of wild animals killed in so-called "sport"; or, lastly, of the unfortunate "vermin"—rats, mice, weasels, hawks, hedge-hogs, &c.—which servants and game-keepers commonly treat mercilessly whenever they find them in their traps.

Can we suppose, finally, that this hateful sentiment is absent from the breast of the Physiologist alone, and that when his doomed victim lies on the torture-trough, and he himself stands over it full of his " joyful excitement," he feels a throb of the pity which is found lacking even in generally humane people when they kill any animal ? It is well-nigh out of question. Perhaps it is best that only One Eye looks into that dark spot of earth— the heart of a Vivisector. It might make us, men and women, hate our kind.

XX.

THE FUTURE OF THE LOWER ANIMALS.

AMONG the problems which have presented themselves with painful urgency to the minds of many Anti-vivisectionists is that of the Future Life of Brutes. So long as we contemplated their humble existences—as Mr. Carill did in a recent number of the *Nineteenth Century*—as containing at least as great a surplus of pleasure over pain as the ordinary life of man, it was natural for us to do little more than wish that their beautiful intelligence and devotion might not be extinguished, and that it might be permitted to ourselves to renew in a perfect world those relations with some of them which have contributed no inconsiderable item to our enjoyment on this earth. Though Mahomet—that typical Semite! —cheerfully announced that only three animals will be admitted to Paradise, to wit, his own Camel, Balaam's Ass, and Tobit's Dog, we, Aryans, have been apt, like the hero of the Mahabharata, to think that a hound who has followed his master faithfully here below might be permitted to attend him on a higher way. Eden itself, to our fancy, would be somewhat incomplete were it only inhabited by lofty intelligences, with no playful beasts or warbling birds to people the lower ranks of life. If music and flowers (or some glorified analogues of them) may lawfully be anticipated, those amongst us who love animals better than harps or roses cannot be blamed for hoping for their presence likewise. Further and more seriously. Many of the wisest of thinkers have maintained that the "Spirit of the Beast" may, on metaphysical grounds, be believed to survive the death of its body; while the intense power of affection which some of them exhibit has

17

furnished another argument, embodied in the touching epitaph on
a dog—

> " O'er this sepulchral spot
> Emblems of hope we twine ;
> If God be Love, what sleeps below was not
> Without a spark Divine ".

But another side of the subject has opened to us since we have
learned that to thousands of the most sensitive animals the gift of
existence has been transformed into a calamity. Optimists as
many of us were before we knew of the crimes of science, our
rose-coloured views of the general happiness of creation have been
all blurred and blotted since we realised the import of the
revelations of cruelty contained in such publications as Weber's
Torture Chamber, Scholl's *Ayez Pitié*, and our own *Light in Dark
Places*. The truth—a bitter drop in the cup of our lives—has
perforce been drunk in ; that Science, by the aid of exquisitely
delicate machinery and far-fetched drugs, and skill, and patience,
and ingenuity worthy of a God-like instead of a Devil-like task, has
achieved the creation of *AGONY* such as simple Nature never
knew—a new factor in the dark problem of evil, never again
to be left out of our view.

The sense thus aroused in many minds of the cruel wrongs of
vivisected animals has led them to review with new interest and
deeper concern the hypothesis of another life reserved for such
creatures when death has relieved them from their undeserved
sufferings. The inquiry " Have they another existence ? " is no
longer merely suggested by tenderness and regret, but pressed on
them with the whole weight of their faith in eternal justice.
Perhaps some one special case of which they have read recurs
continually, challenging some solution endurable to their moral
sense. Perhaps it is Paul Bert's dog left alone at night, with all
the chief nerves of its body dissected out and exposed, and with
the clanking engine still forcing air into its lungs, after the torturer,
wearied with his work, had gone to rest. Perhaps it is one of
those baked to death by Claude Bernard in his stove. Perhaps
some other poor brute, the victim of Schiff, or Roy, or Rutherford,

or Goltz—which has been dealt with by man as man might be dealt with by God if He were to thrust His adoring servant into Hell.   They cannot banish this foully-wronged and tortured animal from their thoughts.   It importunes them by day, and when they lie awake at night they almost see it lying on the vivisecting table in the laboratory.   It brings a pang and a distraction into their prayers.   They implore to be shown how they ought to think of it consistently with their reliance on the Judge of all the earth to do right, and their faith that in His universe there can be no final and remediless injustice.

It is with great diffidence that anyone should presume to speak on such a subject, but, as it is often helpful to know what others think, the present writer will venture to say plainly that, so far as appears, there is no possible solution of this heart-wearing question save the bold assumption *that the existence of the vivisected animal* (and of course, as a consequence, of other creatures of the same rank in nature) *does not end at death.*   It is absolutely necessary to postulate a future life for the tortured dog or horse or monkey, if we would escape the unbearable conclusion that a sentient creature, unoffending,—nay, incapable of offence,—has been given by the Creator AN EXISTENCE WHICH ON THE WHOLE HAS BEEN A CURSE. That conclusion would be blasphemy.   Rejecting it with all the energy of our souls, we find ourselves logically driven to assume the future life of (some, at least, among) the lower animals.

And in that future life we are (by the hypothesis) authorised to conceive of the creature as so happy, so raised in the scale of being, as that its past sufferings will be wholly outweighed and nullified, and its existence, taking it altogether, made a boon and not an evil, a benediction, not a calamity.   This, and nothing short of it, will satisfy our sense of justice ; and it must never be forgotten that though the justice of the Great Lord of All may be, and no doubt *is*, a far more lofty and blessed thing than our poor minds can devise, it can never be a *lesser* justice.   It is impossible that He will ever through eternity do aught which, could we understand it, we should regard with that hatred and contempt wherewith *He Himself* has made us regard injustice.   Neither is it true, as Agnostics frequently argue, that future happiness cannot undo the injustice of past unmerited suffering.   It is quite in harmony with the conception of a Righteous Governor of the world, that He may for good reason permit undeserved pain to fall on a being to whom He knows, with the unerring certainty of Omniscience, that it shall hereafter be abundantly compensated and made up.   This, in fact, is the great distinction between Divine and human justice.   Not that the former is different in kind from the latter, but that it works in unlimited space and time :

> " *Tu n'as qu'un jour pour être juste,*
> *J'ai l'éternité devant Moi*".

Of course the resource of believing in the future life of tortured animals cannot be available to those who are unfortunate enough to have lost faith in the future life of human beings ; and even to those who hold firmly by the creed that "the soul of a Man never dies," there are great difficulties in believing that creatures of a lower grade, who are not Moral Free Agents, should likewise survive corporeal dissolution.   Many of the strongest grounds on which we build our own hopes of immortality are lacking when we would extend them to the brutes ; and there is a special stumbling-block which never fails to be placed in our way, which is briefly this: If we suppose a Dog or Horse or Elephant to live after death, it is impossible (it is said) to limit the privilege to such noble animals.   Below them, shading off by the finest degrees, are humbler and yet humbler ranks of vertebrate, and finally of invertebrate, creatures.   Beneath *Man*, and between him and the Dog or Horse, there is, indeed, a sufficiently sharp line, where Reason and Morality and Religion (in all but some vague and shadowy sense) apparently stop ; and where, accordingly, it is easy to suppose the limits of immortality are drawn.   But if we descend a step below human beings we find no further excuse for limiting the great boon at the bounds of one species or another.   Thus to argue for the immortality of a Dog is (it is contended) to land ourselves in the absurdity of arguing practically for the immortality of a Coral Insect.

The mode of viewing the question which leads us into this dilemma is essentially a physico-scientific, not a moral or spiritual, one. It is true that in the material world there are no breaks in the chain of being—or, if there ever were, Haeckel and his fellow Darwinians fill them up boldly with hypothetical links. But the Life after Death is not a matter wherewith physical science is concerned, or whereto it bears any testimony. It belongs to the moral and spiritual order of things ; and in that order there *are* breaks and chasms, over which we pass *per saltum*, if at all. Not seldom, for example, does a human soul traverse in an hour the measureless moral abyss between the Kingdom of Darkness and the Kingdom of Light ; and undergo a *palingenesia* to which nothing that happens in earth or air or water affords the slightest parallel. And in this particular matter of Immortality, if one single living Man be now an Immortal Being, that man must, at one time or other, have leaped from the Mortal to the Immortal at a bound. There must have been a time, earlier or later, before or after birth, when he was not immortal, but might have perished as an abortion ; and again a time when he had become immortal and would not perish were his body reduced to ashes. It is idle, then, for anyone who believes in human immortality, to object to the possible immortality of a dog on the ground that no line can be drawn between the highly intelligent mammal and a coral insect. We may retort, " Neither can any line be drawn between an adult Man, whom we recognise to be an immortal being, and the first formless embryo which he once was ;"—and which, strangely enough, was (we are told) almost undistinguishable from the embryo of the dog.

Perhaps this parallel between individual human development which slowly brings the child up to the level of Immortality may afford, not only an answer to the above discussed difficulty, but also a valuable rough indication of the ranks of animal life among which we may, not unreasonably, expect to find possible candidates for a future existence. Let us permit ourselves to guess any epoch in the human creature's development when it becomes immortal. Then we may, not too audaciously, extend our hope

of immortality to all animals which have reached *that* stage—
whatever it may be. We cannot for a moment suppose the
tremendous alternative of immortality or extinction to be decided by arrival at any arbitrary or merely *physical* turning
point, such as may occur at various epochs either before birth,
or at the moment of birth, or later. We must believe it to be
determined by entrance on some moral or mental stage, such as
may be represented by the words Consciousness, Self-Conscious-
ness, Intelligence, power of Love, or the like; by the development,
in short, of the mysterious Somewhat above the merely vegetative,
or animated life, for which we believe such life to be the scaffolding.
If then (as we are wont to take for granted) a child of some six or
twelve, or eighteen months old, be certainly an immortal creature,
it follows that the stage of existence which involves immortality
must be an early one, which many a dog has attained. On the
other hand, as those animals which are altogether below the condition of the human infant are not so highly organised or sensitive
as ever to suffer *torture*, our hypothesis allows us to suppose them
to become extinct at death, while it leaves us free humbly to trust
that *every animal subjected to torture*—either by science or any
other agency—will live again in conditions of happiness which
will amply redress the balance of good in the sum of its existence.

Does not every flower of the field offer us a parable which may
serve for man and beast alike? There is a stage of growth when,
if the stalk be cut down or the petals torn away, no seed will ripen.
There is a further stage when the stalk may be broken and the
beautiful petals trodden in the dust, but when the seed will *not*
perish, but live, and bloom wheresoever it may be borne by the
winds of heaven.

II.

Many readers are of course aware that some such belief in the
future life of animals, as above argued, has been occasionally
maintained by thinkers of past generations whose other opinions
carry weight. It is, however, less generally known how very many

eminent men, philosophers of various schools and divines of various churches, have favoured this view, and have stated their reasons for doing so ; albeit usually in a curiously apologetic tone, as if they were conscious that they were on the matter considerably in advance of their contemporaries. Thinking that a collection of extracts of passages of this nature would be interesting I add an instalment of one, for a large part of which I am indebted to the Rev. F. O. Morris, and to an interesting little book, now out of print, *An Autumn Dream*, by the late Rev. John Sheppard (1867), kindly presented to me by the writer's widow. (In some cases the references in this volume are given to *pages* only, the *editions* not being specified.) The collector is unfortunately unable at the moment to supply the deficiency, but the extracts are in every instance *verbatim*.

John Wesley.—" May I be permitted to mention here a conjecture concerning the brute creation? What if it should then please the all-wise, the all-gracious Creator, to raise them higher in the scale of beings? What if it should please Him, when He makes *us* equal to the angels, to make them what we are now—creatures capable of God, capable of knowing and loving and enjoying the Author of their being? If it should be so, ought our eye to be evil because He is good?"—*Sermons*, vol. xi., pp. 128, *et seq.* In Southey's *Life of Wesley*, vol. xi., pp. 189-192, it is stated : " He (Wesley) entertained some interesting opinions concerning the brute creation. Some teachers of materialism had asserted that if man had an immaterial soul so had the brutes. ' I will not quarrel,' said Wesley, ' with any that think they have. Nay, I wish he could prove it, and surely I would rather allow them souls than I would give up my own.' He cherished this opinion (Southey adds) because it furnished a full answer to a plausible objection against the justice of God."

Adam Clarke.—" I. The brute creation never sinned against God, nor are they capable of it, and consequently cannot be liable to punishment.

" II. But the whole brute creation is in a suffering state—they suffer, but who can say they suffer justly ?

"III. As they suffer . . . neither through their fault nor folly, it is natural to suppose that the Judge of all the earth, who ever does right, will find some means by which these innocent creatures shall be compensated for their sufferings.

"IV. That they have no compensation here their afflictions, labours, and death prove; and if they are to have any compensation they must have it in another state.

*   *   *   *   *   *   *

"IX. It is therefore obvious that the gracious purpose of God has not been fulfilled in them, and that, as they have not lost their happiness through their own fault, both the benevolence and justice of God are bound to make them reparation."

Matthew Henry.—"There shall be glory conferred on all the creatures which shall be in proportion to their natures, as suitable and as great an advancement as the glory of the children of God shall be to men. . . . What becomes of the souls of the brutes that go downwards none can tell, but it should seem by the Scripture that there will be some kind of restoration of them."—*Commentary*, Romans viii. 19-22.

Hartley.—"These creatures (the larger animals) resemble us greatly. . . . And if there be any glimmering of hope of an hereafter for them, if they should prove to be our brothers and sisters in this higher sense in immortality as well as mortality . . . this would have a particular tendency to increase our tenderness for them. . . . The future existence of brutes cannot be disproved by any arguments so far as yet appears; let, therefore, those which favour it be allowed their due weight and only that."—*On Man*, vol. ii., p. 231, and p. 404.

Barclay.—"May they not (the animals) be reserved as forming many of the customary links in the chain of being, and by preserving the chain entire contribute there as they do here to the general variety and beauty of the universe? Besides, though some individuals of the human species in that blessed state may no longer feel any interest in them, yet to others of more contemplative mind may they not be a source not only of sublime but perpetual delight."—*History of Opinions*, pp. 398-9.

Hildrop.—" Nor are the boundaries betwixt the human and brute understanding more easily distinguished. Who can determine the lowest degree of human ignorance, and the highest pitch of animal knowledge ? Who can say where the one ends—the other begins ? Shall the eternal purposes of infinite wisdom, love, and power be entirely defeated ? To say that animals shall be annihilated is in effect to say that the Almighty Creator is either unwilling or unable to effect the eternal purposes of His infinite love."—Rev. John Hildrop, D.D. Quoted by Rev. F. O. Morris, Preface, p. 14, to *Records of Animal Sagacity and Character.* Longmans, 1861.

Henry More.—" It is objected that by this manner of reasoning the souls of brutes will not only subsist but also live and enjoy themselves after death. To which I dare boldly answer, that it is a thousand times more reasonable that they do, than that the souls of men do *not*."—*On the Soul*, pp. 302-307.

Lastly—*Bishop Butler.*—" But it is said these observations are equally applicable to brutes ; and it is thought an insuperable difficulty that they should be immortal and by consequence capable of everlasting happiness. Now this manner of expression is both invidious and weak ; but the thing intended by it is really no difficulty at all, either in the way of natural or moral consideration. For first, suppose the invidious thing, designed in such a manner of expression, were really implied, as it is not in the least, in the natural immortality of brutes, namely, that they must arrive at great attainments, and become rational and moral agents, even this would be no difficulty, since we know not what latent powers and capacities they may be endued with. There was once, prior to experience, as great presumption against human creatures as there is against the brute creatures arriving at that degree of understanding which we have in mature age. For we can trace up our own existence to the same original with theirs. And we find it to be a general law of Nature that creatures endued with capacities of virtue and religion should be placed in a condition of being in which they are altogether without the use of them for a considerable length of their duration, as in infancy and childhood. And great part of the human species go out of the present world before they come to the exercise of these capacities in any degree at all. But then, secondly, the natural immortality of brutes does not in the least imply that they are endued with any latent capacities of a rational or moral nature. And the economy of the Universe might require that there should be living creatures without any capacities of this kind. And all difficulties as to the manner how they are to be disposed of are so apparently and wholly founded in our ignorance, that it is wonderful they should be insisted upon by any, but such as are weak enough to think they are acquainted with the whole system of things. There is, then, absolutely nothing at all in this objection, which is so rhetorically urged, against the greatest part of the natural proofs or presumptions of the immortality of human minds."—Butler, *Analogy of Religion*, chap. i., p. 27.

Perhaps to some readers it will be of interest to learn, on the personal testimony of the present writer, that Theodore Parker and Mary Somerville were both ardent believers in the future life of the higher animals.

XXI.

IN THE LONG RUN.

AMONG the many discouragements which fall to the lot of the opponents of scientific cruelty—the perpetual fresh endowments of "research" and erection of new laboratories; the delusive Parliamentary Returns and Reports of Commissions; the persistent boycotting of our meetings by the leading newspapers; the antagonism of nearly the whole medical profession; and (worst trial of all to many of us!) the coldness and incredulity *de parti pris* of friends on whose sympathy we had reckoned—among all these sorrowful experiences there are some reflections of a larger kind which may serve to brace our souls for continued, never-faltering effort.

Looking back through the world's history we see numberless instances of the decay of empires, the disruption and ruin of nations, the return to barbarism of countries once far advanced in civilisation. Nineveh and Babylon, Memphis and Thebes, Baalbec and Palmyra, the cities of the Aztecs and the Incas, and of the races whose very names are lost, who raised the vast piles now hid amid the forests of Cambodia—all these have perished. Of most of them the poet said truly:

> "They rose, while all the depths of guilt
> Their vain creators sounded;
> They fell, because on fraud and force
> Their corner-stones were founded".

But it would appear that among the perishable things of earth are not to be counted the moral truths which, generation after generation, have been slowly acquired by our race; first by a few prophets and sages only, then dimly and hesitatingly by the multitude, and at last fully and frankly by all men. There were " Ages before Morality," as Professor Jowett has called them, for mankind at large, as there are months and years before morality for every child. But since that far-off epoch when even rudimentary ethical ideas were inchoate and unformulated, Man, as the millenniums have rolled by, has grown ever more and more distinctly a Moral Being. To the earliest and simplest moral ideas—such as the condemnation of parricide and perjury, and the few offences which the Greeks deemed deserving of the punishments of Tartarus—he has added the condemnation of Murder, Adultery, Theft, and Falsehood; and then, under the guidance of Christ, has made the great stride forward from the Prohibition of Offence to the Affirmation of positive Duty; from the " Do *not* do to thy neighbour that which thou wouldst not have done to thyself" of Isocrates, to the "*Do* to thy neighbour, what thou wouldst have him do to thee"; from the " Do not kill " of "them of old time" to the "Love the Lord thy God, and Love thy neighbour," which are the "great commandments" of Christianity. Nay more. Not only has the moral law been better taught, but the whole moral ideal has been transformed by Christianity, and the supreme glory has been shifted from Power to Goodness, from Self-aggrandisement to Self-sacrifice. From this loftier standing-ground mankind has taken a new departure, and slowly climbed onward and upward. It has never abandoned the higher level in theory, however much it has fallen below it in practice. It has never receded to earlier and cruder ethics ; and we may feel assured it will never do so.

> " One accent of the Holy Ghost
> The heedless world hath never lost."

As well might our Theology return to Polytheism and Fetishism, as our Morality and Moral Ideal to the Pagan level.

It is true that in our age, owing to the general disintegration and reconstruction actively going on through every department of thought, there appears some danger lest moral ideas, long accepted as part of Religion, may be shaken along with the older theology and perhaps lost. Those, for example, which concern the relations of the sexes will inevitably be subjected soon (as those which concern Property are subjected already) to temporary perilous revision. But let it be noted that it is not the *principles* of Purity or of Justice, or righteousness of any kind which anyone dreams of altering, but only the *application of* them in some supposed yet higher and more perfect manner. Socialist, Agnostic, Comtist, Atheist, Nihilist, all alike urge their theories on ethical grounds which are fundamentally the same as those long adopted by the Christian world; nor would the most revolutionary of them so much as entertain the project of a crusade against Chastity, Honesty, Sobriety, or Veracity. Let us not, then, alarm ourselves lest the human race should apostatise. On the contrary, every order of virtue, it may be confidently hoped, will be better understood and estimated by successive generations. The "magnanimous" Englishman of the nineteenth century is much more truly magnanimous than Aristotle's ideal. Chastity and Truth have purer meaning to us than to men of the past; even as modern Love is an infinitely subtler, more exalted thing than Greek or Roman, Jew or Indian ever dreamed. And in a very special degree the virtues which touch the subject of our work—the charities and sympathies of life—have gone on visibly widening and deepening century after century, insomuch that to revert in imagination to the stage of their development a thousand, or even a hundred, years ago is almost impossible; and every modern novelist who places his scene in bygone times is well-nigh certain to fall into moral anachronism; lending his heroes sympathies with suffering, and regrets for offences and "enthusiasms of humanity" all unknown in their day as were photography and the electric telegraph. Duties of charity—once limited to a man's family, to his tribe, to his nation—have extended laterally in ever-widening circles from Jew to Gentile, from Greek to Barbarian, from Aryan to Negro; and no less obviously have descended perpendicularly through all the social strata till the vilest criminal no longer lies too deep to claim our care.

The mode in which one great step of this extension of the

sense of moral obligation has been effected almost within the memory of living men is so full of encouragement for us in our contention on behalf of the tortured brutes that it may be well to recall it for a moment. Five generations ago our fathers had scarcely conceived the idea (any more than St. Paul seems to have done) that slavery was, *per se*, an immoral institution. The humane Jesuit Las Casas, when he introduced African slaves into the Western Continent, had thought he effected a philanthropic work ; and the pious and evangelical Newton of Olney never to the last gave signs of repenting the hideous cruelties wherein he had been a participator as captain of a slave ship. Even gentle William Cowper (all honour to him !) when he pleaded for " a man and a brother " had little or no notion of the poor, grotesque Sambo really in question, but evolved out of his own conscious- ness a dusky Epictetus, who could argue that " Minds are never to be sold ". Then came the era when William Wilberforce, sitting under the trees in pleasant Kent, made the resolution to bring his first bill into Parliament, and began to plead for the enslaved Negro—even as his grandson, Basil Wilberforce, pleads now for the vivisected dog. Long was the contest, outlasting the generation with which it began. But the victory in the end was greater and more complete than the first warriors dared to hope. And now, when the scourge of " Uncle Tom " has gone to join *in limbo* the rusty racks of the Inquisition, it is noteworthy how the very idea of holding a man or woman in slavery is continually *taken for granted* to be immoral, and shocking to the conscience of mankind. The ethical tide has risen and covered the ground on which Cowper, Wilberforce, Clarkson, Garrison, and Theodore Parker flung themselves in waves of pity and indignation.

Another advance of public moral sentiment is still almost too recent for us to perceive its magnitude or read the lesson of encouragement it teaches us. Not twenty years ago the most wretched fraction of the human race—the women given over to vice—were looked upon as so far outside the limits of sympathy that the most cruel and tyrannical laws might be enforced against them without fear of protest from any quarter. But the doctors (mainly the same who uphold the vivisection of animals) greatly miscalculated the limitations of the public conscience. A band of men and women, overcoming all natural disgust and braving public insult, ranged themselves at once on the side of the trampled victims of " scientific " law, and through years of painful agitation aroused the conscience of England, till—suddenly almost as fell the walls of Jericho in the story—resistance ceased and they carried the day. When Parliament practically abolished the infamous Acts which had been foisted on our Statute Books by the medical clique ; when James Stansfeld (a Vice-President, let us gratefully remember, of the Victoria Street Society, and the Chairman of the first meeting of its Committee) carried his famous Resolution condemning those Acts by an overwhelming majority, even more was done than the rescinding of one frightful piece of legislation. It was demonstrated that the Conscience of the English Nation is a real Power in the State, to which appeal can be made by all men and women ; and that, against that Conscience of England all the sophistries of Science and arguments appealing to cowardice and selfishness are, in the long run, of no avail.

These are practical examples of moral victories which may well afford encouragement to us in our uphill fight. They are instances of the action of that general law of moral progress on which we may rely to put an end eventually to such a practice as Vivisection. In truth, either the moral progress of Europe itself must be arrested and recede far back behind the point attained at the Christian era, or Vivisection must cease. There are, as old Zoroaster proclaimed, " two principles—a Good and a Base ". We must choose the " Good," the humane, the unselfish, the merciful towards weakness ; or else the " Base," the remorseless pursuit of selfish ends. The two cannot both be accepted by civilised mankind and taught to the rising generation. One or other must be discredited and abandoned. It will not be because the victims (*at first !*) are only the poor brutes that the base principle will escape detection. By-and-by it will be universally observed that a certain body of highly educated men, claiming to be in the forefront of mental progress, are defending the practice to which they devote themselves by arguments which, so far as they are not based on egregious falsehoods, are all drawn from motives cowardly and selfish, indicating in those who can use them utter contempt for the claims of the weak, and utter indifference to the suffering of beings sentient like themselves, and, according to their philosophy, having the same origin and the same end. As soon as the dilemma is fairly understood, mankind will choose between the principle of humanity on the one hand, and the principle of selfish cruelty on the other. We can have little fear—after the examples of Slavery and of the vile Acts of Parliament of which we have spoken—on which side the verdict will be given. Were it possible that the nation should abandon all that the world has learned from the beginning of moral progress till now, and, deliberately throwing over the Christian ideal, accept the principle which underlies Vivisection, then it can only be said that the future of England would be doomed. On such a principle no civilisation can flourish. It is a dry rot which, sooner or later, must destroy the very beams and rafters of the edifice of society.

www.ingramcontent.com/pod-product-compliance
Lightning Source LLC
Chambersburg PA
CBHW030730280326
41926CB00086B/978